THE CONQUEST OF
A CONTINENT

THE CONQUEST OF A CONTINENT

OR

THE EXPANSION OF RACES IN AMERICA

BY

MADISON GRANT

PRESIDENT, NEW YORK ZOOLOGICAL SOCIETY
TRUSTEE, AMERICAN MUSEUM OF NATURAL HISTORY
PRESIDENT, BOONE AND CROCKETT CLUB
COUNCILLOR, AMERICAN GEOGRAPHICAL SOCIETY
AUTHOR, "PASSING OF THE GREAT RACE"

WITH AN INTRODUCTION
BY
PROF. HENRY FAIRFIELD OSBORN

Reprinted 2004 by
Liberty Bell Publications
PO Box 890
York, SC 29745
www.libertybellpublications.com
803.684.4408

ISBN: 1-59364-017-X

**Liberty Bell's
Politically Incorrect Classics
Volume 1**

Printed in the United States of America

To
MY BROTHER
DE FOREST GRANT

Madison Grant and the Racialist Movement

By George McDaniel

Perhaps more than any other man, Madison Grant created what we might call the "racialist moment" in America. This was the period beginning approximately with the administration of Theodore Roosevelt and continuing through the administration of Warren Harding, during which the country discarded its old, melting-pot sentimentalism about blacks and foreign immigration. This period also saw the emergence of a new science, eugenics, which promised to banish inherited evils. This era of explicit, intellectual racialism lasted until approximately the Great Depression, then withered under Franklin Roosevelt's massive shift to the Left, and finally collapsed during the war on Nazi Germany.

Madison Grant (1865-1937) worked tirelessly for the racialist movement for almost this entire period. He joined, chaired, and often founded the organizations active within the movement. He counted among his closest associates presidents, top industrialists, best selling writers, and some of the greatest scientists of the century. And he wrote two of the seminal works of American racialism: *The Passing of the Great Race* (1916) and *The Conquest of a Continent* (1933).

Grant was born in New York in 1865, just as the first of the modern white-against-white conflicts was closing. He was descended from Jacobites who came to the colonies from Scotland after the defeat of "Bonnie Prince Charlie" in the Forty-Five uprising (1745), and throughout his life retained the Jacobite brand of conservative fire. He was graduated from Yale in 1887 and received a law degree from Columbia in 1890.

The Passing of the Great Race was published in 1916 to immediate popular success. It established Grant as an authority in the field of anthropology, and laid the groundwork for his research in the emerging science of eugenics. It was read by presidents, dictators, scientists, and common people alike, and even today—excoriated as it is—it has much to teach. The impact of the book can be understood only in the cultural milieu in which it appeared.

Immigration since the War Between the States had proceeded at great speed. The decade of the 1880s saw the arrival of 5,246,613 immigrants, and in 1882 alone,

788,992 were admitted. Two hundred twenty thousand Chinese came from 1854 to 1882. Subsiding a bit in the nineties, the influx rose again after the turn of the century, averaging over 800,000 arrivals each year between 1900 and 1914. Most of these were immigrants from parts of the world to which Americans were unaccustomed: Russia, Poland, Austria-Hungary, Italy, the Balkans, and Turkey. Many newcomers brought Marxist and anarchist ideas alien to the old American stock.

Just as it does today, the American identity faced a two-pronged threat: a large influx of aliens and the presence of a large Negro element. Negro migration to the Northern industrial cities brought a slow awakening to the entire country of the true nature of the race problem, and Thomas Dixon's 1905 novel, *The Clansman*, was one of the first works in the new century to focus on it. The book's sympathetic account of the first Ku Klux Klan encouraged a reappraisal of often-sentimental notions about blacks.

In a sense, this reappraisal came to a head in August 1908 in Lincoln's own Springfield, Illinois. A black habitual criminal attacked a white girl in her bedroom and, while being pursued by her father, turned and killed the man with a razor. At least one other attack on a white woman was also reported, and the white people in Springfield responded by killing two blacks and burning down a crime-ridden black neighborhood called the "Badlands." Thousands of local blacks fled Springfield. It was this event that inspired the creation of the National Association for the Advancement of Colored People in Springfield in 1909.

In 1915, a new entertainment medium widened the audience for the racialist message when D. W. Griffith debuted his film masterpiece, *Birth of a Nation*. Based upon *The Clansman*, and, to some degree, on Dixon's 1902 novel, *The Leopard's Spots*, this movie was hailed as a technical triumph even by its harshest critics. Nevertheless, the NAACP, along with other black and some Jewish organizations, picketed the movie and threatened violence in the cities where it opened.

The success of the film was in some doubt when Dixon contacted his old Johns Hopkins classmate, President Woodrow Wilson, and arranged a special showing at the White House. Wilson is said to have leapt to his feet, exclaiming, "It is like writing history with lightning. And my only regret is that it is all so terribly true."

With the news that the president loved it, audiences flocked to the film. During its opening in Atlanta, William J. Simmons announced the founding of the second Ku Klux Klan, in nearby Stone Mountain, Georgia. This Klan organization went on to sweep the country, becoming especially strong in the midwest.

The Passing of the Great Race was published the next year, in 1916. Grant intended it as a call to American whites to counter the dangers from both blacks and non-traditional immigration. Adopting the then-popular racial taxonomy of William Z. Ripley in *The Races of Europe*, Grant describes the three European subraces of Nordic, Alpine, and Mediterranean. As was common in his day, he unabashedly favored the Nordic and went to great pains to contrast Nordic civilization with that of other races and subraces. For example, he faulted Nordic, altruistic devotion to blacks and other unsuccessful groups, a devotion that always proves self-destructive.

Grant concluded that America should abandon a largely open-door immigration policy. He favored a eugenics program that would promote the Nordic race and discourage the expansion of the colored races in the white world. In particular, he condemned miscegenation.

It is worth noting that one of the reasons Grant and other racialists opposed the new immigration was that it brought alien ideologies. The First World War had seen the triumph of Bolshevism, and continuing immigration from Eastern Europe brought Marxists to the United States. Like most racialists, Grant saw socialism as unfit for the Nordic race he so admired. When he was helping found the Galton Society in 1918, he wrote to the other organizers: "My proposal is the organization of an anthropological society ... confined to native Americans, who are anthropologically, socially, and politically sound, no Bolsheviki need apply."

The Passing of the Great Race became an immediate best-seller, with new editions in 1918, 1920, and 1921, multiple printings, and translations into German, French, and Norwegian.

It was reviewed favorably by *Science*, the journal of the American Association for the Advancement of Science, and by a large number of other periodicals as diverse as the *Journal of Heredity* and *The Saturday Evening Post*. The editor of the *Post*, in fact, George Horace Lorimer commissioned a series of articles on immigration in a similar vein, and in an editorial in the May 7, 1921, issue, wrote: "Two books in particular that every American should read if he wishes to understand the full gravity of our present immigration problem: Mr. Madison Grant's *The Passing of the Great Race* and Dr. Lothrop Stoddard's *The Rising Tide of Color*...These books should do a vast amount of good if they fall into the hands of readers who can face without wincing the impact of new and disturbing ideas."

The Passing of the Great Race did indeed fall into the hands of such readers, turning up in the personal libraries of some of the most important figures of the day. It was typical, for example, that Dr. Rupert Blue, Surgeon General of the United

States, gave a copy personally to the pharmaceutical manufacturer, Sir Henry Wellcome.

Grant was not alone in sounding the alarm. Some of the other books published during this period include: *Mankind at the Crossroads* by E.G. Conklin (1914), *America's Greatest Problem: The Negro* by Major R. W. Shufeldt (1915), *The Rising Tide of Color Against White World Supremacy* by Lothrop Stoddard (1920; Introduction by Grant); *Race and National Solidarity* by Charles Josey (1923), *Applied Eugenics* by Paul Popenoe and Roswell Johnson (1923); and *The Fruit of the Family Tree* by Alfred E. Wiggam (1924). These were all intended for a mass audience, but academic textbooks soon joined them, including *Genetics and Eugenics* by W.E. Castle (1916) and *Evolution, Genetics, and Eugenics* by H.H. Newman (1921).

The effect was felt at both the state and federal level. Twenty-four states passed laws encouraging sterilization of those who were retarded, insane, or had criminal records. At the Federal level, in 1921, Albert Johnson, head of the House Committee on Immigration and Naturalization, began a series of hearings on immigration. He appointed Harry Laughlin, who in 1922 would be one of Grant's co-founders of the American Eugenics Society, as an expert witness on eugenics. In 1922, Laughlin reported extensively on racial differences in IQ as measured by the new army intelligence test.

In 1923, Grant's close friend Henry Fairfield Osborn, the famous paleontologist who coined the term "tyrannosaurus rex," spoke enthusiastically about intelligence testing: "We have learned once and for all that the negro is not like us." This was precisely the kind of thing Grant and others had been saying for years. These ideas helped pass the Johnson Act of 1924, which established national origin immigration quotas of two percent of the number of foreign born already in America as determined by the census of 1890. This greatly reduced the flow of immigrants from non-traditional sources, a policy that remained essentially unchanged until 1965.

Grant called the act a "new Declaration of Independence," and his responsibility for helping pass it was undeniable. The *Dictionary of American Biography* credits him with just such assistance, and, at his death in 1937, the *New York Times* in its obituary said this of Grant's book: "Besides being a recognized book on anthropology, it has often been called to Congressional attention in the passage of restrictive immigration laws. . . . Mr. Grant. . .was also a member of the American Defense Society. As such he helped frame the Johnson Restriction Act of 1924."

Eugenics Congress

Grant remained active throughout the 1920s, serving as president of both the Immigration Restriction League and the Eugenics Research Association. In addition, he was treasurer of one of the most important events in the history of eugenics, the Second Eugenics Congress of 1921. This event continued the pattern of the First Eugenics Congress, which had been held in London in 1912, with Winston Churchill as one of the sponsors and at which Prime Minister Arthur Balfour delivered the inaugural address. The second congress was hosted by the American Museum of Natural History in New York. More than 300 delegates came from Europe, Latin America, Asia, Australia and New Zealand though, interestingly—since German scientists were frequently ostracized from conferences this soon after the First World War—no German eugenicists were invited.

Among the notables in attendance were future U.S. president Herbert Hoover, Alexander Graham Bell (the Congress's honorary president), conservationist and future governor of Pennsylvania, Gifford Pinchot, and Leonard Darwin, son of Charles Darwin. Henry Fairfield Osborn, director of the museum, was president. Harry Laughlin was in charge of exhibits, and Lothrop Stoddard handled publicity. One hundred eight papers were presented on topics ranging from plant and animal genetics to anthropology and political science. The conference signaled the vitality of a young science that was nevertheless destined to die an early death.

Madison Grant continued to lobby for immigration control even after the passage of the Johnson Act. In 1927, he, Robert DeCourcey Ward, and other eugenicists signed a "Memorial on Immigration Quotas," urging the president and Congress to extend "the quota system to all countries of North and South America . . . in which the population is not predominantly of the white race."

Grant continued to write. In 1930, along with Lothrop Stoddard, Harry Laughlin, Charles Davenport, Paul Popenoe, and Henry Fairfield Osborn, and others, he contributed to *The Alien in Our Midst*, subtitled *Selling Our Birthright for a Mess of Pottage*.

Grant himself came up with the idea for this book, which—like *Conquest* a few years later—was written to defend the 1924 immigration act. The idea was to include essays on race and immigration from both contemporary writers and from great Americans of the past such as Thomas Jefferson, Patrick Henry, James Madison, and George Washington. The book was widely distributed to legislators and editors by the American Coalition of Patriotic Societies and was thus instrumental in preserving the 1924 law.

In 1933, Grant's second major work in historical anthropology appeared: *The Conquest of a Continent*, written in part to answer critics of the 1924 Johnson Act. In it, Grant wrote: "A controversy immediately arose over this new basis [the national origins immigration quotas], as it was to the interest of every national and religious group of aliens now here to exaggerate the importance and size of its contribution to the population of the country, especially in Colonial times. . . . The purpose of this opposition was to warp public opinion in regard to the merits of various national groups and to exaggerate the non-Anglo-Saxon elements in the old Colonial population. This book is an effort to make an estimate of the various elements, national and racial, existing in the present population of the United States and to trace their arrival and subsequent spread.

He then embarks upon what Henry Fairfield Osborn in the introduction calls the "first racial history of . . . any nation." Especially interesting today is Grant's analysis of the Negro problem. He writes: "Among the various outland elements now in the United States which threaten in various degrees our national unity, the most important is the Negro." He discusses several proposed solutions. The first, "slow amalgamation with the Whites," he rejects immediately, arguing that this would "produce a racial chaos such as ruined the Roman Empire." He considers repatriation at somewhat greater length, but rejects this as well, for reasons no longer applicable in our time: "Today, [repatriation to Africa] is not possible, because Africa, with the exception of Liberia, is under the control of white states, which certainly would not welcome such an enormous addition to their own color problem . . . ."

The third solution Grant considers is the establishment of a separate black nation within the territory of the United States. This he tends to reject because it would involve the abandonment of large sections of the South. But then he goes on to admit that something of that nature had already occurred in some areas, both in America and—especially—in the West Indies:

"This has actually happened in some places along the lower Mississippi River, where the numbers of the Negroes have become so overwhelming that the few remaining Whites have simply moved out and abandoned the district to them. It has happened and is happening in the West Indies. Haiti and Santo Domingo have been entirely turned over to Negroes and other examples of West Indian Islands almost abandoned to Negroes can be found."

In the final analysis, Grant has no easy answers to the Negro problem. He urges states to adopt laws prohibiting intermarriage and he castigates Christian churches in the North for "trying to break down the social barriers between Negro and White." Social separation is paramount, he says, and to that end public opinion "might well stop exalting the Mulatto and thereby putting its stamp of approval on miscegenation. Negroes should be encouraged to respect their own racial integrity." And, finally, contraception should be made "universally available to them."

Perhaps because *Passing of the Great Race* had been so influential, *Conquest of a Continent* caused an immediate storm of opposition. On December 13, 1933, the director of the Anti-Defamation League, Richard E. Gutstadt, sent the following letter to the publishers of a number of Jewish periodicals:

> Gentlemen:
>
> Scribner & Sons have just published a book by Madison Grant entitled "The Conquest of a Continent." It is extremely antagonistic to Jewish interests. Emphasized throughout is the "Nordic superiority" theory, and the utter negation of any "melting pot" philosophy with regard to America.
>
> We are interested in stifling the sale of this book. We believe that this can be best accomplished by refusing to be stampeded into giving it publicity. Every review or public criticism of the book of this character brings it to the attention of many who would otherwise know nothing of it. This results in added sales. The less discussion there is concerning it, the more sales resistance will be created.
>
> We therefore appeal to you to refrain from comment on this book, which will undoubtedly be brought to your attention sooner or later. It is our conviction that a general compliance with this request will sound the warning to other publishing houses against engaging in this type of venture.
>
> In fact, Grant wrote very little about Jews, noting only his view that they were of Central European, Khazar origin: "It is doubtful whether there is a single drop of the old Palestinian, Semitic-speaking Hebrew blood among these East European Jews.

Nevertheless, by this time, Hitler had begun consolidating power in Germany and was undermining eugenics and scientific racial theory through his excesses. The *New York Times*, in its review of *Conquest*, was quick to make the connection: "Substitute Aryan for Nordic and a good deal of Mr. Grant's argument would lend itself without much difficulty to the support of some recent pronouncements in Germany."

In fact, Grant had occasion to caution others about the National Socialist government. In 1934, he wrote to Laughlin warning that American eugenicists should be careful in their relations with Germany and should "proceed cautiously in endorsing" the actions being taken by the German government.

Conservation

Another aspect of Grant's career that he considered intimately related to his work in racial science was conservationism, and his involvement with nature and wildlife was long and varied. Just as with the racialist movement, he was ever the leader. In 1895, along with Theodore Roosevelt and a handful of others, he co-founded the New York Zoological Society (now the Wildlife Conservation Society), and served as its secretary until 1924. He helped found the American Bison Society in 1905; was president of the Bronx Zoo for many years; was co-founder and president of the Bronx Parkway Commission (which built the road to the zoo); co-founder of the Save the Redwoods League, and a founding member of the Boone and Crockett Club, which helped establish Yellowstone National Park.

In an excellent essay in the April 1995 issue of *Mankind Quarterly*, Roger Pearson writes about the link between conservation and racial thinking:

"The success of the conservationist movement in the United States at this vital period in the nation's history was facilitated by the sympathy of President Theodore Roosevelt, who was deeply concerned about the threat to the quality of both the natural and human stock of America. . . .

"With Madison Grant serving as secretary and later as president, the Boone and Crockett Club was largely comprised of eugenicists and eugenics sympathizers. Renowned as one of the more active members of the eugenics movement, and especially for his efforts to preserve the "Old American" component of the American population, Grant worked just as ardently to preserve the natural heritage for future generations of Americans and should be remembered always with honor as one of the nation's greatest benefactors."

Despite disavowals by American eugenicists, Nazi excesses had already begun to erode support for the eugenics movement by the 1930s. German policies played into the hands of the anti-eugenicist Franz Boas of Columbia, a socialist who embarked on a one-man crusade to destroy eugenics and "undermine the belief in race as a primary factor in cultural behavior." Through his many books and students (including Margaret Mead and Ashley Montague), Boas' views began to prevail.

Even so, Grant's efforts never flagged. In 1932, he again served as treasurer of the third and final Eugenics Congress. This Congress was also held at the Museum of

Natural History, and included as sponsors Mrs. E. H. Harriman, Mrs. H. B. Dupont, Dr. J. Harvey Kellogg (of Kellogg's cereals), and Leonard Darwin.

Conquest was published in 1933, after which Grant served on the advisory board of *Eugenical News*. He continued to write, to plan and to lobby. But the old days were ending. A schism had developed among eugenicists between those who favored "negative eugenics" and those in the "mainstream" who concentrated on "positive eugenics." Moreover, Nazism was rapidly discrediting the science. By mid-decade, Osborn had died, and Grant himself died on May 30, 1937. The man who had devoted so much of his life to preserving his race left no children.

Two years later, Hitler invaded Poland. From then on, eugenics would be equated with concentration camps, Nazi doctors, Holocaust, and war crimes. As a science it was dead. Ironically, Grant's views on nature and wildlife have been largely adopted, and conservation is at the forefront of mainstream thought. Of course, Grant himself receives little credit from today's environmentalist movement. His dreams of racial preservation, which he saw as part and parcel of nature conservation, are reviled today by all but a faithful few. Those few owe it to the rest of the world and to the memory of this tireless champion to carry on his work, to ensure that the ideals of Madison Grant do not perish.

George McDaniel is the editor of A Race Against Time: Racial Heresies for the 21st Century *and the co-author of* Metamorphosis: The Impact of Third-World Immigration on American Culture. *This article originally appeared in the December 1997 issue of* American Renaissance.

All rights reserved.

American Renaissance
PO Box 527
Oakton, VA 22124-0527
(703) 716-0900
(703) 716-0932 (Fax)
www.AmRen.com

INTRODUCTION

THE character of a country depends upon the racial character of the men and women who dominate it. I welcome this volume as the first attempt to give an authentic racial history of our country, based on the scientific interpretation of race as distinguished from language and from geographic distribution.

The most striking induction arising through research into the prehistory of man is that racial characters and predispositions, governing racial reactions to certain old and new conditions of life, extend far back of the most ancient civilizations. For example, the characteristics which Homer, in the *Iliad* and the *Odyssey*, attributed to his heroes and to his imaginary gods and goddesses were not the product of the civilization which existed in his time in Greece; they were the product of creative evolution long prior even to the beginnings of Greek culture and government. This creative principle—the most mysterious of the recently discovered phenomena of evolution, to which I have devoted the researches of nearly half a century—is that racial preparation for various expressions of civilization—art, law, government, etc.—is long antecedent to these institutions.

Ripley missed this point in his superb researches into the racial constitution of the peoples of Europe. Grant partly based his *Passing of the Great Race* on Ripley's researches, but did not carry out the purely anatomical analysis to its logical end-point, namely, that moral, intellectual, and spiritual traits are just as distinctive and characteristic of different races as are head-form, hair and eye color, physical stature, and other data of anthropologists.

In the present volume, which I regard as an entirely original and essential contribution to the history of the United States of America, Grant goes much further and in tracing back the racial origins of the majority of our people he lays the foundation for an understanding of the peculiar characteristics of American civilization, which, all agree, is of a very new type, something the world has never before seen.

Grant supports Ripley in his distinction between three great European stocks—Nordic, Alpine, Mediterranean. He gives very strong additional reasons for one of his own earlier inductions, namely, that the Aryan language was invented by primitive peoples of the Nordic race before its dispersal, in the third millennium B.C., from the Steppe country in the southeast of Russia. This superb and flexible language doubtless aided the Nordic race in its conquest of Europe, in its ever-westward journey across the Atlantic, in its Anglo-Saxon occupation of our continent, in its stamping of Anglo-Saxon institutions on American government and civilization. We all recognize that, like all other languages, Aryan is purely a linguistic and not a racial term, just as French is spoken equally by the Norman Nordics of the north of France, by the Alpines of the center, and by the Mediterraneans of the south.

INTRODUCTION ix

My faith is unshaken in the ultimately beneficial recognition of racial values and in the stimulating and generous emulation aroused by racial consciousness. Let this stimulation be without prejudice to other racial values—which should be duly recognized and evaluated—values we Anglo-Saxons do not naturally possess. Moreover, I set great store by the great mass of documentary evidence assembled by Grant in the present volume. I think it explodes the bubble, of the opponents of racial values, that they are merely myths. The theme of the present work is that America was made by Protestants of Nordic origin and that their ideas about what makes true greatness should be perpetuated. That this is a precious heritage which we should not impair or dilute by permitting the entrance and dominance of alien values and peoples of alien minds and hearts.

Finally I would like to define clearly my own position on these very important racial questions which arouse so much heat, so much bad feeling, so much misrepresentation. I object strongly to the assumption that one race is "superior" or "inferior" to another, just as I object to the assumption that all races are alike or even equal. Such assumptions are wholly unwarranted by facts. Equality or inequality, superiority and inferiority, are all relative terms. For example, around the Equator the black races and certain of the colored and tinted races are "superior" to the white races and may be capable under certain conditions of creating great civilizations. In a torrid climate and under a burning sun witness the marvellous achievements of the Mediterranean race in Mesopotamia, Egypt, North Africa, Cambodia, and India between 4000 B.C. and 1250 A.D. Or, coming nearer home to the cool mountain regions, witness the great achievements of the Alpine race in engineering, in mathematics, and in astronomy.

It follows that racial superiority and inferiority are partly matters of the intellectual and spiritual evolution which guides one race after another into periods of great ascent too often followed by sad and catastrophic decline. In this as in all other interminglings of science and sentiment, let us not extenuate nor write in malice, but always in broad-mindedness and a truly generous spirit.

It is with the greatest pleasure that I have written a few words endorsing this book as the first racial history of America, or, in fact, of any nation. I stand with the author not only in nailing his colors to the mast but in giving an entirely indisputable historic, patriotic, and governmental basis to the fact that in its origin and evolution our country is fundamentally Nordic.

HENRY FAIRFIELD OSBORN.

August, 1933.

ACKNOWLEDGMENTS

First and foremost, the author desires to express his appreciation of the assistance of his research associate, Doctor Paul Popenoe, who collected authorities and statistics during an intensive study lasting over four years.

He also desires to express his appreciation for the sympathy and aid of Professor Henry Fairfield Osborn, and of Charles Stewart Davison, Esq. The latter carefully revised the text and made many valuable suggestions.

The author owes a special debt of gratitude to Doctor Clarence G. Campbell for much assistance and to Doctor Harry H. Laughlin for many of the statistics and analyses used in this book. His thanks are due also to Captain John B. Trevor, whose masterly study of the early population has been a great help, as have the studies of Messrs. Howard F. Barker and Marcus L. Hansen. He also wishes to acknowledge the assistance of Mr. A. E. Hamilton.

Colonel William Wood, of Quebec, has been of great assistance in the data given regarding the origin of the French "Habitants" in Canada.

The writer is also obligated to Professor E. Prokosch, of Yale University, for his assistance on several critical points.

ACKNOWLEDGMENTS

The American Geographical Society and Mr. Ray R. Platt were instrumental in providing the maps used in this volume and the author takes this opportunity to express his thanks to them both.

CONTENTS

		PAGE
INTRODUCTION, BY PROF. HENRY FAIRFIELD OSBORN		vii

CHAPTER
I.	FOREWORD	1
II.	THE CRADLE OF MANKIND	17
III.	THE NORDIC CONQUEST OF EUROPE	39
IV.	THE NORDIC SETTLEMENT OF AMERICA	65
V.	THE PURITANS IN NEW ENGLAND	81
VI.	THE GATEWAYS TO THE WEST FROM NEW ENGLAND AND VIRGINIA	102
VII.	VIRGINIA AND HER NEIGHBORS	130
VIII.	THE OLD NORTHWEST TERRITORY	158
IX.	THE MOUNTAINEERS CONQUER THE SOUTHWEST	183
X.	FROM THE MISSISSIPPI TO THE OREGON	195
XI.	THE SPOILS OF THE MEXICAN WAR	208
XII.	THE ALIEN INVASION	223
XIII.	THE TRANSFORMATION OF AMERICA	235
XIV.	CHECKING THE ALIEN INVASION	268
XV.	THE LEGACY OF SLAVERY	281
XVI.	OUR NEIGHBORS ON THE NORTH	296
XVII.	OUR NEIGHBORS ON THE SOUTH	320
XVIII.	THE NORDIC OUTLOOK	347
	BIBLIOGRAPHY	359
	INDEX	379

MAPS

	FACING PAGE
Ireland	68
Highlands and Lowlands of Scotland	82
Ulster Scot and New England Origins	84
Puritan Emigration from England, 1620–1640	86
Territorial Growth of the United States	122
The Thirteen Colonies	144
Roman Catholics, 1930	160
Congregational Churches	218
Negro Population, 1930	282
Negro Population: Increase and Decrease, 1920–1930	286
Dominion of Canada and Newfoundland	300
Mexico, Central America, and the West Indies	324
Distribution of Mexicans by States	328
South America	334

THE CONQUEST OF
A CONTINENT

I

FOREWORD

AMERICAN public sentiment regarding the admission of aliens has undergone recently a profound change. At the end of the nineteenth century a fatuous humanitarianism prevailed and immigrants of all kinds were welcomed to "The Refuge of the Oppressed," regardless of whether they were needed in our industrial development or whether they tended to debase our racial unity.

The "Myth of the Melting Pot" was, at that time, deemed by the unthinking to be a part of our national creed.

This general attitude was availed of and encouraged by the steamship companies, which felt the need of the supply of live freight. The leading industrialists and railroad builders were equally opposed to any check on the free entry of cheap labor. Restrictionists were active, but in number they were relatively few, until the World War aroused the public to the danger of mass migration from the countries of devastated and impoverished Europe.

As a result of the problems raised by the World War, a stringent immigration law was passed in 1924 and is now in force. This law[1] has for its basic

---

[1] This bill was framed and passed through the efforts of Honorable Albert Johnson of Washington. "A new Declaration of Independence," it has been happily called.

principle a provision that the total number of persons allowed to enter the United States from countries to which quotas have been assigned shall be so apportioned as to constitute a cross section of the then existent white population of the United States. This is the so-called National Origins provision.

A controversy immediately arose over this new basis, as it was to the interest of every national and religious group of aliens now here to exaggerate the importance and size of its contribution to the population of our country, especially in Colonial times. This was particularly true of immigrants from those nations, such as Germany and Ireland, the quotas of which were greatly reduced under the new law. The purpose of this opposition was to warp public opinion in regard to the merits of various national groups and to exaggerate the non-Anglo-Saxon elements in the old Colonial population.

This book is an effort to make an estimate of the various elements, national and racial, existing in the present population of the United States and to trace their arrival and subsequent spread.

In the days of our fathers the white population of the United States was practically homogeneous. Racially it was preponderantly English and Nordic. At the end of the Colonial period we had a population about 90 per cent Nordic and over 80 per cent British in origin. In spite of the intrusion of two foreign elements of importance, both nevertheless chiefly Nordic, our population and our institutions remained overwhelmingly Anglo-Saxon down to the time of

FOREWORD 3

the Civil War. Since that time there has been an ever-increasing tendency to change the nature of this once "American" people into a mosaic of national, racial, and religious groups. The question to what extent this transformation has gone deserves careful study.

The draft lists for the American army in the large cities during the World War showed an amazing collection of foreign names. These lists are most dramatic indications of the substantial modifications of the original Anglo-Saxon character of the population which have occurred. A vivid illustration is found in a war poster issued by an enthusiastic clerk of foreign extraction in the Treasury Department during one of the appeals for Liberty Loans. A Howard Chandler Christy girl of pure Nordic type was shown pointing with pride to a list of names, saying "Americans All." The list was:

DuBois	Pappandrikopulous	Turovich
Smith	Andrassi	Kowalski
O'Brien	Villotto	Chriczanevicz
Ceika	Levy	Knutson
Haucke		Gonzales

Apparently the one native American, so far as he figures at all, is hidden under the sobriquet of Smith, and there is possibly the implied suggestion that the beautiful lady was herself the product of this remarkable mélange.

Similar foreign names are beginning to appear and sometimes predominate in the list of college graduates, successful athletes, and minor politicians. In the words of the late President Theodore Roosevelt, we are becoming a polyglot boarding house.

The modification of the religious complexion of the nation also is very striking. In Colonial times Americans were almost unanimously Protestants. Now the claim is made that one in seven is a Catholic and one in thirty a Jew. To what extent this change is due to immigration and to what extent to the differential birth rate should be carefully considered.

In dealing with racial admixture, we should be certain that we are not considering merely nationality, religion, or language. In popular thought there is such a racial entity as the German, the Russian, the Frenchman, or the Italian. These, however, are not racial, but national terms. In a few cases of still unmixed peoples, like those of Sweden and Norway, nationality, language, religion, and race coincide. But in Germany, for instance, the Germans along the North Sea and the Baltic coasts are Protestant Nordics, while those of Bavaria, of Austria, and of other parts of the south are Catholic Alpines. Italy north of the Apennines is largely Alpine, slightly mixed with Nordic, while Naples and Sicily in the South are purely Mediterranean by race. In France, where there is a mixed Nordic, Mediterranean, and Alpine population, a single language and an ancient tradition have created an intense unity of national feeling, and in recent decades there has been a marked transfer of political control from the Nor-

FOREWORD

dic to the Alpine element, as evidenced by the names and features of the present political leaders. In Belgium there are two languages, in Switzerland four, to say nothing of the medley of languages in the old Austrian Empire. Only in Switzerland is there national unity, in spite of a diversity of tongue.

In America the events of the last hundred years, especially the vast tide of immigration, have greatly impaired our purity of race and our unity of religion and even threatened our inheritance of English speech. If our English language is saved it will be due in no small degree to the growing world power of the language itself and of its literature, as well as to the world-wide ocean commerce of Great Britain and her overseas empire.

In the United States today this unity of language is vigorously opposed by the foreign-language press. In all probability, however, this foreign press is doomed to die out as the older generation of immigrants passes from the scene. The fact that this non-English press represents a score or more of different languages makes it impossible for it in the long run to oppose successfully the English language.

In Canada the fact that the French language is officially recognized in Quebec and, for that matter, in the Parliament at Ottawa, makes the problem there more difficult. It may be here noted that the French language as spoken in Quebec is sneered at and ridiculed by the European French. The use of French speech in Quebec, like the attempted use of Erse in Ireland and Czechish in Bohemia, is merely serving to keep those speaking such language out of touch with modern literature and culture.

The absurdity of attempting to revive an obsolete language such as Erse is shown by its lack of literature of modern type. Sir Harry H. Johnston once said to the author that Erse was a perfectly good language, except for two facts—first, that nobody could pronounce it and, second, that nobody could spell it.

In Louisiana French is still spoken by the Creoles of New Orleans and by the French and Negro mixture called "Cajans." This linguistic diversity will in due course of time also disappear. More serious is the retention and use in New Mexico of the Spanish language by its Mexican-Indian population. Few people know that New Mexico is officially bilingual. Sooner or later this must be stopped, as it has greatly hindered the development of the State.

As to race, as distinct from language, religion, and nationality, we must consider our country today as being in large part a heterogeneous mixture of racial groups and individuals. Since America's first duty is to herself and to the people already here, she must weigh the effect upon the present, as well as upon the future, of such racial admixture as has already occurred and which promises to spread indefinitely.

A striking example of this was shown during the Washington Bicentennial in 1932, when some historians, in their efforts to placate the assertive groups of aliens in our midst, endeavored to show the existence in the colonies of substantial groups of these same aliens. For instance, they claimed that most of the Revolutionary personages of Irish descent were the same as the South Irish Catholics of today. That is wholly error. The so-called "Irish" of the Revolution were Ulster Scots either from the Lowlands of Scotland or from North England, who came to the colonies by way of the North of Ireland after having lived there for two or three generations. These Ulster Scots were reinforced by Protestant English who emigrated from Leinster and both were widely removed, religiously and culturally, from the South Irish Catholics, who did not come to this country in any numbers until the potato famine in Ireland in the 1840's drove them across the seas.

To take an example: In the Convention of 1787, which formulated the Constitution, certain individuals were put down as "Irish." These were Protestant Ulster Scots. In the Senate of today, a few of the senators are put down as "Irish." These are South Irish Catholics. To use the same term for these two different types of population is erroneous. They were widely separated religiously, racially, and culturally. The same thing is true of that part of our population which was referred to as "French." The French of the American Revolution and of our Constitutional Convention were Huguenot French, who, though few in numbers, took a prominent part in public affairs at the time of the Revolution. They were, for the most part, Nordic and were English-speaking. They were a distinguished group which had nothing whatever in common with the "Habitant" French of

Quebec, who are Catholic Alpines. To call them both "French" is erroneous. A similar, but less marked distinction, exists between the North Germans and the Palatines, and they both differ from the South Germans in America, who are mostly Catholic Alpines.

In this connection it should bé clearly understood that in discussing the various European races we are concerned only with such individuals of those races as came to America, and not with the populations which remained in the original homeland.

In Colonial times the Anglo-Saxon American avoided the danger arising from intermarriage with natives, which ruined the Spanish and Portuguese colonies in the New World and threatened the destruction of the French colonies in Quebec. There was some crossbreeding between Englishmen and Indian squaws along the frontier, but the offspring was everywhere regarded as an Indian, just as a mulatto in the English colonies was regarded as belonging to the Negro race. This racial prejudice kept the white race in America pure, while its absence and the scarcity of white women ultimately destroyed European supremacy in the Spanish and Portuguese colonies.

At the time of the settlement of the Spanish and Portuguese colonies, the Roman Church was dominant. Its chief motive was to save souls for heaven rather than to perpetuate the control of Europeans. That church, therefore, favored marriage of the Europeans, Spaniard and Portuguese, with the native women and considered the children to be white.

The same was true of the mixtures of French and Indians in Quebec, and the church recognized the resulting half-breed offspring as French and not native.

This policy of the church was aided by the lack of race dignity which is even today found sometimes among the French, the Spaniards, and the Portuguese. For example, in the South of Portugal there was a large Negro slave element introduced in the sixteenth century which is now absorbed into the surrounding population. Similar conditions exist in South Italy, where there is a substantial Negroid element, probably descended from the Negro slaves introduced by the Romans from Africa some two thousand years ago.

One of the unfortunate results of racial mixture, or miscegenation between diverse races, is disharmony in the offspring, and the more widely separated the parent stocks, the greater is this lack of harmony likely to be in both mental and physical characters. Herbert Spencer, in response to a request for advice, writing in 1892 to the Japanese statesman, Baron Keneko Kentaro, stated this biological fact very clearly when he said:

"To your remaining question respecting the intermarriage of foreigners and Japanese, which you say is 'now very much agitated among our scholars and politicians' and which you say is 'one of the most difficult problems,' my reply is that, as rationally answered, there is no difficulty at all. It should be positively forbidden. It is not at root a question of social philosophy. It is at root a question of biology.

There is abundant proof, alike furnished by the intermarriages of human races and by the interbreeding of animals, that when the varieties mingled diverge beyond a certain slight degree the *result is inevitably a bad one in the long run.* . . . When, say of the different varieties of sheep, there is an interbreeding of those which are widely unlike, the result, especially in the second generation, is a bad one—there arises an incalculable mixture of traits, and what may be called a chaotic constitution. And the same thing happens among human beings—the Eurasians in India, the half-breeds in America, show this. The physiological basis of this experience appears to be that any one variety of creature in course of many generations acquires a certain constitutional adaptation to its particular form of life, and every other variety similarly acquires its own special adaptation. The consequence is that, if you mix the constitution of two widely divergent varieties which have severally become adapted to widely divergent modes of life, you get a constitution which is adapted to the mode of life of neither —a constitution which will not work properly, because it is not fitted for any set of conditions whatever. By all means, therefore, peremptorily interdict marriages of Japanese with foreigners."

The relative diminution of Anglo-Saxon blood in America and the present check to the expansion of the British Empire are due partly to a curious sentimental quality of the Anglo-Saxon mind, the effect of which is almost suicidal.

It is a striking fact that tragic and even fatal consequences may arise from the noblest motives. The abolition of the obsolete institution of slavery occupied the minds of some of the best men of the nineteenth century and serfdom was only stamped out finally at immense cost to the finest elements of our Anglo-Saxon stock. Looking back over these events at a distance of a half-century there appear many considerations which were neglected by those who were too close to the conflict to see into the future. Let us consider the consequences in the world at large of the abolition of slavery and of the breaking down of the barrier maintained by that institution between the Whites and the Blacks.

For instance, in the British Empire, the abolition of slavery a hundred years ago contributed in large part to the decline and finally to the almost complete disappearance of pure Nordic blood in the West Indies, where previously there had been rich and flourishing colonies of white men employing black slaves.

In South Africa the revolt and outtrekking of Boers beyond the Vaal River were due largely to the abolition of slavery and to the sentimental treatment of the slaves by the Home Government. The passions engendered at that time ultimately led to two bloody and useless wars between the Nordic peoples of South Africa.

Other European nations suffered similarly from the abolition of slavery in their American colonies. Undiluted white blood has almost disappeared in Jamaica and Puerto Rico, while the natives of the Virgin Islands are nearly all Negroes and Mulattoes.

The most tragic result of the loss of White control

of the Blacks was shown in the history of Haiti and Santo Domingo. The freeing of the slaves and the disturbances resulting from the French Revolution had as a consequence the massacre or exile of practically every white person in the island. The French doctrinaires were responsible to some extent for this. Even Lafayette was President of the "Société des Amis des Noirs." Today the black inhabitants of this great island have reverted almost to barbarism.

The islands and coasts of the entire Caribbean Sea with much of the coasts of the Gulf of Mexico are fast becoming Negro Land and apparently in the near future the European element will be more and more in a hopeless minority.

In the United States we have a startling example of the effect of sentimentalism upon Nordic survival. The North was entirely right in endeavoring to keep slavery out of Kansas and the new States of the West, to that extent avoiding the color problem there. The sentimental interference with slavery, however, on the part of the Northern Abolitionists helped to precipitate the bloody Civil War and to destroy a very large portion of the best stock of the nation, especially in the South. The Southerners also were greatly to blame for their utter folly in seceding as a means of maintaining their peculiar institution, as they termed it.

If the question of slavery had been left alone, the issue of the preservation of the Union would have been postponed for at least a generation. In time the overwhelming numbers and wealth of the North would have made any serious question of secession an absurdity. As a consequence of the Civil War hundreds of thousands of men of Nordic stock were cut off in the full vigor of manhood, who otherwise would have lived to propagate their kind and populate the West. Besides this, slavery as an institution was outside of the pale of civilization long before the Civil War and it would have been peacefully abolished in a few decades through economic causes.

The Blacks themselves were raised by slavery from sheer savagery to a feeble imitation of white civilization, and they made more advance in America in two centuries than in as many thousand years in Africa. The presence of slaves, however, was injurious to the Whites. Serfdom has been a curse wherever it has flourished in the New World and it has had a profoundly demoralizing effect on the masters.

American democracy at the start rested on a base of population that was, as already said, homogeneous in race, religion, tradition, and language, and in a relative equality of wealth. All these features are things of the past and democracy has virtually broken down in spite of the fatuous ecstasy which characterizes the utterances of sentimentalists, who even claimed that the World War was fought "to make the World Safe for Democracy."

It seems strange that this so-called liberal point of view is so short-sighted that we have in our midst today organizations and groups who, with the best intentions, are encouraging the Negro within and the black, brown, and yellow men without, to dispute the dominance over the world at large of Christian Europeans and Americans. Throughout the world, there has gone forth a challenge to white supremacy and this movement in Asia, Africa, and elsewhere has been fostered by the Christian missionaries. It has even gone so far that it is openly stated that any assertion of race supremacy, or even discussion of race distinctions in this country, should be suppressed in the interests of the spread of Christianity in foreign countries—notably Japan. In the long run, however, these doctrines will work great injury to the Protestant churches if they persist in taking an anti-national point of view. While many of the individual ministers are well-meaning and kindly, their education is undeveloped in world affairs and their advice in such matters, on which they are uninstructed, is often very dangerous.

Sentimental sympathy for other races of mankind is manifest today all over the world, but especially among Anglo-Saxons. It received a great impetus from President Wilson's doctrine of the right of Self Determination. The fruits of this doctrine can be seen in the rise of so-called nationalism everywhere, as in Ireland, Bohemia, Poland, Egypt, the Philippines, China, and India.

The racially suicidal result of all this is the undermining of the control of the Nordic races over the natives. The upper classes and, in many cases, the peasantry in eastern Germany, for example, are Nordics. One of the tragic consequences of the

World War was the taking of political power in this region from the Nordics and transferring it, under the guise of democratic institutions, to Alpine Slavs. In Soviet Russia, also, through the massacre and exile of the Nordic upper classes, political power has passed into the hands of Alpines, exactly as in France during the Revolution the Alpine lower classes destroyed the Nordic nobility and assumed control of the state. The Revolutionary and Napoleonic Wars which followed killed off an undue proportion of Nordics in France and are said to have greatly shortened the stature of the French soldiers.

The revolt against European control, especially in the Orient, is becoming more and more pronounced. As said above it has been encouraged unintentionally by the missionaries, who, in educating the natives, succeed only in arousing them to assert their equality with the European races. Probably the greatest tragedy in the world today is the corrosive jealousy of the fair skin of the white races felt by those whose skin is black, yellow, or brown. The world will hear more of this as the revolt of the lower races spreads.

One of the manifestations of this jealousy of the fair skin of the Nordics is shown in those numerous cases where members of the colored races, or even dark-skinned members of the Nordic race regard the possession of a blonde woman as an assertion and proof of race equality. This has been true historically since the earliest times. It is more than ever in evidence at the present day.

All the foregoing points to the value of a critical consideration of the racial composition of the original thirteen colonies and an analysis of the situation as it is today.

II

THE CRADLE OF MANKIND

MAN is an immensely ancient animal. Over a million years have elapsed since he first made fire and more millions since he became a bipedal prehuman. He left the forests, at the latest, at the end of the Miocene, not less than seven million years ago and ventured out into the plains of Central Asia as a savage, powerful, clever biped, hunting in packs, or by sheer wit securing his prey single handed by pitfalls and other devices, the invention of which marks the development of growing intelligence.

Man's initial differentiation from his simian ancestry probably began when he came down from the trees and began to walk erect. The hand was then liberated from its use as an instrument of locomotion and was devoted primarily to defense, attack, discovery, and invention. It is by means of the opportunities afforded by the hand that the human brain has evolved into man's most important factor in racial survival.

Clear evidence of man's remote arboreal ancestry is offered by his stereoscopic or double-eyed vision. The great majority of ground animals, especially those living in the forest, have eyes on the sides of their heads; but in man's arboreal ancestors, by the recession of the intervening nasal and facial bones, the eyes were brought around to the front of the face. The resulting stereoptic vision enabled him to judge distance far more accurately than most mammals. Such power of determining distance is of course vital to an arboreal animal. Failure to judge accurately the length of a leap from branch to branch would be fatal.

One often hears it stated that man has lost his sense of smell; but this sense was probably never better developed within the human period than it is now. In the trees a sense of smell is not of much value. The monkey can sit on a branch and jabber with impunity at the leopard on the ground below. To forest animals, like the deer or boar, however, the sense of smell is the surest protection against attack and is much more highly developed than the sense of sight, which latter is often quite feeble. In fact, in the thick jungle it is almost useless (and at "black night" completely so).

Eurasia, where it is probable that mankind originated, was the greatest land mass on the globe in Tertiary times. Modern Europe and North Africa formed relatively small peninsulas in the extreme west of this Tertiary land mass. It is probably from Eurasia that man spread out to the uttermost parts of the habitable globe, carrying with him his language and such cultural features as had developed at the time of each successive migration. No race or language or cultural invention seems to have entered Eurasia

THE CRADLE OF MANKIND 19

from adjoining land areas. All went out. None came in. While the original center of dispersal of the Hominidæ or human family was probably Eurasia, it was at a later date also the center of the evolution of the higher types of man.

To the northeast of Eurasia lay the ancient land connection with North America via Alaska, over which various species of animals passed back and forth, some of them having their origin in Asia and others in western North America. It was undoubtedly over this land connection that man first entered America at a relatively recent period and probably he came in successive waves. The American Indians appear to have been derived from the Mongoloid tribes of northeastern Asia before the latter had developed some of those extreme specializations which characterize the typical Mongols of Central Asia and China proper today. Judging from the culture which these American Indians brought with them, this migration began before 10,000 B.C.

The existing races of mankind, and those either entirely extinct or now absorbed in other races, had their distinctive areas of differentiation and periods of radiation from Eurasia over the habitable globe. The most primitive types are now found farthest from this original centre of distribution in countries where through isolation they escaped competition with the higher types which evolved later.

The weight of evidence appears to show that Africa, or Ethiopia, lying far to the southwest of Eurasia, was peopled in earliest times, by way of Arabia, by a most primitive negroid type of mankind. While north of the Sahara migrations from Asia have continued until recent times, the south was left for a vast period in possession of the Negro. Even today, aside from the recent infiltration of Whites and Browns, Africa south of the Sahara belongs to three negroid groups; the Negroes proper, the Pigmies or Negrillos, and the Bushmen and Hottentots. These three human types are characterized by very dark or yellow skin, tightly curled hair, very scanty body hair, flaring nostrils, flattened noses and an absence of supraorbital ridges.

Again, Australia, Tasmania, and some of the adjoining islands are, or recently were, inhabited by what used to be considered one of the great divisions of mankind, the Australoids. These people have the black skin and certain features of the Negro; but differ from him in the possession of abundant body hair and of marked supraorbital ridges. Also the Australoid head hair is wavy, and not closely curled, a most important characteristic. The profound cleavage between the Negroes and the Australoids is now questioned in some quarters.

The differentiation of the human species into types so distinctly contrasted as Whites and Blacks and the problems of the evolution of higher types of man from original stocks bring us to a new classification of the genus Homo. Some anthropologists still maintain that all human beings are included in the species *Homo sapiens;* but this is an old-fashioned grouping. Sooner or later a new system must be

THE CRADLE OF MANKIND 21

formulated based on the same fundamental rules that are applied to the classification of other mammals. For instance, the physical differences between the Nordics and the Negroes, the Australoids and the Mongols, if found among the lower mammals, would be much more than sufficient to constitute not only separate species, but even subgenera, and they are now so regarded by some anthropologists.

Race is hard to define. It consists in the presence of a collection of hereditary characters common to the great majority of individuals in a given group. It lies in the preponderance of such characters as color of skin, hair, and eyes, facial and nasal contour, shape of skull, and even mental characteristics, which are more difficult to classify, but which are distinctly typical of specific human groups. Many individuals possess all the hereditary characters of a given race. But man is so ancient a being and intermixture has been so widespread that nearly every race shows signs of blending with others. This is especially true in Europe, where the intermingling of peoples has been extensive during the past twenty centuries.

Just as the classification of man according to race needs revision in the light of recent discoveries, so the definition of race must be understood anew in the light of genetics. Thirty years ago we talked glibly about the Aryan or Indo-European race, or the Caucasian or Germanic race. All these terms must be discarded. Aryan, Indo-European, and Germanic are only linguistic terms and Caucasian has no meaning except as used in America to distinguish between whites and colored.

Language or culture may spread quickly and widely among the peoples of the earth irrespective of race. For example, the bow and arrow may have originated with some specific race of mankind, yet we find this invention in use all over the globe and in the hands of the most diverse peoples. The use of firearms and of horses by the American Indians indicates nothing more than their contact with the Whites. It is unsafe to attribute the inception of any cultural feature to a given race.

Civilization itself, that is, agriculture and the domestication of animals, probably arose in West Central Asia, spreading east, south, southwest, and west. Although the earliest remains of the dog, the first animal tamed, are found in the Maglemose in Denmark approximately 8000 B.C., it may have been domesticated far earlier in Asia.

There were two centers of the development of civilization—two foci. The first was in southwestern Eurasia: the Valley of the Syr-Daria; Mesopotamia and its city states; Chaldea, Babylonia, Assyria; then Egypt, Crete, Greece, Rome, and modern Europe. There is the possibility, or even the probability, of finding in the unexplored portions of southern Arabia, connecting links of early culture between the Valley of the Euphrates and the Valley of the Nile. Recent discoveries indicate a very early civilization in the Valley of the Indus, which apparently had been brought down from the north. All

THE CRADLE OF MANKIND 23

these regions formed a single group and were the first center.

The second focus was an independent, but similar and parallel expansion of civilization in southeastern Asia, now China. There was apparently little intercourse until modern times between the Far East and the Far West of Eurasia, except by caravan routes across Central Asia. The Romans knew the silk of China and there was a certain amount of trade in jewels, precious metals, and spices down through the Middle Ages, but the extraordinary fact that these two cultures developed independently with slight mutual influence of the one on the other is little appreciated. Both cultures seem, as said, to have had their origin in West Central Asia and to have radiated southwest, south, and east.

One of the periodic cycles of drought desiccated the central area, and separated the Western and Eastern worlds by an almost impassable series of deserts, like the Gobi Desert of Mongolia. In the west, even as late as the time of Alexander the Great, Bactria and Sogdiana, northwest of India, were populous and flourishing states. Here it is that future exploration may uncover the first beginnings of agriculture and the domestication of animals—perhaps, also, the first written language.

Language, like culture, is not identical or co-extensive with race to any great degree. Witness the neighboring islands in the West Indies where Negroes speak Spanish in one, French in another, and English in a third. The language of a given group at a given time, however, being possibly a much more recent acquirement than its cultural inventions, does show either that it was originated by those who speak it or that it was imposed upon them by another race long in contact with them.

Since we are to deal principally with the racial groups of Europe, namely the Nordic, Mediterranean, and Alpine, we might glance for a moment in more detail at this distinction between race and language. The Mediterraneans of Arabia speak a Semitic language, while the Berbers of North Africa, also a people of Mediterranean stock, speak a Hamitic language. This same Hamitic tongue was probably spoken all around the coast of the inland sea and up the west coast of Europe to the British Islands before Aryan speech was brought there by Nordic invaders from the north and east. Meanwhile the Alpines spoke languages related to Turki, a Ural-Altaic language—of course, non-Aryan—as they still do in Turkestan, Hungary, and Finland.

As to the Nordics, it would appear that this race originated the so-called Aryan or Indo-European group of languages. The Aryan tongue was probably developed in South Russia before the long isolation from Asia had been broken. At a period in the third millennium B.C. the Aryan language split into two groups: one, the Western or Centum group, which pushed west and north; the other, the Eastern or Satem group which pushed south and east. The Centum group included the Greek, Latin, Celtic, and Germanic languages. Curiously enough, an out-

THE CRADLE OF MANKIND 25

lying member of this group, the Tokarian, was spoken in Turkestan as late as the seventh century A.D. The Satem group, sometimes called Iranian, included the Lithuanian, all the Slavic languages and those of ancient and modern Persia and the various forms of Sanscrit spoken in India and Burma.

Light-skinned invaders from the northwest appear to have entered India in successive waves and to have introduced the Aryan language known as Sanscrit. They were probably the Sacae or Scythians from South Russia. These Nordics in India can properly be called "Aryans." As used otherwise, however, the term Aryan is purely linguistic. Originally all the tribes who spoke the languages of the Centum and Satem groups were members of the Nordic race.

According to recent discoveries in the Valley of the Indus, a very elaborate civilization flourished at least five thousand years ago at Mohenjo-Daro, four hundred miles north of the mouth of the river. This civilization was as elaborate as the corresponding culture of Mesopotamia or of Egypt. The racial characters found in the bodies in the burials indicate that the mass of the population was then, as now, of Mediterranean race, but that the ruling class was long-headed and long-faced, and of a tall stature and sturdy build—a type clearly Nordic. In the earliest graves of Ur, in Mesopotamia, the skulls are very clearly of a race akin to those on the Indus. All this would tend to throw back the date of the invasion of men from the north by another thousand years or more. The same appears to be true of the invasions into Greece of the Achæans and of the Osco-Umbrians into Italy.

The wide distribution of the Satem or Iranian group to the south and west of Asia shows that the Nordics in great numbers conquered the aboriginal inhabitants of these countries and imposed on them the Aryan speech. They invented the caste system to maintain the purity of their blood. In fact, the Hindu word "varna" means both color and caste. In spite of all their efforts, however, the conquering invaders died out almost completely in India and Persia—leaving behind them only their language, and, in some cases, their religion.

With this brief review of the essential difference between race and language or culture, we may return to a consideration of humanity in terms of essentially racial characters.

The world as a whole can be roughly mapped racially according to the most obvious human differentiation—namely, color: white, yellow, red, black, and brown. The white race at the present day dominates Europe, northern Asia in part, Australia, and North America as far south as Mexico, with outposts scattered all over the globe. Eastern Asia is yellow. Southern Asia and northern Africa are brown. Africa south of the Sahara Desert is black, and there is a black tinge across southern Asia, as we shall see. The red men, or Amerinds, with but a small remnant in the United States and Canada, inhabit Latin America, where in some cases their blood is mixed

THE CRADLE OF MANKIND

with that of the descendants of Negro slaves, and, of course, to a still larger extent with that of South Europeans.

Color, however, is not the only character upon which a racial map of the world could be based. Perhaps a more satisfactory division could be made according to the cross section of human hair. However, in dealing with the racial groupings of Eurasia, we find different types of humanity arranged in definite zones according to certain outstanding physical characters.

Farthest south on the great land area of Eurasia lies a belt of Negroids, extending from Ethiopia with intervals through Arabia to the South Seas. The principal racial characteristics of these people are very dark or black skin, dark eyes, tightly curled black hair, and long, *i.e.*, dolichocephalic skulls. In southern Persia the population shows a Negro admixture, and a distinctly Negroid type is numerous among the Pre-Dravidians of India. The Hindus themselves are very dark brown with wavy black hair.

A few decades ago there was much talk of the English officer and the Hindu in the ranks being of the same Aryan blood, because they both spoke widely diverse forms of the great group of Aryan languages. This, of course, did not imply the slightest trace of blood relationship—the Aryan speech of the Hindu had been imposed upon him by his conquerors from the north. Such fallacies were common a generation ago.

To the eastward we find remnants of Negro types in the Malay Peninsula and in the large islands to the east as far as the Philippines. This Negroid type extends also eastward through Melanesia. From this discontinuous distribution it would appear that the Negroes and Negritos were the original population of southern Eurasia. It is probable that from this region the true Negroes migrated westward into Ethiopia.

At a date far earlier than this hypothetical migration westward, an earlier type of Negroid pushed southeast to Tasmania, which was thereafter cut off from the land mass of Australia. In Australia itself these Tasmanians were absorbed or exterminated by the later coming Australoids from whom they differed materially.

The racial tangle in Australia, Papua, and the islands of Melanesia presents great difficulties in classification, but the basic element appears to be Negro with a large admixture of later Mongoloids coming from Asia.

The next zone of human population, superimposed in many cases upon the Negroids, but south of the great central mountain ranges of Eurasia, is constituted by the Mediterranean race. This race is characterized by black, wavy hair, very dark eyes, oval face with fairly regular features, dark olive skin, relatively short stature, and a somewhat slight skeletal and muscular structure. This last character is in sharp contrast with the powerful and sturdy build of the next two races to be considered, the Alpine

THE CRADLE OF MANKIND

and the Nordic. The principal character of the Mediterranean race, however, is its long (dolichocephalic) skull. The Negroes, as we have said, have long skulls, but of quite a different type.

The range of the Mediterraneans extends from the western part of the British Isles, through Spain and along both coasts of the Mediterranean Sea, down the east coast of Africa to Somaliland. In Asia it embraces the Arabs, South Persians, most of the Hindus, with an eastward extension. In Northeast Africa and India it is strongly mixed with Negro.

Spreading everywhere throughout Europe north of the territory dominated by the Mediterranean race, and often mixed with it, we find the Alpines. This race is characterized by a somewhat short, stocky build much sturdier than the Mediterranean, abundant dark, but not straight, head and body hair, dark eyes and round (brachycephalic) skull.

The center of origin of the Alpines was somewhere in Central Asia west of the true Mongols, north of the Mediterraneans, and east of the Nordics—possibly in Turkestan. The Alpines and Mongols are both characterized by a round skull but, as in the case of the long-skulled Mediterraneans and the long-skulled Negroes, the type of skull differs appreciably.

The Mongols and Alpines have been in close contact for ages. The Mongols have issued again and again from East and Central Asia and submerged the Alpines, driving them westward into Central Europe. There has been a great deal of intermixture and the

Slavic Alpine population of eastern Europe frequently shows distinctive Mongol traits. However, the two races, while perhaps remotely connected, differ widely. The Alpines, like the Australoids and to a less extent like the Nordics, have abundant body hair and copious beard, while the Mongols (like their derivatives, the American Indians) are beardless and without body hair. Alpine hair is wavy, that of the Mongols and Mongoloids straight. Alpine features are rather coarse, often with a large prominent nose, while true Mongols have an exceedingly flat face, depressed nose, and a broad space between the eyes. This depressed nose, in adult Mongols, is the retention of an infantile character, as babies of all races are born with bridgeless noses. As to stature, most Alpines are of moderate height, although those from the Tyrol to Albania, the so-called Dinaric race, are decidedly tall.

It was a branch of tall Mongols, with a slight admixture of Alpines, that crossed into America from Asia and became the ancestors of the American Indians, who are of substantial height, often with prominent, almost hawklike noses and high cheek bones.

We might mention here the Malays, who are essentially Mongols and who pushed down into Indo-China and throughout the Malay Peninsula. There are many traces of their blood in Polynesia. This expansion was relatively recent and in those localities there are everywhere indications of earlier races, especially of the very ancient Negroid types known as

THE CRADLE OF MANKIND 31

Negritos. These Malays extended through the Philippines as far north as Japan, where they met and mingled with a stream of northern Mongoloid immigrants from Korea.

The Alpine domain at the present time extends from the center of France eastward in an ever widening wedge as far as the Himalayas. It includes the bulk of the population of Central France, North Italy, South Germany, Switzerland, the provinces of the recent Austrian Empire, and extends through the Balkan states, Russia, Asia Minor, and far into Asia. This race penetrated into and overran Central Europe during relatively recent times, probably at about the beginning of the Bronze Age, approximately 1800 B.C.

East and north of the Carpathians, about 400 A.D., the Alpines had a period of great expansion, chiefly at the expense of the Nordic race, whose distribution we shall discuss presently.

As the Nordic tribes moved into the Roman provinces, the lands they vacated were occupied by Alpine Slavs. All these movements may have been caused by the pressure from the east of Asiatic Mongols, who, like the Huns, were beginning their drive toward Europe. Our word slave coming from Slav reveals the social relation of these Alpines to West Europeans.

The westernmost of the Alpine Slavs were called Wends. In Charlemagne's time they occupied what is now Germany as far west as the Elbe. In its easternmost range these Alpines were called Turanians and were confused with the Mongols of Central Asia, who had again and again conquered them. The remnant of Wends in East Germany, the Bohemians, most Poles and South Slavs are all Alpines. The great mass of Russians are of this type, as well as the ancient Avars, Hunagars, Magyars, Cumans, and the Bulgars, all more or less mixed with Mongols. The Armenians are Alpines of an especially pronounced type and are probably descended from the ancient Hittites. The East European Alpines are saturated everywhere with Mongol blood, dating for the most part from their conquest by the Tatars during the thirteenth century.

The fact that Asia, north of the main mountain ranges, is pre-eminently the home of round skulls is very significant and suggests remote relationship between Alpine and Mongol.

The Alpine skull reaches a most extreme form among the Armenians, who have a very high skull, greatly flattened behind and somewhat like a sugar loaf in shape.

The division of the races of mankind based on long and round skulls is extremely ancient. We find both types among the fossil and semi-fossil skulls at the end of the Paleolithic.

The first definite appearance of round skulls mixed with long skulls is found in the burials at Offnet in Bavaria in the Azilian period at the very end of the Paleolithic, some twelve thousand years ago.

From that day to this in France, Bavaria, and elsewhere in western Europe as well as in eastern

THE CRADLE OF MANKIND 33

Europe the round skulls have expanded their range. This steady increase of round-skull Alpines everywhere in Central Europe in recent centuries is one of the most ominous racial facts that confront us.

The great French anthropologist, deLapouge, stated in a recent letter to the author that in France the cranial index has risen two points a century since the Middle Ages, so that France is no longer a Nordic land. This transformation is due, in the opinion of some observers, to a mixture of race in which round-headedness is dominant over long-headedness. In the opinion of the writer, however, it is due to the replacement of one race, the Nordic, by another, the Alpine. The Nordics not only incur disproportionate loss in war, but are also highly nomadic in habit, while the Alpines, on the other hand, stick close to the land and breed persistently.

Of the European races, there remains to be considered the Nordics, a people greatly specialized, who have developed a fair skin, light-colored eyes, tall stature of sturdy build, and long, *i.e.*, dolichocephalic skulls, and definite mental traits. The slow but long-continued physical development of the Nordics has culminated in a powerful skeleton and musculature in sharp contrast to that of the Mediterranean race, to which the Nordic is more closely related than to any other. In fact, the mixture of Nordic and Mediterranean in the British Islands may possibly be one of the few advantageous racial crossings.

As to the homeland of the original Nordic race, we have as yet only guesswork on the part of the anthropologist. When we shall know more about the condition of Central Eurasia during the glacial period and immediately thereafter, we may get nearer to an answer to the question of where and how this race originated and developed. It is certain, however, that the Nordics were originally located west of the Alpines and Mongols and north of the Mediterraneans.

We have fossil records of five or six extinct species or genera of man and more are constantly coming to light in Asia and outlying regions of the Old World. The impulse that forced the ancestors of man to develop his high energy and intelligence probably arose from the onset of the Pleistocene glaciation a million or more years ago. Mankind was then forced apart into widely separated areas where specific characters developed in isolation. The Nordics were most likely cut off from Asia by the Caspian and Aral Seas, which extended far to the north, where they met the oncoming ice. It was west of this barrier that the Nordic race developed its peculiar characters.

Later, when the ice retreated and this watery barrier disappeared, the Nordics were inundated again and again by floods of Asiatics, first Alpines and then Mongols. Sometimes the Nordics became the aggressors and expanded eastward in turn, conquering Persia, India, and Burma. Blond invaders of East Asia, called "the green-eyed devils," attacked the Great Wall of China as late as 200 B.C. They were also called "Wusuns," a Tatar word meaning "the tall ones." In the long run, however, the Nordics were forced westward.

When the retreating glaciers left habitable land in Scandinavia, it was into this region that the first westward migration of the Nordics found its way. This was probably as early as 8000 B.C. There it was, through the fogs and long winters of the north, that they developed in complete isolation their great stature and musculature, their fair or flaxen hair, and their blue eyes. The continental Nordics, however, who moved westward to settle around the Baltic and North Seas, retained the more generalized characters of brown hair of various shades, and eyes which tend to either brown, gray, or, to a less extent, blue. The light eyes of the Nordics include light brown or hazel, and may be of any and all shades of gray and green to the deepest violet blue.

The racial characters which most noticeably distinguish the Nordics are the colors of the skin, hair, and eyes. As sharply contrasted with the skin of the Mediterranean peoples, the color of the blood shows through the fair Nordic skin except when tanned by exposure to the sun. The light-colored hair is almost always blond in youth, turning darker with age, although in many individuals extreme blondness is retained through life. The brown hair, characteristic of the Nordics of the British Isles and America, runs from light to very dark brown; but blue-black hair, so rare in England and among native Americans, is never Nordic. The blond hair may tend towards golden red. In fact, in classic times, red hair seems to have been more common than now and may be more characteristic of the Celtic Nordics than of the Teutonic Nordics. In race mixtures between blond and black-haired peoples, the blondness tends to be lost.

On the other hand, light-colored eyes are much more persistent, and this sign of Nordic admixture is found about ten times more frequently than is blond hair among such peoples as the Albanians, where all other Nordic characters except stature seem to have been lost.

For thousands of years, Europe has been an arena of racial mixtures. Over great territories, as we shall see, the Nordic race has been dominant for the past thirty centuries, so that the majority of Alpine and Mediterranean types shows the impress of Nordic characters. For example, in Bavaria are found short, stocky, round-skulled Alpines with extremely blond hair and blue eyes. The French, who are to-day preponderantly Alpine, show outcroppings of profound Nordic characters throughout the population. Thus, while pure types exist everywhere in sufficient numbers to enable us to define race, nevertheless there has been so much intermixture in the past that it is hard sometimes to assign a given individual to a specific race. The definition of race, in fact, cannot be based on any one character, but on a preponderance of many racial characters which make up the resultant type.

We have now considered the main races of mankind, but should devote space to the Mongols

THE CRADLE OF MANKIND

and their derivatives. The Mongol is undoubtedly a very ancient and major subdivision of the Hominidæ, but appears to be intrusive in much of its present range. In Southeast Asia and in the Malay countries and islands it arrived later than the ancient Negroids.

The Mongoloids, as stated above, are characterized by a short, stocky build and generally a round skull, very straight black hair with a round cross section, a broad flat face with projecting malar bones, and a slanting eye often marked by the Mongol fold. The last characters distinguish them from the Alpine race, but are sometimes to be found in such members of that race as have a Mongoloid admixture.

These Mongolian characters occur often in Bohemia, in Moravia, and especially in Galicia, in which last province they probably date from the Mongol invasions of the thirteenth century. Such traits, however, are not found among the Alpines of southern Germany or France.

In the American Indians, Mongoloid blood undoubtedly predominates but the high-bridged nose of some of the tribes and their high stature undoubtedly point to admixture with other races.

The Mongol is not inferior to the Nordic in intelligence, as is the Negro, but represents such a divergent type that the mixture between Nordics and Chinese or Japanese is not a good one. The overflow of these Asiatics into our Pacific Coast might have Mongolized the States there, had not the American laboring man taken alarm and secured legislation forbidding their immigration.

With the foregoing as a simple and generalized description of the primitive races of mankind as we know them today, and with special emphasis on the three principal European variants of the "white" race, we shall proceed to consider the distribution and racial influence of the Nordics in western Europe.

III

THE NORDIC CONQUEST OF EUROPE

About 1300 B.C. a blond, blue-eyed race of Libyans appears in Egyptian sculptures. Whence these blonds came or how they got into Libya is not known, but it is interesting to note that blond Berbers are to be found today in the Atlas Mountains of North Africa. These, however, are probably more recent arrivals from the north.

About 1800 B.C. traces of Nordic infiltration appeared among the Hittites. These Nordic conquerors later entered Mesopotamia as the Mitanni and the Kassites, although it may be that they were only the ruling classes of these peoples.

In recorded history the Nordics first appear in the West as Achæans. They came from the North from the Dacian Plains and conquered Greece and Phrygia about 1400 or 1500 B.C.

About 1200 or 1300 B.C. a Nordic people, the Osco-Umbrians, sweeping down from the northeast, entered Italy. They were kindred to the Achæans and were the ancestors of the Latin tribes, including the early Romans. The aboriginal Mediterraneans were driven into southern Italy, where, in Calabria and Apulia, they persist to this day. The contrast between the peoples of North and South Italy is still profound.[1]

The Continental Nordics, as Celtic tribes, entered Gaul in the ninth century B.C. From the evidence of place names, they passed through South Germany. All Gaul except Aquitania, in the southwest, was overwhelmed.

Spain was conquered by Celtic Nordics about 600 B.C., but their domination was never complete and they soon mingled with the natives. The mixed inhabitants of the peninsula were called Celtiberians by the Romans.

During this same period the British Isles were overrun and thoroughly occupied by Celtic Nordics named Goidels and the Celtic tongue was imposed upon the Mediterranean population, although the latter survived as a race in large numbers, especially in the western parts of England and Ireland. These Celtic-speaking Mediterraneans were, until recently, called "Iberians"; but fifteen hundred years ago the

---

[1] In *Geographical Lore of the Time of the Crusades*, by J. K. Wright of the American Geographic Society, p. 320, the author says: "In these authorities we find that the differences between the inhabitants of the northern and southern parts of Italy were fully appreciated in the twelfth century. 'The Lombards,' Gunther says, 'are a keen, skillful, and active people; foresighted in counsel; expert in justice; strong in body and spirit, full of life and handsome to look upon, with slight, supple bodies that give them great power of endurance; economical and always moderate in eating and drinking; masters of their hands and mouths; honorable in every business transaction; mighty in the arts and always striving for the new; lovers of freedom and ready to face death for freedom's sake. These people have never been willing to submit to kings. . . . But what a contrast the people of Apulia in the south present to the Lombards. Dirty, lazy, weak, good-for-nothing idlers that they are.'"

THE NORDIC CONQUEST OF EUROPE 41

invading Saxons called all the people they found in England "Welsh."

In about 300 B.C. a new wave of Celts entered Gaul and Britain. This time they came from the German plains, speaking a somewhat different form of Celtic. On the Continent they were known as the Belgæ and in the British Isles as the Brythons. They gave their name to the British Islands. By Cæsar's time they had conquered the northern third of Gaul and all of England; but the Roman armies put an end to their farther advance. They did not reach Ireland.

Roman writers describe the Celts in Gaul as pure Nordics and speak of them as forming the ruling classes and military aristocracy until their virtual destruction by Julius Cæsar in his ten years of conquest. His campaigns in Gaul are said to have destroyed a million men, chiefly of the warrior caste.

At the time of their greatest expansion the Gauls sacked Rome (387 B.C.). They pressed no farther south and soon retreated to and remained in Cisalpine Gaul, that is, the valley of the Po and the country north of the Apennines.

The Nordic Gauls or Galatians—to use the Greek form of their name—devastated Greece about 297 B.C. and passed over into Asia Minor. There they settled in what was long known as Galatia, now Angora, the present seat of the Turkish Government. These Galatians were the last Nordics to enter Asia Minor, if we except the armies of the Crusaders.

From the description of the physical characters

of the Celtic-speaking tribes they closely resembled the Germanic tribes that followed them into the Roman Empire. Some French anthropologists find that the present-day population of France is nearly four-fifths Alpine and they have decided to call the Alpines "Celts," to avoid admitting that the Celts were physically the same as the hated Germans. This error is not shared by the leading French anthropologists, such as deLapouge, but it has been accepted by some anthropologists.

Careful study of the references to the Celts by classic writers leaves no doubt that the Gauls, Galatians, Belgæ, and Brythons were Nordics as were their successors the Visigoths, Suevi, Alemanni, Burgundians, and, above all, the Franks. In fact, France down to the time of the Reformation was a Nordic land.

Soon after the time when the Belgæ first appear in Europe, Nordic tribes speaking a Germanic dialect are mentioned in history. The first of these tribes to come in conflict with the Romans were the Teutones and Cimbri, who after defeating several Roman armies, were utterly destroyed in 103 B.C. These people were the forerunners of many tribes and nations which emerged, one after another, from the swamps and forests of the north. The original home of most of them seems to have been in Scandinavia, where they had been developing for several thousand years. These newcomers were the latest and final linguistic group to appear in the history of Europe. As Teutonic Nordics they have dominated

THE NORDIC CONQUEST OF EUROPE 43

the scene ever since. The use of the word Teutonic is here purely linguistic in order to distinguish these late comers from the earlier, Celtic-speaking Nordic tribes.

The Teutonic Nordics formed a substantial element among the Belgæ and Brythons and their expansion may well have been the cause of the westward thrust of the latter. The Teutons began to press southward on the Roman Empire early in the Christian era and this pressure continued for some three centuries until the Empire collapsed under their successive invasions.

As said above, the Celts and the Teutons were identical physically and the use of the word "Celtic" cannot be justified as a racial term at the present day. Among living Nordics, those of Celtic origin cannot be distinguished physically from those of German or Scandinavian extraction. Possibly red hair and the psychical peculiarities associated with it may be rather more Celtic than Scandinavian. We find in classical writers the names and description of the barbarians beyond the borders of the Empire. They were all described as blue-eyed, fair or red-haired giants. Height, however, must be considered as relative to that of the Romans, whose legions in the later years of the empire were apparently composed of small men. With each generation the names applied to the barbarian tribes change, but the description of physical characters remains the same.

The finest of these Teutonic barbarians were the Goths who, according to their historian, Jordanes, crossed over from Sweden about 300 B.C. and settled on the banks of the Vistula, whence they expanded into South Russia, which they occupied for centuries. In fact, a remnant of their language (Krim Götisch) was spoken in the Crimea until the seventeenth century. The Gepidæ were a branch of the Goths who lay to the west of the main body, and the Alans, a closely related tribe, were located well to the east. It is interesting to note that some of the Alans, fleeing from the Huns, took refuge in the Caucasus where the Ossetes to this day show occasional Nordic physical characters.

The main body of the Gothic nation was split in two in 375 A.D. by the invasion of the Huns, a Tatar people from Central Asia. Those who took refuge in the west, in South Germany and Gaul, were called Visigoths. A part of the Visigoths, however, fled across the Danube, devastated the provinces of the Byzantine Empire and slew the reigning emperor, Valens, in 378 A.D.

The eastern branch, or Ostrogoths, were conquered by the Huns and remained in Dacia. Later, after Attila's death and the disruption of his empire, the Ostrogoths, under the great Theodoric, invaded Italy and came near to building a unified Italian nation nearly fourteen hundred years ago.

The Visigoths, who had been long in contact with Roman civilization, occupied Gaul. When Attila crossed the Rhine in 451 A.D. they fought on the side of the Romans at Chalons, one of the decisive battles of history, and their king, the Visigothic Theodoric,

THE NORDIC CONQUEST OF EUROPE 45

fell in the battle. The Ostrogoths, on the other hand, were the best troops of the Hunnish host.

The Visigoths entered Spain in 412 A.D. Their allies, the Suevi, conquered and ruled Galicia and the provinces on the Atlantic which now constitute Portugal. The invasion of Spain by the Visigoths resulted in the expulsion of a closely related Teutonic people, the Vandals, who, with their allies, a remnant of the Alans, crossed over into Africa in 428 A.D. On the site of Carthage the Vandals erected a kingdom which lasted a hundred years. They ruled the African coast westward to the Atlantic, conquered and settled in Corsica and under their king, Genseric, sacked Rome in 455 A.D.

These Vandals, originally from Sweden, first appear in history on the Baltic coast, thence they passed down through Central Europe and westward into France and thence into Spain, where they settled and remained until they were driven into Africa. They may have left behind some of their blood to mingle with the later-coming Germanic tribes in Spain. It is possible also, though not probable, that to them are due some of the blond characters still found in the Atlas Mountains. As a race, however, their disappearance is complete.

The Visigoths maintained their control in Spain until 711 A.D. when the Mohammedan Arabs crossed the Straits of Gibraltar and completely defeated the Visigothic armies. Why the power of this people collapsed so suddenly and completely is one of the mysteries of history, but after the great seven days' battle on the Guadalquivir in which their king, Roderick, was slain, the whole peninsula was easily conquered by the Arabs. At this time, it is true, the blood of the Visigoths had been greatly mixed with that of the subject races, resulting perhaps in a weakening of their fighting power.

One of the reasons for the easy conquest of the Visigoths by the Moors lay in the hatred for them as Arians by the old Orthodox Catholic population who regarded their conquerors as heretics, and the assistance rendered by the Jews whom the Visigoths had treated harshly and who are reputed to have induced the Moors to make their invasion.

A remnant of the Visigoths fled northerly into southern Gaul, which was called Gothia Septimania. There the name Visigoths was corrupted into Vigot or Bigot, which was a term of reproach used by the orthodox natives.

It is important to note that the relations between the populations of the Roman Empire and the invading Teutonic Nordics were greatly affected by the fact that the latter were the followers of the schismatic monk Arius who, about 350 A.D., converted the Goths to a Unitarian form of Christianity. The denial of the Trinity by the Barbarians roused a fierce hatred among their subject peoples. Ostrogoths and Visigoths, Vandals and Alans, Burgundians and Lombards, all were Arians. The Franks alone among the Barbarians were converted directly to Orthodox Christianity. This greatly facilitated their conquest of Gaul. In consequence, France for

THE NORDIC CONQUEST OF EUROPE 47

more than a thousand years was regarded as the eldest son of the church.

Down to our time, the aristocracy of Spain, and more especially that of Portugal, shows a marked inheritance of blondness coming down largely from Visigothic and Suevic ancestry. The province of Galicia still retains very appreciable marks of Gothic blood, especially in a high percentage of light-colored eyes.

The Visigoths left behind them in Spain a legacy of names which now are regarded as most typically Spanish, as for instance Rodrigo, Alfonso, Alvarez, Guzman, and Velasquez. In the same manner we find a Nordic legacy of names reaching from Italy into France even where little Nordic blood is left. In other words, while blood dies out, names persist.

At the time of Spanish greatness the predominant blood in the peninsula was still Gothic,[2] and the adventurers who went overseas and were lost to the

[2] The Spanish popular heroes, Don Rodrigo and the Cid Campeador, were Gothic, to judge by their names, as was the brave crusader, Count Raymund of Toulouse. L. Wilser has called attention to the number of Gothic names still in use in the Iberian peninsula: Alfonso or Affonso, Alonzo (Gothic Athalafuns), Alvaro and Alvarez (Gothic Alavair) Bermuy (Gothic Berimud); Bertran (Gothic Bairhtram); Diego and Diaz (Gothic Thiudareiks, Dietrich); Esmeralda; Fernando and its genitive Fernandez (Gothic Ferdinanths); Froilaz and Fruela (Gothic Fravila); Gelmirez (Gelimer); Gomez (Gothic Guma); Gonzalo and Gonzalez (Gothic Gunthimir, Gundemar); Guilfonso (Gothic Viljafuns); Guzman (Gothic Godaman, Gutmann); Ildefonso (Gothic Hildifuns); Isabella; Marques (Gothic Markja); Menendez (Gothic Herminanths); Mundiz and Munnez (Gothic Mundila); Pizarro (Gothic Pitzas); Ramiro (Gothic Radomir or Ragnimir); Ramon and Renmondez (Gothic Ragnimund); Rodrigo and Rodriguez; Ruiz (Gothic Rudoreiks); Sesnandes (Gothic Sisenand); Vasco and Vasquez (Nordic Wasce); Velasquez (Gothic Vilaskja?). See p. 107, vol. II, of book *Die Germanen*, by Doctor Ludwig Wilser.

race were of this blood. In Portugal, the one great poet, Camoens,[3] and in Spain Cervantes, who was his contemporary, were descendants of the old Gothic nobility and had marked Nordic characteristics, as had the Cid Campeador. The case was the same in Italy[4] at this period. The great men were from the northern part of the peninsula. Dante, Michaelangelo, Leonardo Da Vinci, and virtually all of the leading men of the Renaissance were blond Nordics. Columbus himself, supposed to have come from Genoa, is described as having blue eyes and fair hair. In southern France, in the so-called Gothic Septimania and in the country around Toulouse, the home of the Troubadours, Gothic names abound.[5] A simi-

[3] Describing Camoens, George Edward Woodberry (*The Torch*, pp. 203-4; New York, 1920) says: "He was of the old blue blood of the Peninsula, the Gothic blood, the same that gave birth to Cervantes. He was blond, and bright-haired, with blue eyes, large and lively, the face oval and ruddy—and in manhood the beard short and rounded, with long untrimmed mustachios—the forehead high, the nose aquiline; in figure agile and robust; in action 'quick to draw and slow to sheathe,' and when he was young, he writes that he had seen the heels of many, but none had seen his heels. Born about the year 1524, of a noble and well-connected family, educated at Coimbra, a university famous for the classics, and launched in life about the court at Lisbon, he was no sooner his own master than he fell into troubles."

[4] Wilser cites Woltmann's essay, "Have the Goths disappeared in Italy?," which shows that even in the latter part of the Middle Ages many people lived according to Gothic law; that in some cities there even existed Gothic sections; and that many Gothic names can be traced, as Stavila, Nefila, Leuuia, Hermia, Hilpja, Ansefrida, Gilliefredus, Totila, Vila.

[5] In fact, almost all the names of the Troubadours are Teutonic, says Wilser, giving the following examples of French names, with the Teutonic original in parentheses: Arnaut (Arnold); Aimeric (Emerich); Bernart (Bernhard); Bertrand (Bertram); Gaucelm (Walchelm); Gautier (Walther); Guillem (Wilhelm); Guiraut (Gerold); Gunot (Wido); Jaufre or Joffre (Gotfrid); Raimon (Raginmund); Rambaut (Raginbald); Rudel (Rudolf); Savaric (Sabarich). See p. 107, vol. II, of *Die Germanen*, by Doctor Ludwig Wilser.

THE NORDIC CONQUEST OF EUROPE 49

lar condition prevails throughout France. French names are Gothic, Frankish, or Burgundian today, though disguised by their spelling, as, for example, Joffre from Gotfrid. In the opinion of Count deLapouge, France as late as the settlement of America was more Nordic than is the Germany of today.

The main body of the Visigoths who survived the conquest by the Arabs took refuge in the northwestern part of Spain where they maintained some small kingdoms which ultimately coalesced and became the nucleus of a Christian Spain, which in the course of a seven-hundred-year crusade gradually reconquered the peninsula and finally expelled the Moors in 1492.

The Arabs who conquered Spain, and the Islamized Persians and Moors, had a wonderful period of intellectual expansion during the seventh and following centuries. This amazing outburst of genius, which preserved for us much of the science and learning of the Greeks, came to an end when the Mediterranean Mohammedans began mixing their blood with that of their Negro slaves. Mohammedanism has always appealed to the lower races, especially the Negro, because when they became followers of the Prophet they were admitted to social and racial equality with the superior race. This and the lure of the Negro women ruined the Arab race. Today, all through Africa and Egypt and in parts of Arabia, the so-called Arabs are often Negroid in appearance. In this case polygamy was a racial curse because the richer and abler men had the most slave women and left a larger progeny of half-breed children than did their poorer countrymen.

The exact reverse happened in the case of the Turks, who were originally Alpines from Central Asia strongly mixed with Mongol. They conquered Asia Minor and the nations of Southeast Europe up to and including Hungary. Everywhere they seized the most beautiful women and, being polygamists, the ablest Turks had the most children by the finest women of the subject countries. Thus the Turks bred up as the Arabs bred down. To this day the Turks are the superior race in Asia Minor and have eliminated, at least from the ruling classes, practically all the physical traces of their Asiatic origin.

The women of the Caucasus, especially the Circassians and Georgians, who retain some remnants of the Nordic Alans, have always been noted for their physical beauty. They were in great demand in Turkish Harems.

Incidentally the Kurds are, or rather were, Nordic and it is interesting to note that Saladin, of Crusading fame, was a Kurd.

Concerning other Teutonic Nordics, we need mention only those whose blood enters largely into modern nations. Of these, one of the most interesting peoples were the Burgundians, who settled on the western bank of the upper Rhine in what is now Alsace, and in Burgundian France and French-speaking Switzerland. They were a very promising and flourishing nation until their overthrow in the

THE NORDIC CONQUEST OF EUROPE 51

middle of the fifth century by Attila and his Huns, a tragedy which supplies the subject matter of the Niebelungenlied. Appollonius Sidonius refers to the Burgundians as being seven feet high; while this is an obvious exaggeration, it is interesting to note that in the old Burgundian provinces we find the tallest stature in France today.

When the Lombards first appear in history about 165 A.D. they were in northern Germany. They entered Italy in 568 A.D. and conquered the Peninsula even more thoroughly than had their predecessors, the Ostrogoths. They not only occupied Italy north of the Apennines for three hundred years, but also established several large duchies in the south. The valley of the Po, where they settled, had been for centuries Cisalpine Gaul, and this Lombard territory is today the backbone of modern Italy. The percentage of light-colored eyes around Milan is high, and blondness through this district is as common a characteristic of the peasantry as it is of the aristocracy throughout the rest of Italy.

The Lombards were Arians and were in constant conflict with the Popes and their Orthodox followers and were consequently generally maligned. Just as a similar situation facilitated the conquest of Spain by the Moors, so the destruction of the Lombard Kingdom by the Franks was made the easier by this antagonism.

In passing, we need only remark that there were small bands of other Nordics, who entered Italy as Saxons, Alemanni, and Suevi, and who entered

France as Alans and Saxons. These small bands differed in few respects from the larger Nordic peoples and were quickly absorbed in them. All these barbarian tribes were closely related racially.

Before we leave the Alemanni who occupied southwest Germany with Alsace and German-speaking Switzerland, we may note that their name, Alemanni, did not mean 'All Men' in the sense of a mixed company, but rather *The Men* "par excellence,"—the German *"All"* being the analogous of the Greek *"Pan."*

We come next to the Franks, who appear in history about the time of the Battle of Chalons in 451 A.D. in which they took an unimportant part, but in the following centuries they rapidly gained the ascendency throughout Gaul and western Germany. The conquests by the Franks were the most important and enduring of those of the Teutonic Nordics in Continental Europe. We know very little about the Franks from the Romans, although they may have been the Varini, who were located in northwestern Germany in classic times. As a result of the Crusades, Roman Orthodox, as contrasted with Greek Christians, are known as "Ferangi" to this day in the Levant. Being Orthodox Christians and not Arians, the Franks had the support of the Roman Church in all their conquests.

The Flemings of Belgium are remnants of the original Franks who retained their own language. Most of these invaders, like the Franks, Visigoths, Lombards, and Normans, adopted the Latin lan-

THE NORDIC CONQUEST OF EUROPE 53

guage of their subject peoples when they settled within the confines of the Roman Empire.

Except in eastern England and northern France the numbers of the conquering Nordics were not sufficient entirely to evict and replace the conquered populations, but they everywhere formed the upper classes and land-owning aristocracy and to this day these same classes in all European nations continue to show, in more or less purity, the physical characters of the Nordic race.

During the Middle Ages, the dominating and warlike Nordics paused long enough from fighting each other to carry on the Crusades and to beat back the onrush of the Saracens at Tours in 732 A.D. They saved Europe from the Mongols in 1241 A.D. at the Battle of Liegnitz (now Wahlstatt) in Silesia where the Duke of Liegnitz and the Nordic nobility, outnumbered five to one, lay dead upon the field of battle; but checked the advance of the Asiatic hordes and saved the budding civilization of Europe from the fate of Asia.

This race supplied the navigators of the expansion period, when the world was for the first time opened up in the fifteenth and sixteenth centuries, and since then they have formed the fighting men, soldiers, sailors, explorers, hunters, adventurers, and frontiersmen of Europe and her colonies.

After mastering the north of France, the Franks subjugated the remnants of the Burgundians and destroyed the Visigothic kingdom which still flourished in the south of Gaul. They also conquered the country on the east bank of the Rhine known as Franconia, and under Charlemagne seized northern Italy. In 800 A.D. Charlemagne revived the Western Roman Empire, which under various guises lasted down to 1807.

Charlemagne's greatest and most difficult conquest, however, was that of the Saxons, who were pure Nordics. They occupied the districts of northwest Germany, centering in Hanover, and even today this part of Germany is still the most Nordic portion of that country.

When Charlemagne reached the Elbe in his conquests he found beyond it the heathen Alpine Wends and from his day down to the World War, the history of Central Europe has been the pushing back of the frontier of Alpine Asia from the Elbe eastward toward the Urals.

These eastern lands were conquered and little by little Christianized and civilized from the west. This process went on as far as the Vistula, where it met the culture, and Greek Orthodox religion, of the Byzantine Empire, which had followed up the rivers of Russia from the Black Sea and had given to Moscovia and to the Ukraine their religion, alphabet, and art.

The Northmen were the last of the Nordic barbarians to appear on the scene. In the ninth and tenth centuries they raided the coasts of Europe from England to Greece. They established themselves as permanent settlers on all the Scottish islands and on many parts of the Scottish coast. In

THE NORDIC CONQUEST OF EUROPE 55

Caithness, the northernmost corner of Scotland, Norse was spoken as late as the seventeenth century. They formed settlements and left place names all around the coasts of Wales and England. In the tenth century as Danes they subjugated northeastern England and imposed their rule east of the line of Watling Street, which runs from London to Chester. These Danes had barely been overcome by the Saxons when a new group of Nordics arrived as Normans from France and conquered England in 1066.

Ireland was attacked by the Norse who came in from the north and by the Danes who entered from the south. The island was overrun by these two peoples who have left many traces in the place names and in the blood of Ireland.

On the Continent the coasts of France and Germany were harried by the Northmen and the country since called Normandy was conquered by them in 911 A.D. The Danish conquest of England, referred to above, must have been largely Norse while, in France, Rollo's followers were probably to an overwhelming extent Danes.

The Norman element in England and to some extent in America down to this very day has supplied a very large proportion of the conquerors, seamen, explorers, and frontiersmen. This same ruling and restless strain showed itself in the individual adventurers who went to South Italy and Sicily, which they thoroughly conquered in the twelfth century. They even attacked the Byzantine Empire. To this day blue eyes in Sicily are called "Norman eyes" and are to some extent characteristic of the upper classes there.

It was in this period that the Norse rovers under Leif Ericson discovered the northeast mainland of America about 1000 A.D., nearly five hundred years before Columbus, who probably knew of their voyages, crossed the Atlantic.

At the time of this Norwegian and Danish expansion, there was a similar outpouring of Swedes who, as Varangians, crossed the Baltic into Russia, which they conquered and ruled for many centuries. The name Varangian is strongly suggestive of Varini or Franks and the name "Russian" means "rowers." The Varangians came across the seas precisely as their ancestors, the Goths, had done a thousand years earlier. After the expansion of this so-called Viking period, Scandinavian activities came to an end.

Man undoubtedly crossed back and forth on dry land from Europe to England in Neolithic and earlier times. In fact, some of the earliest records of man have been found in England and the recent discoveries in Norfolk of chipped implements and hearths show that man made tools and used fire in England before the appearance of the first glaciers —something over a million years ago.

These early species and genera of men largely died out or were exterminated and were succeeded at the beginning of Neolithic times by invasions of

THE NORDIC CONQUEST OF EUROPE 57

the small, dark, long-skulled Mediterranean race which for many thousands of years formed the basis of the population of England, Scotland, and Ireland.

About the beginning of the Bronze Age, some 1800 B.C., a tall, round-skulled type from the Continent called the Beaker Makers appeared on the scene in England. They resembled somewhat the present Dinaric race, a tall, round-skulled branch of the Alpines now found from the Tyrol southward to Albania on the east side of the Adriatic. It is clear that the Beaker Makers entered from the east across the narrow seas and their remains indicate a tall, masterful type which seems to have disappeared to a large extent, although some of the round-skulled, heavily built Englishmen, found numerously among the commercial classes, may be their representatives today.

The racial composition of the British Isles when the Nordic first appeared on the scene may be safely said to have been composed of small, brunet Mediterraneans interspersed with a small number of round-skulled types and including, very probably, remnants of still earlier races.

The Celtic-speaking Nordics appear to have crossed the Rhine into France and the countries to the southwest about 800 B.C. At about the same time they forced their way into the British Isles which they thoroughly conquered. These Nordics were called Goidels or "Q" Celts and their language is represented today by the remnants of Erse in Ireland, Gaelic in Scotland, and Manx on the Isle of Man. These "Q" Celts, as contrasted with the later coming "P" Celts, are now represented by the Macs (meaning son) just as the later Cymric or Brythonic Celts are called "P" Celts because in their language Ap means son.

The aborigines were called Picts in Scotland. These Mediterranean Picts spoke a language related to Hamitic or Egyptian, and many place names of this origin are still to be found.

It is not definitely known whether the Gaelic speech of Scotland is a remnant of early Goidel invasion or whether it was reintroduced from Ireland in the early centuries of our era. The latter appears probable, because the second conquest by the Celts was nearly complete throughout Britain, although it did not reach Ireland. This second subjugation of Britain was by the "P" Celts or Brythons, speaking a Cymric form of Celtic. It occurred in the fourth century B.C. and was so thorough that it is not probable that remnants of the earlier Goidelic speech could have survived in Scotland.

These Brythons were represented on the continent by the Belgæ, who, in Cæsar's time, occupied Gaul between the Rhine and the Seine. A remnant of their speech survives in Brittany as Armorican.

The "P" Celts gave their speech to all England and remnants of it are found in the recently extinct Cornish in Cornwall and in the Cymric of Wales. Both the "Q" Celts and the "P" Celts were, on their arrival in Britain, pure Nordics, but in many cases

THE NORDIC CONQUEST OF EUROPE 59

they soon merged with the aboriginal population. They were everywhere the ruling military class, in Britain as well as in Gaul.

Having imposed their language on the conquered people, they died out almost completely, leaving, as in Wales, their speech on the lips of the little Mediterranean native. Whatever truth there is in the legends of King Arthur and his resistance to the Saxons they clearly indicate a blond, Celtic aristocracy ruling over an underclass of small Mediterraneans. The same condition is indicated in Irish legends where the Celts appear as a distinct, fair-haired military class.

The next Nordic invasion of Britain was by the Saxons from the country around the present duchy of Holstein and by the Angles and Jutes from farther north on the mainland of Denmark or Jutland. These tribes which entered England in the fifth century were probably more purely Nordic than the continental Teutons and this also was true of the Norse and Varangians of a later date. Their conquest was almost completed during the century after their arrival but there was sufficient resistance in the western part of England to postpone its final subjugation for several centuries. However, gradually the population of practically all England and the lowlands of Scotland became purely Nordic. This racial stock was reinforced by the invasion of Danes, who occupied most of northeast England.

The Norsemen settled around the coasts of Ireland, Scotland, England, and, especially, Wales, and added a very considerable contribution to the pure Nordic element of the population.

The next and last invasion of Britain by the Nordics was the Norman conquest in 1066. The Norman leaders and soldiers were pure Nordics from the most Nordic part of France. In fact, the Normans were heathen Danes speaking a Teutonic tongue when they arrived in Normandy in 911 A.D. so that on coming to England they had been in France only a little over one hundred and fifty years. In those years they had accepted Christianity, had learned French, and had become the exponents of the highest culture in Europe. Into England they brought with them many followers of Alpine origin, and the clergy whom they imported was also composed very largely of Latinized Alpines.

At this point we may remark that Wales, especially along the coasts, has a very large Nordic population. It is absurd to distinguish between England, Scotland, North Ireland, and Wales as is done in the census of the United States. We might just as well distinguish between North England and South England on the ground that the first is Anglian and Danish and the other Saxon and Jutish. The lowlands of Scotland are pure English territory and have been such for a thousand years. The Ulster Scots who came to America were only two or three generations removed from the Scottish and English borderers and had not mixed with the native Irish. It is also to be remarked that the Norman conquest of England was that of one Nordic people by an-

THE NORDIC CONQUEST OF EUROPE 61

other, and that Great Britain and Ireland constitute a group, the membership of which is overwhelmingly Nordic in its racial inheritance.

At the time of the discovery of America, all Europe was far more Nordic than it is today. Germany at that time had not witnessed the expansion of the Alpines of the south and east which is characteristic of the present era. In England, before the industrial revolution created a demand for little brunet Mediterraneans to drive spindles, the Nordic had the field to himself. As farmer, soldier, sailor, explorer, and pioneer he was pre-eminent. The brunet Mediterranean element, formerly called Iberians, had been forced back into the extreme west of England and into Wales, and was not an important economic or political factor. Nor was there any considerable immigration of that racial stock into the American colonies. These were settled primarily by the descendants of the Normans, Saxons, Anglians, and Danes coming from the distinctly Nordic districts of the mother land.

Norfolk and Suffolk were settled by the Angles and afterwards formed a part of the Danish kingdom. As said above the lowlands of Scotland and the English borders were Anglian and Dane, while the coasts and islands of Scotland were everywhere Norse. The Highlands were Celtic with an admixture of Norse, Anglian, and Norman. There were also remnants of the old Mediterranean populations, probably Picts. Curiously enough these Mediterraneans contributed their dark eyes and hair color, but not their short stature. The population of West Scotland has the greatest height of all the peoples of Europe.

Ireland, like England, was settled as we have seen originally by the Neolithic Mediterraneans. They in turn were conquered by the Goidelic or "Q" Celts, blond Nordics who imposed their language on the aborigines. In the ninth century, Ireland was overrun by the Norse and Danes, whose descendants today constitute a very considerable portion of the population. The very name Ireland is Danish. Most of the big blond Irish of today, although they like to claim "Celtic" descent, are, in fact, of Norse, Danish, Saxon, Norman, or Scotch derivation.

The Nordic elements in Ireland were reinforced again and again by the English and Normans, who, from the days of their original entry into the island down to our day have formed the great majority of the nobility and upper classes of the country. The Celtic Goidel in Ireland today is a negligible quantity which cannot be racially identified. The brunet elements in western Ireland, though to some extent Celtic in speech, are descended from the old Neolithic or Mediterranean population of the British Isles, mixed with a primitive, aboriginal race of great antiquity, the Firbolgs.

Ireland has shown a singular power of absorbing its conquerors. The descendants of Danish, Norman, and English settlers consider themselves pure Irish "Celts." It is a strange fact that the English, Scotch, Norman, Danish, and even the French Hu-

THE NORDIC CONQUEST OF EUROPE 63

guenots who have settled in Ireland have acquired and have handed down an extraordinary temperamental unity. As to language, by the time of Elizabeth the English Pale constituted a part of eastern Leinster, and there English was uniformly spoken. The English language ultimately spread over the whole of Ireland, leaving only a few remnants of Celtic speech in the extreme west.

From the times of James I to those of William III, large numbers of English and Scotch borderers passed over to the northeast corner of the island into the province of Ulster. They were fervent Presbyterians and hated the native Catholic Irish. It was the sons and grandsons of these immigrants who came to America in the eighteenth century and are sometimes miscalled the "Scotch Irish." They had special grievances of their own against England on account of economic restrictions imposed upon their industries.

Before this time a large number of Cromwellian soldiers had settled in Leinster, but not having their own women with them they intermarried with the Catholic Irish and their descendants today are most intensely Irish in national feeling. The Reformation never had much hold on Ireland, so that the Catholic Irish today represent the mixed population of Ireland before the sixteenth century, together with numerous converts from the Scotch and English immigrants.

With this brief survey of the distribution of the Nordic race in Europe down to the time of the discovery of America and the beginning of emigration to the colonies of the New World, we can pass on to one of the most dramatic mass-migrations of man.

From West Central Asia where it was in contact with the Mongoloids on the *east,* the Nordic race pushed across Europe to the extreme western coasts. We shall show how it traversed the Atlantic Ocean and then in three centuries subdued a continent. Generation after generation it fought its way westward, until it reached the Pacific Ocean, where today it stands confronting Asia and its immemorial rivals, the Mongols, this time on the *west.*

IV

THE NORDIC SETTLEMENT OF AMERICA

BEFORE considering the question of the origin of the English settlers of the Atlantic seaboard, it is important to understand the motives that actuated the newcomers.

The impelling motive of the settlers who crossed the ocean to America from the earliest Colonial times down to 1880 was land hunger, and just as we speculate in stocks today, so down to one hundred years ago our ancestors speculated in lands on the frontier.

It is difficult to realize the extent to which the ownership of the land in Europe was monopolized, largely through the exercise of Royal favor, by the upper classes in the seventeenth and eighteenth centuries. This established English tradition and practice, brought to America by the early settlers, coupled with the favoritism of the royal governors in land grants, was one of the causes which led to the Revolution. After the American victory much land was confiscated on the plea that the owners were Loyalists.

The distribution of free land in the United States came substantially to an end about 1880, when the public domain became exhausted. Up to that date, the immigration into America had been assimilated readily. Certain exceptions will be dealt with later. Practically all of it was from northwestern Europe, and the immigrants came mostly of their own volition. It took some degree of enterprise to leave home, cross the Atlantic, and establish oneself in a new country amid strange surroundings. Settling new land meant clearing the forests and destroying the game, as well as buying off or fighting the Indians, whose ideas about land ownership were vague. To the frontiersman in early days, the term "a clearing" was synonymous with "a settlement."

Religious motives and the desire for political and economic independence, of course, were also great factors in the Pilgrim and Puritan migration to New England from 1620 to 1640.

The New England Puritans represented only a part and relatively a small part of the exodus from England. They were pure English from the most Anglo-Saxon part of England and consisted largely of yeomen and the lesser gentry, who found the religious and political conditions in England under the Stuarts intolerable for freemen. They were essentially dissenters, who refused to bend the knee to prelate or to king.

In 1640, under the Commonwealth the Puritans seized the reins of government in England and only permitted the return of royalty in 1660 under conditions which established for all time the supremacy of Parliament. In fact, during the Commonwealth the power of Parliament had become so great that many of the best minds of England felt that a restoration of the monarchy was needed as a check.

The settlers of New England may be regarded as essentially rebels against established religion and established authority when the religion and authority were not of their own choosing. This non-conformist spirit persisted in the successive new frontiers as they were settled by New Englanders. The early New England settlers of western New York and the old Northwest Territory gave birth to an astonishing number of new sects, religions, "isms," and communities, ranging all the way from Mormonism to Shakers and the Oneida Community. They were, however, law-abiding in their own way and murders and crimes of violence were relatively infrequent.

This is in sharp contrast to the southern frontiersmen, who were and are addicted to killings and physical violence. That, however, is chiefly true of the inhabitants of the Appalachian valleys, who always have been lawless. The dissent and predisposition to rebellion among the New Englanders dates back to the Puritans in England and the lawlessness and violence of the Ulster Scots to the endless border warfare on the Scottish frontier. The southern frontiersman was originally a Presbyterian, but he found his religion too intellectual for isolated communities and turned in many cases to the more emotional creeds of the Methodist and Baptist. The hatred of England by the Ulster Scotch frontiersmen dated back to the unjust and oppressive interference with their industries in the north of Ireland, as well as to a deep-seated impatience of all authority.

After the Revolution this hatred of authority was transferred to the tidewater aristocrats and was accentuated by the debtor complex, which has characterized all our frontiers.

The character of the frontier from the very beginning remained the same. Each generation of the restless, the discontented and the failures pushed West, carrying with them some of the fine qualities of the original settlers of the seaboard, but more often developing a new complex of intolerance for the restraints and usages of the older communities.

There is an amusing and significant evolution of these traits in families who settled around Massachusetts Bay and then moved to the Connecticut Valley; thence to Vermont, western New York, Ohio, Illinois, Iowa, and Los Angeles, where they now flourish.

At the time of the Revolution the intense hatred in New England of the mother country was due partly to a desire to confiscate the lands of the Loyalists and partly to that which they considered unfair restrictions on their overseas trade, as well as to an unwillingness to being taxed to pay a part of the great cost of conquering Canada.

The net result of these forces was a widespread anti-British and, later, anti-governmental complex, which has characterized our country ever since. In contrast to England and to Canada, we are an essentially lawless people.

Ireland.

THE NORDIC SETTLEMENT OF AMERICA 69

In the North the Revolution was largely a movement of various Calvinist communities. The few Episcopalians in New England and the more numerous adherents of that church in New York, Pennsylvania, and Maryland were almost all Loyalists. In Virginia, however, and further to the south the numerous Church of England planter class took the American side and as a result retained their leadership as an aristocracy down to the time of the Civil War. Even at the time of the Revolution this church contributed more than its quota of leaders. Of fifty-six signers of the Declaration of Independence, thirty-four are classified as Episcopalians, twelve as Congregationalists, five as Presbyterians, two Quakers, one Baptist and one Roman Catholic. Of the Continental Congress which ratified this Declaration, nearly two-thirds are said to have been Episcopalians.

In the North following the expulsion of the Loyalists, the Church of England was left prostrate, and it was some time after the Revolution before it was successfully reorganized and was definitely designated as the *Protestant* Episcopal Church to become, after a century, the fashionable church of the Atlantic seaboard. The Protestant Episcopal Church has never had any substantial hold in the Middle or Far West and even today it is there largely a missionary church with a tendency towards ritualism, which has checked its normal development.

The Roman Catholic population of the colonies was negligible. In 1790 out of a white population of a little over 3,000,000, there were not more than 35,000 Catholics in the United States. This number included 5000 Negroes and some Germans. They were located for the most part in Maryland and Pennsylvania, showing that the South Irish Catholics had not come over in appreciable numbers during Colonial times. Many of the colonies legislated against Roman Catholics.

The Revolution itself was political and social, carrying to an extreme development the political theories of the English Whigs. The distrust of officialdom in power, engendered by the Revolution, led to all manner of constitutional and legal restrictions, in place of a reliance on the personal character of office holders as in England.

During Colonial times two distinct types of population developed. First, the older communities along the tidewater districts, closely in touch with Europe and having a long tradition of culture and wealth. Second, a type grew up on the frontier which from the very beginning showed itself intolerant of the control of the older and richer settlements. This found its expression in Shays's Rebellion in West Massachusetts in 1786–87, in the Whiskey Rebellion in Pennsylvania in 1794, and, still earlier, in 1770, when the "Regulators" in North Carolina were in open rebellion. After the Revolution this tendency became more and more marked until the then West under Andrew Jackson took over the control of the country and, with many unfortunate results, carried Jefferson's ideals to an extreme.

THE NORDIC SETTLEMENT OF AMERICA 71

The Revolution emphasized this second attitude of mind and resulted in the loss, by expulsion, of some of the best Nordic blood in the country. The Loyalists from Boston, for instance, comprised many of the oldest and most distinguished families. The representative families of that city today are not descended wholly from the aristocratic Colonial families, but largely from the population of the small towns and villages in its neighborhood. It is said that a total of eighty to a hundred thousand Loyalists left the colonies and went to Canada and England and to the English West Indies.

New England to a greater extent than any other colony had been at war with France and her Canadian Indians for the best part of one hundred and fifty years, but the memory of this prolonged and bloody struggle was obliterated by the Revolution. In its place there arose in America a sentiment for France, caused largely by the romantic personality of Lafayette, which survives to this day. The Jeffersonian emotional sympathy with the French Revolution also played a large part. The fact nevertheless is that we had a naval war in 1798 with the French, although no formal war was declared. It was caused by French depredations on American commerce, resulting in several duels between American and French frigates. All this is conveniently forgotten or ignored in some of our school textbooks.

The earliest permanent settlements of importance

in New England were around Massachusetts Bay, and in Virginia along navigable streams. From such centers settlements spread up and down the coast until all the desirable lands accessible to salt water became occupied. In New England the coasts of southern Maine, of Rhode Island, and of Connecticut were quickly occupied. Migration then went overland from Massachusetts Bay, westward to the Connecticut River. This was our first real northern frontier, and it took more than a century to populate southern and western New England.

The settlement of Connecticut westward was blocked by the colony of New York, while the Indians delayed the advance of Massachusetts to the north. Connecticut in turn threw out colonies at an early date, such as Newark in New Jersey in 1666.

Vermont was not settled until just before the Revolution, owing to the danger from the Indians and a serious dispute between New Hampshire and New York as to its ownership. At the time of the Revolution it was a typical frontier with all of its bad features. At that time it was about as rough and tough as Kentucky or Tennessee. After the Revolution some of the best of its population migrated to western New York, along with settlers from all over New England who went for the most part through Vermont.

Early in the eighteenth century nearly all the desirable lands within reach of salt water had been occupied from New Jersey southward, and later coming immigrants were forced back into the uplands

THE NORDIC SETTLEMENT OF AMERICA 73

of the West beyond the so-called Fall Line at which the Atlantic rivers cease to be navigable.

New York interposed an absolute bar to westward migration because the Iroquois Indians held almost all the fertile lands to the west of the Hudson River. The east bank of the Hudson was more or less filled up with New Englanders and the west bank with its undesirable lands was turned over to late coming immigrants, chiefly Germans. The Dutch population of New York was but small. The total population of the colony at the time of its seizure by England in 1664 was little more than 10,000 and there were already many English among them.

The English settlers occupied both banks of the Delaware around Philadelphia, forcing the later-coming Germans and Ulster Scots to the west. The Swedish settlement along the river was trifling and was soon absorbed. There is very little trace of it left in place or personal names. On the upper reaches of the Delaware River, in Pennsylvania, and in New York, there were some small settlements of French Huguenots, who suffered severely from Indian depredations during the Revolution.

Delaware and the country east of Chesapeake Bay are purely English, as was Maryland, except that western Maryland was really part of western Pennsylvania and western Virginia.

Virginia itself was the mother of States and in Colonial times extended in fact, as other colonies did in theory, to the Mississippi, without mentioning claims to the South Sea. The tidewater population of Virginia differed profoundly from that of the western part of the State, including the Shenandoah Valley, which was settled largely from western Pennsylvania.

There was a marked difference between the settlement of New England and that of Virginia. To New England the earliest settlers brought their women and families, while in Virginia the early arrivals were nearly all males. Women were afterwards sent over by the shipload, but this was only during the early days of the colony.

Like Virginia, North Carolina in Colonial times extended nominally to the Mississippi. Its population lacked the tidewater aristocrats of the Old Dominion and contained many Scots, straight from the Highlands, who, strangely, took the British side during the Revolution, as well as a very large number of Ulster Scots in the western mountains, and in the counties which were afterwards Tennessee.

Kentucky and Tennessee were both settled from the colonies immediately to the east, but largely by the Ulster Scots, coming from western Pennsylvania through the mountainous districts of Virginia and North Carolina. These Ulster Scots came south along the Appalachian valleys, which trend in a southwesterly direction. They were reinforced by the numerous groups of the same people, who came up from South Carolina. Kentucky was much more purely English than Tennessee.

It is a fact but little understood, that the frontier was not much reinforced from the coast but extend-

THE NORDIC SETTLEMENT OF AMERICA 75

ed itself. In other words, the frontier from the beginning was pushed onward by the backswoodsmen, each generation advancing a little farther westward and making new clearings.

The people along the coast, after a couple of generations of severe privation, became relatively rich as compared with the frontiersmen. The inhabitants of the coast cities for the most part preferred a seafaring life rather than the hewing out of a homestead in the wilderness. There have been many cases in our Colonial history where men went from the coast towns to the wilderness, but for the most part they were content to stay at home.

As to the original racial complexion of the colonies, New England was purely Nordic and English. The handful of Ulster Scots in New Hampshire was not to be distinguished from the English, and the individual Huguenot families around Boston were only trifling in number. This remained true of all New England during the Colonial period.

In New York, however, conditions were different. Dutch New Amsterdam, afterwards English New York City, was always an important port and attracted to itself from the earliest times a substantial number of foreigners. In addition to the Dutch founders a considerable number of French Huguenots were among the earlier settlers. There were also a few Germans and Portuguese.

The west bank of the Hudson was less accessible and desirable than the east bank, but there were some substantial colonies of Palatine Germans settled there and up the valleys of the Mohawk and its connecting streams. These last played a creditable part in the heavy fighting which raged in this district with the British settlers, who were for the most part Loyalists. There were also some small colonies of pure Scotch along the Mohawk.

One of the results of the Revolution was the expulsion of the Iroquois Indians, who had occupied New York westward from near Albany to Buffalo. They had sided with the British and had committed many atrocities. Their lands were immediately occupied by New Englanders, coming chiefly from or through Vermont, so that New York State west of Albany became little more than an extension of New England, except that the settlers had become Presbyterians.

Many of the colonists who came to New York from Holland were refugees from the provinces now included in Belgium—in other words, they were either Flemings or French Huguenots. The real Dutch in the province came from the north of Holland and were mostly Nordic Frisians.

In addition to the large migration from Ulster very many English Protestants from Leinster came to America by way of New York immediately after the Revolution. The Catholic Irish did not come in any numbers until after 1845.

The Huguenots were predominantly Nordic. For example, New Rochelle in New York was settled directly from Old Rochelle which is, even today, one of the purest Nordic districts remaining in France.

THE NORDIC SETTLEMENT OF AMERICA 77

It is entirely safe to say that the Huguenots from Brittany, Normandy, and Picardy, who came to the American colonies by way of England and Holland were overwhelmingly Nordic. Some of those from southern France were probably Mediterranean.

Outside of the Port of New York the Dutch population was confined to the Hudson River towns, chiefly on the east bank, up to and including Albany and Schenectady. The Dutch element of New Jersey was very small.

New Jersey was almost all English, except a few Scotch settlements. It was settled directly from England by way of Perth Amboy, Elizabeth, and Freehold in the north. South Jersey was settled from Pennsylvania. There were a few German communities scattered throughout the north-central part of New Jersey, but, on the whole, the State can be counted as purely English.

The case of Pennsylvania was somewhat different. The original settlers on the west bank of the Delaware, around Philadelphia, were English Quakers with a certain number of Welsh, who probably were for the most part Nordic. This section was the most cultured and important part of Pennsylvania. Philadelphia was the port of entry of two important migrations in the eighteenth century. First, the Ulster Scots, who came in great numbers after 1720. In fact, most of the Ulster Scots in America entered the colonies through Philadelphia and, to a less extent, through Charleston, South Carolina. These late comers found the desirable land along the Delaware had been taken up, so they moved westward to the Indian frontier. They were a restless, brave, and pugnacious people, and immediately assumed the burden of the Indian fighting, often without the support or even the sympathy of the Philadelphia Quakers. They were numerous and soon spread along the foothills and valleys of the Appalachians southwestward through western Maryland and Virginia into North and South Carolina, whence they again crossed the ridges westward, until, by the time of the Revolution, they had laid the foundations of Kentucky and of Tennessee. They were, of course, pure Nordics and of North England and Lowland Scotch origin. They had resided for two or three generations in North Ireland. Being fervent Presbyterians, they had not mingled with the Catholic Irish.

In 1790 these Ulster Scots in the colonies numbered about 200,000 and the pure Scots about 300,000 and taken together they were, next to the English, the most important element. They were, as said above, pre-eminently pioneers and Indian fighters and the same fact appears in the history of practically every frontier of British colonies during the next century. They were a highly selected group when they first went to Ireland, which was at that time to all intents a frontier. Since that time the Scots and the Ulster Scots have everywhere shown the characteristics of the ideal pioneer. They played a predominant part in the settlement of the southern part of the Middle West.

THE NORDIC SETTLEMENT OF AMERICA 79

The next most important racial element was the Germans. In fact, it was the only non-British element of importance in the colonies. At the time of the Revolution the Germans numbered about a quarter of a million and by 1790 they have been computed to have been about 9 per cent of the total population of the colonies. They settled in the districts of Pennsylvania immediately west of Philadelphia around York and Lancaster, where they are to be found today. They were a peaceful and industrious people, and have to some extent retained their language and customs down to the present time. A very few of them joined their neighbors, the Ulster Scots, in the migration to the Southwest. They were not particularly loyal to the American cause during the Revolution nor in the preceding French Wars, and their presence in the colonies excited much hostility. They were refugees, who had fled down the Rhine from Alsace and the Palatinate to escape the French when Louis XIV invaded and devastated their country. With them were many refugees from German-speaking Switzerland together with Hussites from Moravia. While there were some Lutherans and Calvinists among them, most of the "Pennsylvania Dutch," as they were called by the English colonists, belonged to small and obscure sects. Dunkards, Schwankenfelders, Amish, and Mennonites still maintain their special religious communities. Their language is Alemannish and this German dialect is still spoken in Alsace and Switzerland. In addition to their colonies in Pennsylvania, there was a small settlement of Moravian Brothers in the western part of North Carolina.

Maryland was originally settled under a charter to Lord Baltimore as a refuge for English Catholics, but from the beginning these latter were very few in number and by 1690 were so thoroughly outnumbered that they were deprived of the franchise.

Virginia, the most important of the colonies next to New England, if the latter be taken as a whole, was pure English in the tidewater district, that is, as far west as Richmond. Beyond were many Ulster Scots, who, it must be remembered, were very largely English.

North Carolina was much the same, except that the Ulster Scots were relatively more numerous.

South Carolina had an English planter aristocracy and was much purer English and had less Ulster Scotch than her northern neighbor. It had also a considerable French Huguenot element, by far the largest and most influential in the colonies. These Huguenots, while not very numerous, were nearly all men of culture and social standing and played a large part in the development of the country.

Georgia was substantially of the same racial complexion as South Carolina.

V

THE PURITANS IN NEW ENGLAND

TAKING up the settlement of the colonies more in detail, we may commence with New England. The first inhabitants of Massachusetts were predominantly from the eastern half of England. This contains the counties in which Nordic influence had probably been the strongest, and the early settlement of Massachusetts was by an overwhelmingly Nordic stock, judging alike by place of origin and by family and personal names. A study of the origin of the pioneers of Plymouth, Watertown, and Dedham shows that two-thirds of them came from a region along the English coast between London and the Wash and mostly from the southern part of that stretch of territory.

Although given an important position by historians because of its priority and the romantic incidents connected with its founding, Plymouth Colony, because of its small size, played only a minor part in the early development of the American nation. Its settlers, as shown by the detailed accounts available concerning many of them, were people of the lower and middle classes, mostly of good character but attracting to their numbers also adventurers and men of more doubtful quality.

Within five or six years after the landing at Plymouth Rock, the Plymouth settlers were already outnumbered by other settlers in New England, while Plymouth itself was the parent of a number of other settlements that outstripped it. During the decade 1630–40 it became a province of eight small towns, seven of them stretching for fifty miles along the shore of Cape Cod Bay, from Scituate to Yarmouth, with Taunton lying twenty-five miles inland. The entire colony would probably have moved to the Connecticut River valley, had not the competition of settlers from Massachusetts Bay been too strong. Two generations after the original settlement there the number of inhabitants of Plymouth was no greater than it was at the start.

In the decade of 1620–30 there was a rapid but sporadic settlement of small towns on or near the Massachusetts coast, but the first great migration was that represented by the arrival of Governor Winthrop's fleet in Massachusetts Bay in 1630. The new arrivals settled Boston, Charlestown, Medford, Watertown, Roxbury, Lynn, and Dorchester. During the next decade the Puritan emigration from England continued, again largely from the northern and eastern counties, overwhelmingly of as nearly pure Nordic stock as Great Britain could show.

The difference in antecedents of the Massachusetts Bay Colony from that of Plymouth is reflected in the differences in geographical and social origin. The Pilgrim Fathers, as every one knows, took their start from Scrooby in Yorkshire at the point where

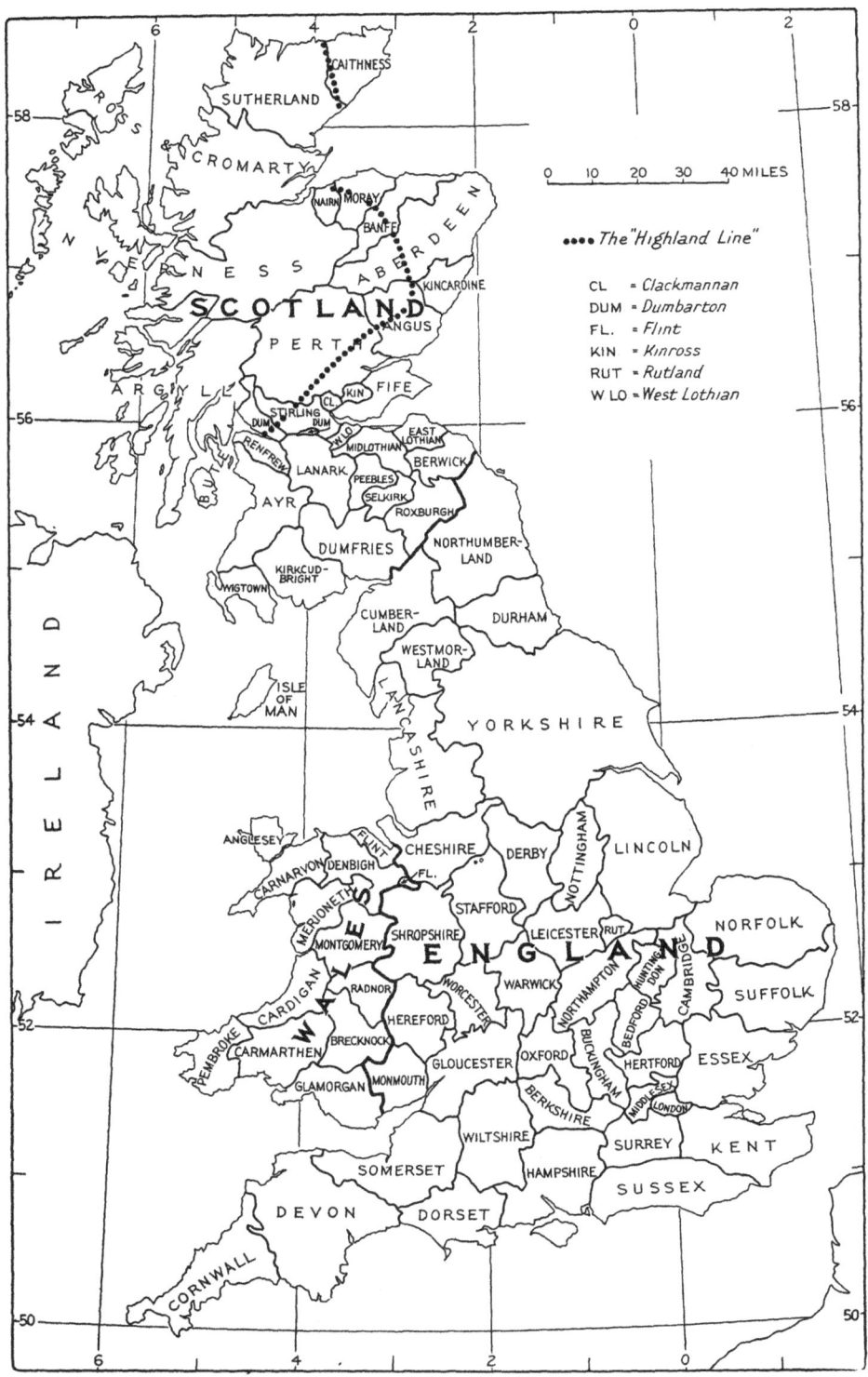

Showing Highlands and Lowlands of Scotland.

this county joins Lincolnshire and Northamptonshire, under the leadership of Bradford, the local post-master and Robinson the clergyman. The capital for the enterprise was almost all subscribed in London, and only one-third of the first settlers were members of Robinson's congregation. The part of Scrooby and Holland in that colony has therefore often been exaggerated. The English founders of the Massachusetts Bay Colony were on the other hand not merely religious dissenters, but powerful members of the Puritan nobility. The group attracted to their enterprise was therefore one of a somewhat wider social outlook. It was distinguished for the same reason from most of the later emigration.

The people who settled in the Massachusetts Bay Colony in the decade of 1630-40 doubtless had every desire to better their condition, and their zeal in seizing land from the Indians showed that they were able to put this desire into effect successfully. Their motive in emigrating, however, was more political than was that of many later colonists, most of whom came frankly to find fortune in a new country.

There were among them a sprinkling of members of the important county families and even a few representatives of the Puritan gentry. Alumni of Cambridge were liberally represented among the clergy, together with a few from Oxford, although few other professional men seem to have been in the group. Many of the settlers were from families of merchants, among whom Puritanism had made great progress in England. The bulk, however, consisted of more or less well-to-do yeomen and artisans.

Since a large part of this Puritan migration, which probably amounted to 20,000 between 1620 and 1640, came in groups often following their local clergymen, it is fairly easy to determine from what parts of Great Britain the early population of Massachusetts came. The evidence all indicates that little of it was from the far north of England where Puritanism had made comparatively slight progress. The greater proportion of the settlers came from the Puritan stronghold of East Anglia comprising the counties of Suffolk, Essex, Norfolk, and eastern Hereford. Next to this was the emigration from Wessex including Dorset, Somerset, and eastern Devon. Following came contributions from Kent, from the midland counties of Buckingham, Northampton, and Leicester, a considerable group from the borders of Wiltshire, Hampshire, and western Berkshire with some from as far west as Gloucestershire near the Welsh border. A large Boston group came from Lincolnshire (which was the home of the ancestors of the Boston-born Benjamin Franklin) and of course there was a strong contingent from London, which was largely Puritan and Presbyterian. Towns in Massachusetts tended to be settled by people who were all from the same region in England; and as the expansion of Massachusetts was very largely in the form of congregations from given towns, these populations often kept together for a long time. Frequently the town's name indi-

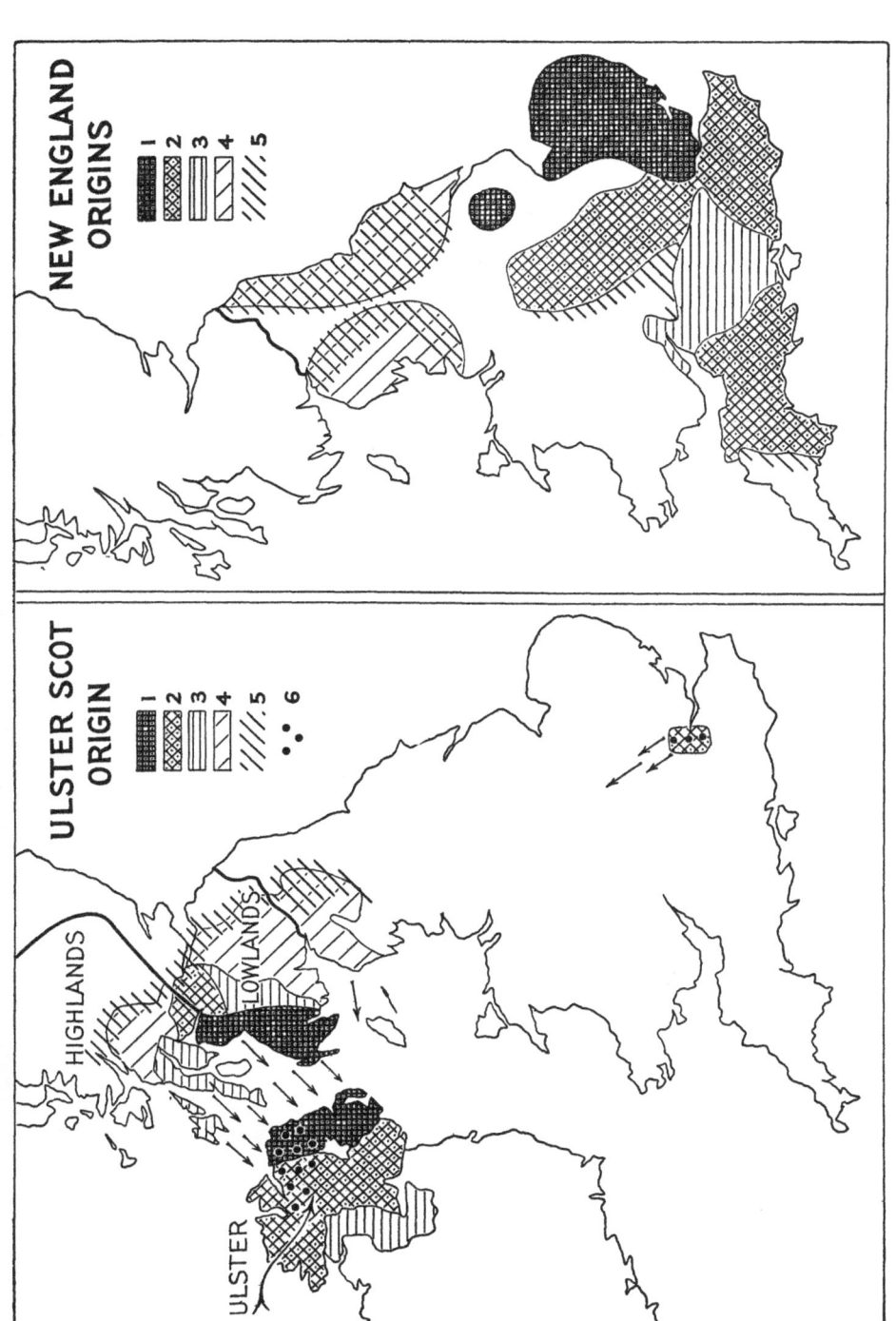

Ulster Scot and New England origins—1, heaviest; 2, heavy; 3, light; 4, very light; 5, uncertain; 6, English definitely present.

THE PURITANS IN NEW ENGLAND 85

cates the old home. Thus Gloucester was settled by men from that county and Dorchester was named for the town in Dorset from which its early settlers came with the Rev. John Maverick, although it contained an element of Lancashire people from the neighborhood of Preston, Liverpool, and Manchester.

Along with the desire of these settlers to better themselves, to acquire the ownership of land, and to seek fortune in new countries, the disturbed political conditions in Great Britain particularly urged Puritans to migrate. British documents of the period throw many sidelights on the nature and scope of this movement. Thus Lord Maynard, in a memorandum to Archbishop Laud in 1638, laments "the intention of divers clothiers of great trading to go suddenly into New England." He hears daily of incredible numbers of persons of very good abilities who have sold their lands to depart and says there is danger of divers parishes being impoverished.

Since some of them liked the Massachusetts government no better than the one at home, the tide of emigration turned strongly toward the West Indies, the British islands of which were rapidly filled with Nordic stock. The history of Nordic settlement in the West Indies is little known and is exceedingly instructive in connection with a study of the peopling of the New World. Bermuda was colonized in 1612, Saint Kitts in 1623, Barbadoes and Saint Croix in 1625, and Nevis three years later. By 1640 Massachusetts had about 14,000 settlers; but Saint

Kitts had almost as many and Barbadoes decidedly more. The number of Englishmen who migrated to the West Indies was perhaps three times as large as the number who went to all New England.

Down to the end of the eighteenth century the West Indies were flourishing, populous, and wealthy, but these islands then ceased to have any world-wide importance—not merely because of economic and agricultural changes, such as affected the sugar industry, but because the white man in the tropics could not compete on even terms with the Negro. It will be pointed out later that these islands are now virtually Negro territory, and they have become centers of emigration into the United States of a black populatation of low economic and social status—the Nordics having died out, or lost their original characteristics, or gone elsewhere.

From 1640 the emigration from Great Britain to New England almost stopped and the tide turned the other way; many settlers in Massachusetts either returning to England or going to the West Indies. The natural increase of the population from then on accounts for most of the growth of the New England colonies. Even here, however, the Bay State fell behind Virginia in rate of increase of white population.

Almost as soon as they had established themselves around Massachusetts Bay, groups of settlers began to push out in all directions, partly to get better or cheaper land, and partly to get greater independence of action. In this way the settlement of Connecticut

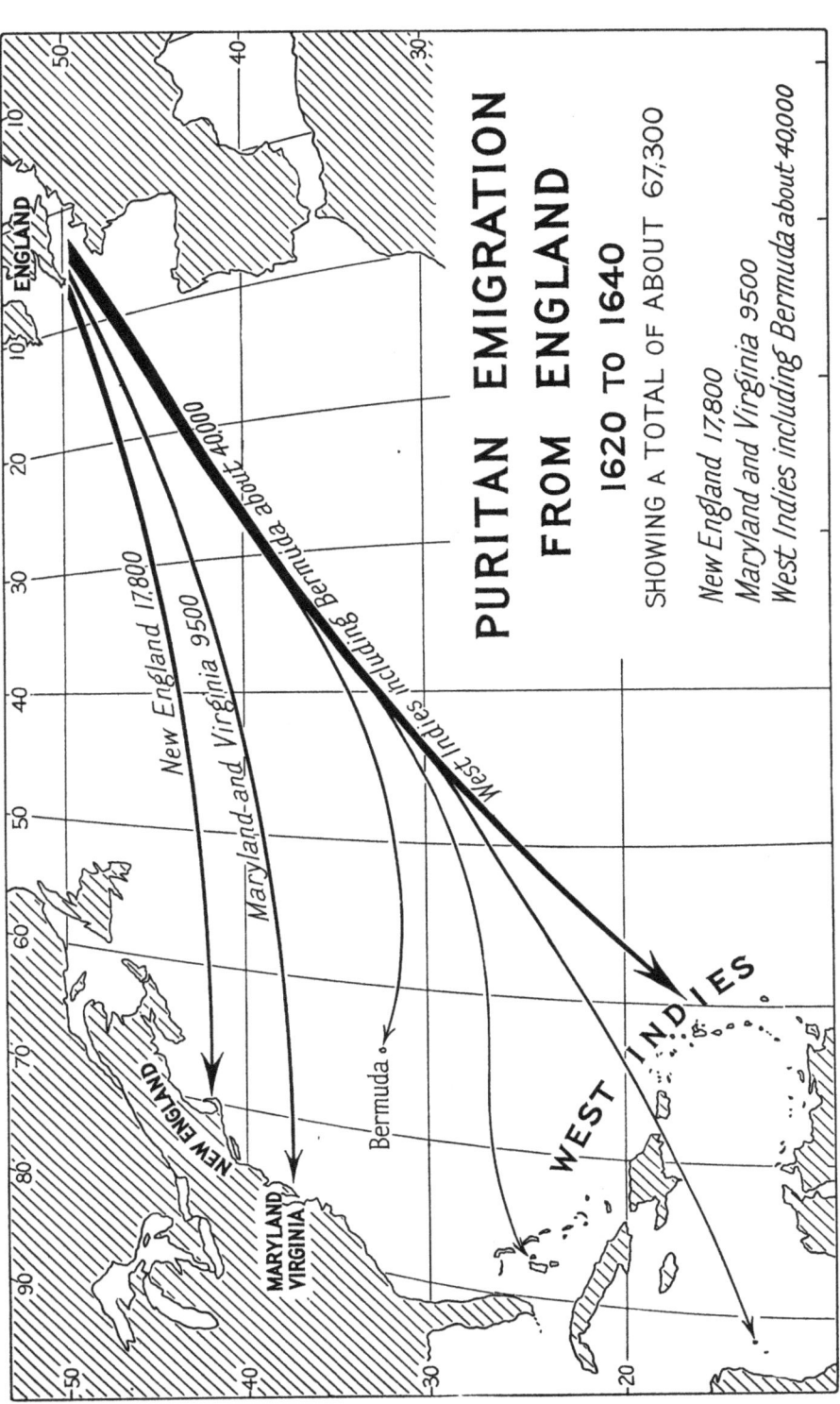

THE PURITANS IN NEW ENGLAND 87

was begun as early as 1634. In the next year emigrants arrived in Connecticut from Dorchester and Watertown in Massachusetts and in 1636 from Newton. They established settlements in the Connecticut River valley bearing the names of the Massachusetts towns from which they came until the names of Windsor, Wethersfield, and Hartford were substituted. In 1638 came the settlements at New Haven, Guilford, Milford, and elsewhere. Stratford, Fairfield, Norwalk, and Stamford were established not many months later as a challenge to the Dutch from New York who regarded that part of Connecticut as their own domain. By 1640, at least a couple of thousand settlers were in Connecticut; Hartford, New Haven, and New London becoming in their turn the main gateways of immigration into the whole back country. The settlement of New England was, in general, however, from south to north, proceeding along the river valleys.

The fisheries and the excellent supply of timber for naval construction led to scattered settlements on the coast of Maine even earlier. The lack of navigable rivers delayed penetration into the interior—but during the seventeenth century the Massachusetts people had settled along most of the river valleys. Even to this day the interior of Maine is very largely backwoods. This territory was claimed by Massachusetts as a part of its own dominion, from which it did not separate until in 1820 when it was admitted as an independent State to offset Missouri in Henry Clay's famous compromise.

As Indians were gradually dispossessed, the population of Massachusetts continued to push westward. In 1676 the end of King Philip's War removed the fear of Indians for a time and led to particularly active movements of population inland. Meanwhile settlements had been made in New Hampshire and Rhode Island. The first settlement in New Hampshire had been made by David Thomson, a Scotsman who established himself on the coast; but its population came from Plymouth Colony and later from other parts of Massachusetts. The spread of the English in the New Hampshire mountains and forests, where the Indians continued hostile for a long time, was slow, and even at the time of the Revolution, New Hampshire contained few settlements of any size. The greatest development came toward the end of the period here considered. In 1700 it held but 5000 or 6000 souls. Up to 1760 only the coast towns had any considerable population, but the peace of 1763, which finally removed the French and Indian menace, resulted in a rapid penetration of settlers largely from Connecticut. In the next fifteen years 30,000 people are said to have entered New Hampshire from Connecticut alone, and a hundred new towns had been planted.

Rhode Island already had a few settlers before Roger Williams founded Providence (1636), though that is generally regarded as the beginning of the colony. Portsmouth was founded in 1638, Newport and Warwick in 1639, and in 1644 these settlements were united under one government. Because of its

THE PURITANS IN NEW ENGLAND 89

small size, Rhode Island plays in a sense only a minor part in the history of the formation of the early population of North America. But it served as a place of entry for colonists from all sources, and it likewise attracted settlers from the other colonies, due to its conspicuous policy of political and religious toleration. In another way the small size of Rhode Island led to its being a source of colonization. Its available land resources were so small that large families soon exhausted them and there was no recourse except to get out of the colony. It was therefore an incubator for colonists and furnished more emigrants in proportion to its population than did other colonies which had greater resources wherewith to care for their own people. It may be said that while Massachusetts is the parent of all New England, the whole of New England is in some sense a parent of Rhode Island. In either case, the racial homogeneity of the population is conspicuous, the little groups of settlers who represented other than Nordic stock being insignificant in numbers however much they may appeal through sentiment to the pride of their descendants.

Vermont was settled late, its main occupation not coming until after the Revolution. At first a part of New Hampshire, it attracted occasional settlers from that State and its neighbors, but there could hardly be said to have been a permanent settlement until Brattleboro was founded in 1740.

The settlement of Massachusetts west of the Connecticut River began in 1725, when the Berkshires were invaded and Sheffield established. Settlers steadily pressed north and west, and gradually took possession of the territory between the Connecticut River and Lake Champlain. The Connecticut River was the first American frontier, as Alaska was the last.

At the time of the Revolution Vermont was very much of a frontier, in which a lawless and defiant lot known as the Green Mountain Boys held possession and yielded allegiance to no one. Within six weeks after the collapse of Shays's Rebellion, more than 700 families are said to have migrated from western Massachusetts into Vermont. Many New England soldiers who had fought over this ground in the Revolution had marked it as offering desirable home sites, and came into it to take up land and clear it, to bring their families, and establish isolated settlements which gradually coalesced into something like a settled country. The increasing influx of New Englanders led to the surrender of New York's claims on the territory, so that it took its place as an independent State in 1791, the first to be added to the original thirteen.

The picture of New England then is that of a community which received the bulk of its foundation stock in a very short period of time, 1620 to 1640, and almost wholly from a single source; that is, England, and specifically from the most Nordic districts of England. It was no mere figure of speech when Captain John Smith bestowed upon the region the prophetic name of New England. During the eighteenth century, scattered groups of other origins came to add themselves to the descendants of these early settlers; but in most cases they represented only drops in the bucket. Doubtless one of the reasons why the study of genealogy and the pride of ancestry have flourished most conspicuously in New England is that so large a proportion of the old population traces its ancestry back to the same period and to the same group of people. Even as early as the Revolution, the great bulk of the settlers of New England represented families that had been four or five generations on American soil.

If there was a conspicuous absence of immigrants of very distinguished families into New England at that time, it may be said, on the other hand, that the general level was sound and intelligent. The immigrant population of New England was composed of a small group of families dominant in business and the professions, and an overwhelming proportion of representatives of the English yeomanry, owners of small freeholds, whose sons often sailed ships or went to the fisheries. This same type made up the bulk of the population of the middle colonies and peopled the back country of the southern colonies. As most of the settlers in New England in the early migration were men who brought their families, the foundation stock thus established was on a better level than that in some other colonies where men arrived without bringing wives and therefore were forced to marry women of any kind whom the colony could furnish. The definitely Nordic character of New England stock, its early establishment, and the survival of the able and vigorous in a region where nature took a heavy toll of weaklings, have produced in New England a population that has left its stamp on subsequent American history as has no other group.

As to the Ulster Scots we must bear in mind that the Irish question was as serious a thorn in the side of English statesmen in the sixteenth and seventeenth centuries, as it was before or since, and numerous attempts were made to alleviate the situation, if not to end it, by the colonization of Protestant people in Ireland. In 1611, James I began to encourage the emigration of people from the lowlands of Scotland, particularly from the western part, and from the north of England, into Ulster. He looked forward to establishing in Ireland a staunch Protestant population that might ultimately outnumber the Catholics and become the controlling element politically. For this reason the settlers were picked with some care. The plan succeeded so well that in a generation or a little more, about 300,000 people had been colonized in the northern part of the island, and by the end of a century their number had risen to nearly a million.

These are the "Scotch Irish" of American history. The name is a grotesque misnomer suggesting to the popular mind a sort of hybrid origin and hybrid character which has no basis in reality. They were not Irish in any sense of the word, and while most of them were Scotch a great many were English. They are designated in this book as "Ulster Scots."

Following the planting of Ulster in the north of Ireland, there was a heavy British emigration into the east of Ireland. This was due partly to economic factors and partly to the desire of Cromwell, in his turn, to solve the Irish problem by colonization, after the precedent which James I had established. These English Protestants in eastern Ireland have too often been ignored. They, too, had nothing in common with the older Roman Catholic population of the eastern part of the Island. Many of the Protestant "Irish" were Quakers.

These adopted children of Ireland also migrated freely to the American colonies and have been assumed far too easily to have been Roman Catholics. While it is extremely difficult to arrive at exact figures on this point, there is some reason to believe that the number of Protestant English in the east of Ireland during the seventeenth century was as large as the number of Protestant Scotch in the north, and this former group contributed its quota of English population to the colonies. It was this group which imposed the English language on the Irish. Until the later 1840's the Leinster Protestants and the Ulster Presbyterians were practically the only immigrants from Ireland to this country.

The great movement of Ulster Scots to America, although of an entirely different degree of magnitude, has been perhaps second only to that from the English counties in its influence on the subsequent history of the Continent. It began in the latter part of the seventeenth century but did not reach its height until the first quarter of the eighteenth. Five shiploads arrived in the summer of 1718, giving Cotton Mather the chance to note in his diary with anticipatory pleasure the merit that would accrue to him from showing "kindness to ye indigent." Thereafter, one finds in most histories such items as "In 1719 there came one hundred and twenty Presbyterian families from the north of Ireland who settled in Massachusetts" or "In the years 1719 and 1720 more than one hundred Presbyterian families came from the north of Ireland and settled at Londonderry in New Hampshire," and so on.

The Congregationalists of the seaboard were not too hospitable to these Presbyterians, and forced them to move inland in almost every case, away from the long-settled territory over which the Boston theocracy attempted to maintain its rule, and mostly to New Hampshire and Connecticut. Londonderry recalls its origin by its name and the Scotch who settled it not only introduced their manufactures into New Hampshire but brought along with them a still more valuable importation, the so-called Irish potato, which, having been taken from South America to Ireland long before, had, in this round-about way, been brought back to its own hemisphere. Other groups went to Worcester, to Pelham, to Palmer, to Andover, and to other communities in small numbers; while many others went to Maine. The total numbers, however, were very small.

THE PURITANS IN NEW ENGLAND 95

Massachusetts had a definite policy at this time of encouraging, if not requiring, immigrants of this sort to settle on the frontiers. They furnished less competition in this way and played a useful part in keeping off the Indians.

The emigration of the Scotch and North English who had been in Ulster for a generation or two or at the most for three generations, was due to discontent with their situation there. They had built up an important manufacture of woollens and linens which has ever since been famous throughout the world; but in 1698 the jealousy of rival industrialists in England led to Parliamentary legislation which crippled the industries in Ulster and threw many men out of employment. In 1704 and the following years a religious persecution of these Presbyterians was also carried on. These economic and religious handicaps were so great that after a few years of patient waiting the population gave up hope, and within half a century about half of the entire number had moved to the New World. The most important stream went into the middle and southern colonies and will be traced later.

This exodus was a cause of alarm in the old country as well as in the new. "The rumour [of going to America] has spread like a contagious distemper," laments an Irish letter writer in 1728; "and the worst is that it affects only Protestants, and reigns chiefly in the North"; while another laments that "there are now seven ships at Belfast, that are carrying off about 1000 passengers thither; and if we knew how to stop them, as most of them can get neither victuals nor work at home, it would be cruel to do it."

Reference will recur frequently to this immigration of Ulster Scots. At this point it is necessary to emphasize in the first place that it was little different in racial background from the preceding English settlement, both groups being definitely Nordic in their make-up. In the second place it was a valuable addition to the colonies in the quality and energy of its members. In the third place it was always small in proportion to the English element.

New England in 1790, regardless of numerous non-English groups, many of them of good individual quality though insignificant in total numbers, is to be considered definitely as a transplanted English population, most of which had been settled in North America so long that its habits of thought and action had become differentiated—one might say definitely American rather than English.

A third source of New England settlers during this period, small in numbers but valuable in quality, is represented by the French Huguenots who arrived for the most part in the decade or two following the Revocation of the Edict of Nantes.

The Huguenot migration to America falls in two general epochs. From 1555, when Admiral Coligny had a vision of a Protestant France in the New World, to the Revocation in 1685 of the Edict of Nantes, the French charter of Protestant liberty, is the first epoch, during which the immigration was scattering. From 1685 up to about 1750 is the second epoch, when the Huguenots, fleeing from oppression and death, sought refuge in many countries. During this period their immigration to North America reached considerable proportions. Providence and Boston were points of entry for many, though more went to the Southern colonies, and to them many an American family of the present day is proud to trace its ancestry.

These French Huguenots seem to have come predominantly from the middle class or artisan stratum of the population with a mixture of the lesser gentry. But their energy, ability, and character earned for them an important rôle in their adopted country, out of proportion to their small numbers. Unlike some of the other non-English groups they did not tend to establish colonies or settlements of their own, but scattered widely and merged freely into the general population. This was the less difficult in that they came from the most Nordic parts of France and in racial composition are scarcely to be distinguished from the English.

In the same way those northern and eastern counties of England, which supplied a large part of the migration to America, had, during the preceding century, received a continuous infusion of continental Huguenots to a total sometimes estimated as high as 250,000, who there also became by admixture and hereditary similitude indistinguishable from their neighbors.

The Indian population of New England though

never great was largely exterminated by war, disease, whiskey, and the breaking up of their cultural and economic background. In the century before the settlement of Plymouth, smallpox, introduced from the Spanish Main, had flickered up and down the New England coast and had so decimated the natives that only a weakened remnant remained to oppose the Whites.

In contrast, in the eleventh century the Norsemen who attempted to found settlements on the New England coast had met with savage resistance from the natives, whom they called Skrellings.

Intermarriage between Whites and Indians was almost unknown save in the occasional case in which a colonist was carried into captivity. The antipathy of the English settlers to the Indians was far too great to lead to the sort of miscegenation which was encouraged by the French in their part of the continent, and to which reference will be made later. In the British colonies the half-breed was looked upon as an Indian, whereas in the French colonies, as generally in all Colonial countries that had the Roman imperial tradition and the Roman Catholic religion, the half-breed was assimilated to the European group. Some of the remaining Indians along the Atlantic coast mixed with the runaway Negro slaves, but few of them contributed to the white population, and the term "half-breed" was in general a term of contempt. It was not until within the lifetime of those now living that an infusion of Indian blood became a subject of pride, particularly in Oklahoma, unless one makes exception for such isolated tales as the somewhat grotesque Pocahontas tradition in Virginia.

The predominant influence of Massachusetts at the time of the Revolution is easy to understand. It possessed, to an unusual degree, unity in the various fields in which unity is most valuable to a nation—unity of race, unity of language, unity of culture, unity of religion, unity of institutions—and, more than anywhere else in the United States, its unity was attained through a long-continued, independent growth on American soil.

The French and Indian menace held back the rapidly multiplying population of New England for at least a generation. The agricultural areas were carrying more population than they could support, and they were waiting for a favorable opportunity to spread out. This opportunity came in the overthrow of Montcalm at Quebec in 1759. The Peace of Paris in 1763 left the road open, and the New England population began to push north, west, and south with a vigor that was reflected in the activity of the communities at home. The succeeding half-century is correctly regarded as the golden age of New England. Its country districts were more densely populated when the first census of the United States was taken in 1790 than they have been since. The decline, which will be traced in the next section, then began and decade after decade thereafter the New England towns and villages are found in a surprisingly large percentage of cases either standing still or actually declining in number of inhabitants.

The history of American colonization is usually written only in terms of the additions to population. The subtractions from it may be no less important. Subtractions by migration westward were less significant because in many cases the frontier merely proliferated itself by sending its surplus out without diminishing its own standards or numbers.

The first national loss of population occurred after 1640 when the changing political conditions in England, and the tyranny of the Massachusetts Bay authorities, drove many people out of Massachusetts. This loss, serious as it was, is insignificant compared with the tremendous loss of superior stock at the time of the Revolution. The Loyalists made up an undetermined part of the population, perhaps as much as one-third. Those who had been most conspicuous or most active were obliged in many cases to flee, and persecution with the confiscation of their property was carried on even after the war. Most of the Loyalists who left the colonies went either to Canada or to the West Indies. Altogether the loss from this source may have been as great as 100,000 people representing on the whole a superior selection of the population. It is comparable in the racial damage done the American population with the loss which France suffered from the expulsion of the Huguenots.

By the Revolution, the colonizing impulse of New England had not merely begun to fill up western New York, as will be described shortly, but had led to the formation of speculative land companies for settlement in the Wyoming Valley of Pennsylvania, and even on the lower Mississippi. The hard times following the Revolution led to a great increase in migration, which, in general, has been rapid in hard times, slower in periods of prosperity. Vermont, as already said, felt the impulse markedly. Maine also seems to have grown most rapidly in the decade or two following the Declaration of Independence, though Portland and Falmouth were the only towns worthy of the name. New Hampshire, likewise, slower in its development than other parts of New England, had begun to catch up by attracting those ready to better themselves by a change of location. Connecticut had made a steady growth and had fewer non-English elements than almost any other of the New England colonies, small as these elements were everywhere. The growth of Massachusetts had been largely in the interior, Boston having made less progress than many other cities. People were moving from Massachusetts to other colonies. Many were moving through Boston but not staying there. Politically and culturally important, the Hub of the Universe stagnated industrially until the beginning of the manufacturing era.

VI

THE GATEWAYS TO THE WEST FROM NEW ENGLAND AND VIRGINIA

In 1609, the English navigator, Henry Hudson, had explored the river which now bears his name, acting on behalf of the Dutch East India Company. During the next decade, small Dutch settlements, trading posts, were established along the river; but the first real settlement is generally dated 1623 when thirty families of Walloons arrived. These were people from northern France and the southern Netherlands who had been driven into Holland by religious persecution and wanted to escape from the unsympathetic treatment which they were receiving in the southern part of Holland. Their language was not Dutch but French.

Speaking at large the Dutch settlement of New Netherland was, at the beginning, a trading venture and was based on a stronghold at the mouth of the river and another one at the head of navigation. For many years the latter settlement, originally called Fort Orange and later Albany, was much more important than the little town of New Amsterdam on Manhattan Island.

Restrictions on land tenure held back colonization, and at no time during the Dutch occupation did its reach extend much beyond the fertile farm lands of the Hudson valley northerly to Fort Orange, though an outpost to the west was established at Schenectady and scattering settlements had also been made in New Jersey and on Long Island.

In all these outlying regions, the pressure of New England migrants was too strong for the scanty Dutch population to withstand, and even in Manhattan the New Englanders had become early an important part of the population.

The immigration of respectable Dutch families did not begin in general until after 1638 when the monopoly of the West India Company was abolished. Many of the families who became great land owners in the northern part of the Hudson River valley were from Gelderland, east of the Zuyder Zee, the town of Myjerka being one of the principal centers of emigration. While many of these Dutch families were of excellent mercantile stock, it is a mistake to suppose that they represented the social élite of the home country.

Although the Dutch have left a permanent mark on the Hudson River valley, the contribution which they made to the future population of the State was small. When England captured the colony in 1664 and the Dutch immigration ceased, there were probably not many more than 10,000 inhabitants in the whole region, and of these from a quarter to a third were English.

Holland at the time was not at all a colonizing nation. Its overseas ventures were for the purpose of trade, and it had not sufficient surplus population to settle colonies permanently.

The amount of Dutch and Huguenot blood that was perpetuated in the later history of the colonies was, therefore, small by comparison with the English, but was for the most part of the same racial stock. Six or seven thousand Dutch in the present State of New York in 1664 are to be compared with 35,000 English in Virginia and 50,000 in New England at the same date.

There was no further general and organized emigration from Holland to America until the close of the Revolution. At that time some of the Amsterdam bankers, who had loaned millions of dollars to the Revolutionary government, decided to try to capitalize their investments and bought nearly 4,000,000 acres of land in New York and Pennsylvania. Most of the settlers on this tract were not Dutch; and while Dutch names may still play an important part in the Social Registers of New York and Albany, Dutch blood is insignificant in the present makeup of the population of the United States.

The southerly tide of New Englanders, which washed over the Dutch colony and others to the South, was in the first instance made up largely of those who did not find the religious convictions of their associates in Massachusetts and Connecticut to their liking.

The little "Forts" of the Dutch in the Connecticut valley were swamped shortly after 1630, and by 1639 the Connecticut people of English ancestry had established themselves at Greenwich within thirty miles of New Amsterdam and in other towns even nearer. Long Island was settled from the same source, and Thomas Belcher took up a tract upon the present site of the City of Brooklyn in the same year in which the English began to build at Greenwich. Brooklyn, until the twentieth century, has been a typically New England community, entirely distinct from the other boroughs of Greater New York. The eastern end of Long Island was long separated from the western end and was settled directly from Connecticut. The Hamptons are virtually still a part of New England.

The development of the southern part of New York State, and particularly of the Hudson River valley, was delayed indefinitely by the great land holdings of the so-called "patroons" or great landlords. New York City continued to be a cosmopolitan and nondescript town, built up on commerce and trade and without any particular racial complexion. Even at the time of the Revolution, it was inferior alike in size and in influence to Philadelphia and Boston, and New York State was but seventh in population among the thirteen colonies.

The real foundation of the greatness of the Empire State was the New England colonization of northern and western New York, which created a territory that was, and has ever since remained, quite distinct in political complexion and economic and social interests from the Hudson River valley and the metropolis at its mouth.

The commercial greatness of the City of New York dates from the opening of the Erie Canal in

1825, which made New York the outlet of the lake States. Meanwhile, however, several other foreign invasions had taken place.

The French Huguenots, racially Nordic and almost identical with the British, began to arrive in Colonial New York after 1685, founding the town of New Rochelle to commemorate the French city from which so many of them had come. Here, as elsewhere, their influence was far in excess of their proportionately small number.

In 1711, Governor Hunter of New York became imbued with grandiose ideas about developing the resources of his Province and began to look for a source of cheap labor for its exploitation. He found this in the German districts on the Rhine, broadly known as the Palatinate, where various national elements, not merely German and Alsatian, but French, Swiss, Moravian, and miscellaneous, were gathered, and where the religious persecution to which they were subjected as Protestants, and the excessive hardships which they were compelled to endure from invasions of the armies of Louis XIV, had reduced them to great misery.

The population was ripe for emigration and furnished the only substantial element of non-Nordic origin in the Colonial history of America. It is not necessary to trace in detail the innumerable petty sects and national elements, often two or three times removed from their original home, of which this "Palatine" emigration was composed. For the present purpose it was predominantly German-speaking,

THE GATEWAYS TO THE WEST 107

and largely of the round-headed Alpine stock in racial makeup.

About 1709, these Palatines began frantic efforts to escape from their misfortunes, and within a few years some 30,000 had gone over into Holland and even into England, where they were not welcome. The British Government was only too glad to subsidize their further emigration, and several thousand of them were transported to the Hudson River valley. They soon became discontented there and were finally colonized on the Schoharie River in New York. Here, in turn, they were ousted by what they considered political jobbery and many of them moved on to the Mohawk River, a tributary of the Hudson, while others continued down the Susquehanna River to Pennsylvania. On the whole, therefore, the Palatines are to be considered merely temporary inhabitants of New York State. Although a good many of them remained, the reports they sent out as to their treatment were so unsatisfactory that thenceforth the Palatine immigration mostly avoided New York and landed in Pennsylvania, where it will be encountered later.

The next influx, particularly after 1719, was of Ulster Scots, similar to that already mentioned as invading New England. Much of Orange County on the west of the Hudson River was settled by these Ulstermen, beginning as early as 1729, and for the next half-century the infiltration of this Nordic element was continuous, although more of it came through New England than directly into New York harbor. By the time of the Revolution the Ulster Scots had spread over much of the eastern part of northern New York, having enough representatives in Albany in 1760 to establish a Presbyterian church there.

At about the same time Sir William Johnson, who had received a grant of 100,000 acres of land north of the Mohawk River for his valor in defending the colonies against the French at Crown Point and Lake George in 1755, began to look about for suitable tenants and hit upon the idea of importing Scotch Highlanders of Roman Catholic faith. Some hundreds of these arrived just before the Revolution, and like Sir John Johnson, son of Sir William, espoused the cause of the Loyalists. After the Revolution, they moved northward to Ontario where the town of Glengarry recalls their earlier home in Inverness. There, such families as the MacDonnells, McDougalls, Camerons, McIntyres, and Fergusons became an important element of strength to Canada.

As noted, New York State at the time of the Revolution was still distinctly an unimportant colony, and its greatness dates from the invasion of New Englanders immediately after the war. Connecticut, by virtue of its proximity, was the principal source of these settlers, although almost every part of New England contributed. The crossing over of the Ulster Scots has already been mentioned, but it must not be inferred that that was the principal element in the settlement of the State. The main immigration was of the old Puritan English stock which still dominates all of upper New York, except where subsequent colonies of recent immigrants in some of the larger industrial cities have altered the local scene.

The western shores of Lake Champlain and some of the older towns of the Hudson River valley could scarcely be recognized, after a few years, by those who had known them previously. A mere Dutch farm in 1784 had been changed in four years to the thriving city of Hudson, a typical New England commercial town with warehouses, wharves, Yankee shipping, and stores filled with Yankee notions.

A visitor to Whitesborough on the Mohawk River, in 1788, reported that "settlers are continually pouring in from the Connecticut hive." Binghamton was settled jointly by Connecticut and Massachusetts. The same spirit caused a mixing up of the population within the limits of New England so that, to take a single illustration, the men of Middlefield, a small hill town in western Massachusetts, were found on inquiry to come from nearly sixty different towns in Massachusetts and Connecticut.

After the Revolution the more enterprising young men of Massachusetts and Connecticut began to leave their home towns. Of those who departed, a half went to other places in New England, a quarter to western New York, and a quarter to Ohio and other points in the then "Far West."

The extreme western part of New York State had not begun to develop as early as the period of which we are speaking. Canandaigua was the largest town in 1790, and it had but a hundred inhabitants. Pioneers came from New Jersey and Pennsylvania by way of the Susquehanna and Tioga Rivers, went to Seneca Lake, and thence to Cayuga; others from Connecticut had entered the valley of the Mohawk by way of Albany and Fort Schuyler. Small settlements sprang up at Bath, Naples, Geneva, Aurora, Seneca Falls, Palmyra, Richmond, Fort Stanwix, and Marcellus. The Erie Canal was as yet undreamt of.

The population picture of New York State in 1790 is then a double one. The great bulk of the State, so far as area is concerned, was a colony of Anglo-Saxon origin almost identical with the New England States. The Hudson valley formed a less important appendage to this, with New York City at its mouth—a miscellaneous settlement of people of all sorts whose interests were largely commercial.

New York was one of the States that lost most heavily by the Loyalist migration at the end of the Revolution. This superior Nordic element left in two great streams; one by sea to Nova Scotia, and the other overland to Canada. Long Island was a particularly heavy loser, 3000 people going in one fleet in 1783. The influx of Loyalists into Nova Scotia, amounting to some 35,000, was a severe burden on that little colony. Those who went into Canada overland from New York were more easily assimilated, and many of the important settlements along the northern shores of Lake Erie and Lake Ontario,

THE GATEWAYS TO THE WEST 111

such as Kingston, date from that time. To these Ontario settlers was given, by Order in Council in 1789, the honorary name of "United Empire Loyalists," and they formed the backbone of Upper Canada, as the Province of Ontario was then called, and were a main element in defeating the plans of American strategists in 1812 to capture Canada and annex it to the Union.

Although New York is generally credited with having more Loyalists during the Revolution than any other colony, she also furnished more troops for the patriot army than did any other State except Massachusetts.

New Jersey, in contrast to its neighbors on either side, was one of the most thoroughly English of all the colonies. The settlements of the Dutch in the north, and the squabbles of a few hundred Dutch, Swedes, and Finlanders in the south, left little trace on the population when colonization once started in earnest. The real history of the colony begins in 1664 when the English proprietors, to whom it had been granted, began to colonize it seriously.

Northern New Jersey was a chaos of rugged hills and forests which offered little to the settler and is still largely waste land. The southern part of the State is also largely waste land, consisting chiefly of pine barrens so that early settlement was virtually limited to two areas. On the North River, as the Hudson was called, the lands along the meadows opposite Manhattan Island were inviting, and on the South River, as the Delaware was originally designated, there was a broad strip of fertile farm land which attracted the early settlers. Among other centers New Haven had established a colony there about 1640, but had been driven off by the Dutch. There was also some extremely fertile land around Freehold and other towns on the line between New York and Philadelphia.

Since these two areas were so inaccessible to each other by direct communication, the State grew up in two distinct settlements; that along the western side of New York harbor, then known as East Jersey, and that on the Delaware, known as West Jersey. While these two were consolidated administratively in 1702, they have never been wholly consolidated in actual character, and the two ends of the State are, even today, diverse enough to show their somewhat divergent origin.

The land along the Delaware was colonized, for the most part, directly from England by the Quakers who had secured an interest in it, and who established the only two towns of importance in West Jersey during the Colonial period—Burlington in 1667 and Salem in 1675. Those who established Burlington were mostly from Yorkshire with a large group also from London, and they took opposite sides of the town, the Yorkshire people spreading north and the London people spreading south. Geographical difficulties checked the southward spread so that Cape May was settled separately by people from Connecticut and from Long Island. Later, some of the French Huguenots went down into West Jersey, but it always remained essentially an English colony, largely of Quaker complexion and influenced by the close proximity of co-religionists in Pennsylvania.

East Jersey, like western New York, represents more directly a New England outpost. Elizabethtown had been established in 1665 by emigrants sent direct from Great Britain, but Newark had at almost the same time been colonized by people from Connecticut, who at first gave to it the name of their old home, Milford. The Elizabethtown Association somewhat later sold part of its territory to people from New Hampshire and Massachusetts who established the two hamlets of Woodbridge and Piscataqua, now New Brunswick.

In 1666, Connecticut Puritans also established on the Passaic River first Guilford, and later Branford, both of which with Milford merged in the town of Newark. The New England overflow continued until the shores of Newark Bay had become another New England colony. Such communities as the Oranges were chiefly transplanted Puritan towns.

The proprietorship of East Jersey shortly passed into the hands of Scotsmen and a steady immigration of these began about 1684. The capital of East Jersey, Perth Amboy, was named for one of the proprietors, James Drummond, the Earl of Perth. The colony soon became, and has ever since remained, one of the strongholds of Scotch Presbyterianism in America, which found its intellectual center in the establishment of Princeton University.

For a long time the two sections of New Jersey

were of about equal size and importance. As the country between them gradually filled up, the State grew slowly until at the time of the Revolution its population was estimated at about 120,000. Another fifteen years saw a healthy growth, the first census, in 1790, showing 184,139 inhabitants. The somewhat complicated details of its development should not obscure the fact that New Jersey was one of the most purely white, Protestant, Nordic settlements in the colonies.

Although prior to the arrival of William Penn there were several thousand settlers on the Delaware River, in the territory now covered by Pennsylvania and Delaware, the real settlement of that region is generally dated from the beginning of his operations in 1681, when Upland, now Chester, was settled as his headquarters. A year later Philadelphia was founded, and in spite of this late start grew so rapidly that William Penn, the Quaker, at his death, had the satisfaction of knowing that the City of Brotherly Love was the largest in North America.

While the foundation stock was made up of English Quakers, Penn had ambitious ideas of establishing a headquarters for other like-minded persons, and with this idealism was apparently mixed a solid commercial ambition which led him and his agents to advertise the merits of the colony widely. The land system, unlike that of Virginia or New Netherlands, favored the settler with small means. English and Welsh farmers rapidly appropriated to themselves the country along the west side of the Delaware River from Trenton to Wilmington.

Penn maintained friendly relations with the Protestant leaders in southern Germany, and he and his agents seem to have had an extraordinary flair for finding obscure and peculiar sects and getting them to emigrate to the new colony. A mere list of the odd religious denominations that soon flourished in Pennsylvania is bewildering, and an attempt to define the characteristics, which to them seemed more than matters of life and death, is quite beyond the capacity of the present-day student not steeped in the knowledge of seventeenth-century theology.

Germantown was established in October, 1673, the first outpost of the Alpine race in the present territory of the United States. It founders were Mennonites; but they were later joined by Dunkards or Tunkers, that is, Dippers, who held to the efficacy of baptism by immersion.

Generally speaking, the Germans who came to Pennsylvania during the first quarter-century of its settlement belong to these distinctive sects, while after that time the immigration was made up of a somewhat more uniform mass of adherents of either the Lutheran or the Reformed Church. This difference soon became a recognized one for an easy division of "the Pennsylvania Dutch," as this mixed group of Alpines came to be called, not very correctly, from an assimilation of *Pennsylvanische Deutsche*. One would ask, on hearing such a person mentioned, "Does he belong to the sects or to the church people?"

A few of these such as the Labadists from Friesland who settled in New Castle County, Delaware, were either from Holland or parts of Germany bordering Holland, but the great bulk of the "Pennsylvania Dutch" came from the Rhine Provinces, particularly from Alsace and the Palatinate, with a liberal sprinkling of northern French Protestants who had been forced over the border, while others came from Austria and Prussia and even from northern Italy. As a matter of fact, down to the time of the World War, Americans called, colloquially, all Germans "Dutchmen."

While the Palatinate furnished only a part of the immigration its name was soon given to all similar newcomers, so that the term Palatine became a general description for a German-speaking immigrant; and one even finds in the old records such anomalies as an allusion to "a Palatine from Hamburg." An important centre of their dispersion was the town of Crefeld near the border of Holland.

The colonies in general, being overwhelmingly and typically British, looked with suspicion on any alien groups, and New England, in particular, probably would not have encouraged these Alpines to enter at all. Virginia with its Church of England establishment and its self-conscious English attitude was likewise not disposed to be hospitable to such a large group of foreigners.

Governor Oglethorpe attracted some of them to Georgia, but not very successfully, as will be mentioned later. One important group of his settlers, in particular, the Moravians, left Georgia about 1739 because they were required to take up arms against the neighboring Spanish in Florida. They moved to Pennsylvania where they founded, in 1741, the town of Bethlehem, which has been their headquarters ever since.

While New York originally welcomed the Palatines, it soon treated them so badly that thereafter almost all the vessels bearing German immigrants came directly from Dutch ports to the Delaware, and if by chance an occasional ship was forced to make a landing in New York, its passengers quickly made their way across the Jerseys into more hospitable territory.

Even in Pennsylvania the invasion of the Germans eventually began to cause alarm among the English-speaking and dominant part of the population. In Virginia this attitude of exclusion of supposedly alien races had been maintained ever since the first permanent settlement. Inspired by visions of building up a great industry, the proprietors of that colony had sent out with their "second supply" a little group of eight artisans from Germany and Poland who were skilled glassmakers. The English colonists charged them with treasonable dealings with the Indians and the Chronicler of the settlement refers to them disgustedly as those "damned Dutchmen."

Benjamin Franklin, who, in 1753, expressed his opinion of some of his fellow citizens in a letter to Peter Collinson, was merely reflecting an attitude which the English stock had more or less generally taken when he declared:

"Those who come hither are generally the most stupid of their own nation, and, as ignorance is often attended with credulity when knavery would mislead it, and with suspicion when honesty would set it right; and as few of the English understand the German language, and so cannot address them either from the press or the pulpit, it is almost impossible to remove any prejudices they may entertain. Their clergy have very little influence on the people, who seem to take a pleasure in abusing and discharging the minister on every trivial occasion. Not being used to liberty, they know not how to make a modest use of it. And as Holben says of the young Hottentots, that they are not esteemed men until they have shown their manhood by beating their mothers, so these seem not to think themselves free, till they can feel their liberty in abusing and insulting their teachers. Thus they are under no restraint from ecclesiastical government; they behave, however, submissively enough at present to the civil government, which I wish they may continue to do, for I remember when they modestly declined intermeddling in our elections, but now they come in droves and carry all before them, except in one or two counties.[1]

"Few of their children in the country know English. They import many books from Germany; and of the six printing-houses in the province, two are entirely German, two half German, half English, and but two entirely English. They have one German newspaper, and one half-German. Advertisements, intended to be general, are now printed in Dutch and English. The signs in our streets have

[1] He is writing of Pennsylvania.

inscriptions in both languages, and in some places only German. They begin of late to make all their bonds and other legal instruments in their own language, which (though I think it ought not to be) are allowed in our courts, where the German business so increases that there is continued need of interpreters; and I suppose in a few years they will also be necessary in the Assembly, to tell one-half our legislators what the other half say.

"In short, unless the stream of their importation could be turned from this to other colonies, as you very judiciously propose, they will soon so outnumber us that we will, in my opinion, be not able to preserve our language, and even our government will become precarious. The French, who watch all advantages, are now themselves making a German settlement, back of us, in the Illinois country, and by means of these Germans they may in time come to an understanding with ours; and, indeed, in the last war,[2] our Germans showed a general disposition, that seemed to bode us no good. For, when the English, who were not Quakers, alarmed by the danger arising from the defenseless state of our country, entered unanimously into an association, and within this government, and the Lower Counties raised, armed, and disciplined near ten thousand men, the Germans, except a very few in proportion to their number, refused to engage in it, giving out, one amongst another, and even in print, that, if they were quiet, the French, should they take the country, would not molest them; at the time abusing the Philadelphians for fitting out privateers against the enemy, and representing the trouble, hazard, and expense of defending the province, as a greater inconvenience than any that might be ex-

[2] The French and Indian War.

pected from a change of government. Yet I am not for refusing to admit them entirely into our colonies. All that seems to me necessary is, to distribute them more equally, mix them with the English schools, where they are not too thickly settled, and take some care to prevent the practice, lately fallen into by some of the shipowners, of sweeping the German gaols to make up the number of their passengers. I say I am not against the admission of Germans in general, for they have their virtues. Their industry and frugality are exemplary. They are excellent husbandmen, and contribute greatly to the improvement of a country."

By 1727, the English in Pennsylvania had become sufficiently alarmed over the proportions of the Palatine invasion to demand a careful record of the numbers arriving each year so that from then on there is full official record of all foreigners entered at the port of Philadelphia. By that time there were probably fifteen or twenty thousand Germans already in the province, and the record mentioned indicates that between 1727 and 1745 approximately 22,000 arrived by ships. To this number should, of course, be added the high natural increase of those already settled.

Since the English had pre-empted much of the desirable land along the Delaware and around Philadelphia, the Germans, with whom the acquisition of farming land was a dominant passion, mostly went westward of the English settlement and formed a belt where their language was and, in scattered groups to this day, is spoken. They filled the Lehigh and Schuylkill valleys and occupied a band of fertile soil beginning in eastern Pennsylvania on the Delaware, passing westward toward the Susquehanna through the towns of Allentown, Reading, Lebanon, Lancaster, and thence down to the Cumberland valley on the Maryland border where they had a natural outlet to western Virginia and to the south. The tier of counties north of this belt and along the borders of New York was comparatively neglected by them, and was filled largely by settlers from Connecticut. The influx of English and German sectaries was so rapid that within three years from its founding, Penn's province had made a growth as great as that of New Netherlands in its first half-century.

The early Quakers who belonged to the privileged group grew prosperous, and many of them finding the strict ordinances of their sect somewhat oppressive became Anglicans. Thus the Church of England gained an important position in Philadelphia which it retained up to the Revolution. In general, it represented the Loyalist element and therefore partly disintegrated when they left at the end of the war. The Revolution was largely Calvinistic, and the Established Church was in most of the northern colonies regarded with disfavor as "loyalist."

The invasion of Ulster Scots into Pennsylvania began shortly after the German immigration was well under way. Within a few years the great majority of the Ulster immigrants to America were making directly for the Delaware shores. Presbyterian congregations existed in the important towns of the colony about 1700, and within the next decade the Scotch had made numerous settlements in New Castle County, Delaware, and on both sides of the Pennsylvania-Maryland boundary at its intersection with the Delaware line.

When the great tide of emigration from Ulster set in about 1720, the Scotch found the best and most accessible soil in Pennsylvania occupied by the English and the next belt held firmly by the Germans. In general, therefore, they were obliged to pass over these two territories and settle still farther west, particularly in the Cumberland valley of which Gettysburg, York, and Carlisle are now important centers. In this district geographical isolation led later to the establishment farther south of a distinct church, the Cumberland Presbyterian, somewhat different in its tenets from the Presbyterianism of the Philadelphia region and Delaware.

The number of Scotch who thus left Ulster for Pennsylvania is uncertain, but may have exceeded 40,000 or 50,000. Taken in connection with the Palatine immigration at the same period the influx to Pennsylvania in the 1730's formed the largest migration from Europe to the New World that ever took place until the steamship era arrived.

Seeking newer and freer land, the Scotch together with some Germans began to follow the mountain valleys trending southwestward from Pennsylvania. They not only filled the Shenandoah Valley in a few years, but filtered down to the back country of the

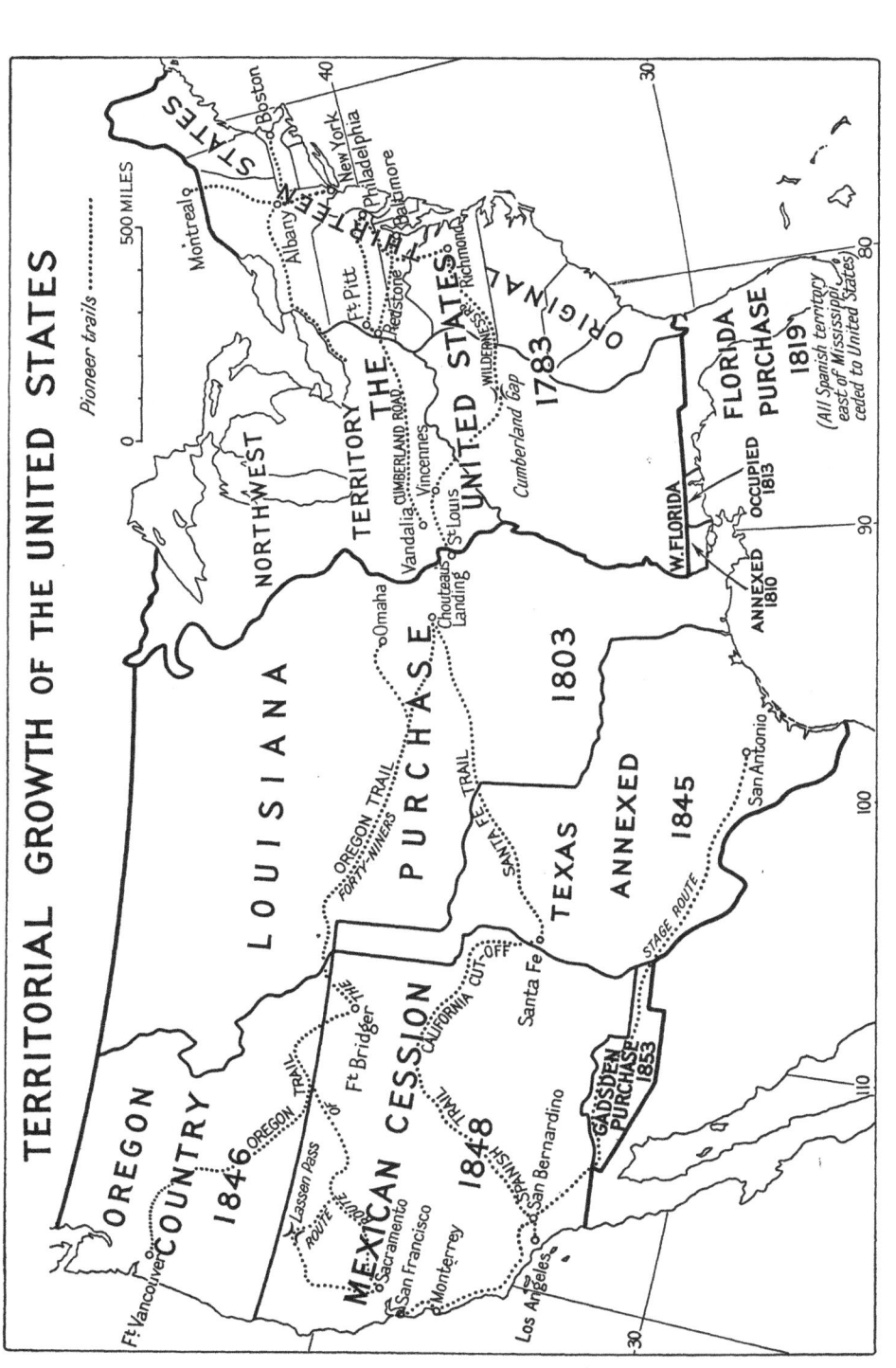

southern colonies and to the eastern portion of what is now Tennessee.

A good illustration of this migration is Daniel Boone, himself of English stock, who was born on the Delaware only a few miles above Philadelphia. The Boone family soon moved to Reading. Thence drifting southwestward with his compatriots, Daniel Boone settled in the North Carolina uplands, along the valley of the Yadkin, then passed beyond into Kentucky, and, after that location began to be civilized, went on as a pioneer to Missouri. His son appears a little later as one of the early settlers of Kansas, his grandson as a pioneer in Colorado.

When the land west of the Alleghanies was opened for settlement about 1768, the Ulster Scots began to throng the mountain passes. In addition to their aptitude for frontier life, and the insatiable desire to find new and cheap land, they wanted to get away from their neighbors, the Pennsylvania Dutch, with whom they usually did not live on very good terms. Pittsburgh rapidly became a Nordic territory settled mainly by the Ulster Scots.

These streams of immigration were sufficient by 1740 to enable Pennsylvania to overtake and pass the population of every other colony except Maryland, Massachusetts, and Virginia, although most of them had been started a generation earlier than Penn's settlement. A decade later Maryland was passed and just after the Revolution Massachusetts was outstripped, while Philadelphia remained the metropolis of the United States until finally excelled by New York City in the first half of the nineteenth century.

Benjamin Franklin's offhand estimate that at the end of the Colonial period one-third of the population of his adopted State was English, one-third Scotch, and one-third German, was not far from the truth. Though the population was then by a safe majority British in origin and English-speaking, the Germans remained an element impossible to assimilate, so long as they continued to be segregated in their own communities of which Lancaster was the largest inland town in the thirteen colonies.

Such of the Germans as went to the frontier States were assimilated by the Nordic groups without much difficulty; but the experience of the Pennsylvania Dutch farming communities is like that of some of the city slum districts of the last century, in presenting groups almost impossible to Americanize. Even at the present time this Alpine island of population still retains many of its alien characteristics. For this, among other reasons, the German element in Pennsylvania at the time of the Revolution played a relatively unimportant part in the affairs of the State, as suggested by the quotation from Franklin above. The dominant element was formed by the group around Philadelphia composed mainly of the original English Quakers; but the Pennsylvania-Dutch, on their farms, and the Scots on the frontier, furnished a large contingent with which the politicians had to deal, though they were seldom represented in the government and leader-

THE GATEWAYS TO THE WEST 125

ship of the colony. The German element was inclined to follow the leadership of the Quakers under whose invitation it had come to Pennsylvania. The Scots, on the other hand, were apt to be in a state of rebellion when occasion arose, as conspicuously in the Whiskey Rebellion, which formed one of the first tests of the power of the Federal Government under Washington's presidency.

The claim that half of the Ulstermen were adherents of the Established Church, rather than Presbyterians, is doubtless extreme, but emphasizes the typically non-Irish and Protestant character of this whole element of the population, as also the fact that many of the Ulstermen were not Scots, nor even Lowland Scots, whose ancestors had moved northward across the border from England; but were direct emigrants from England to Ireland, some indeed as late as and even after the time of Cromwell.

Delaware has been dealt with incidentally in what has been said concerning Pennsylvania, because it was part of Pennsylvania during the first period of colonization. Unimportant attempts had been made by the Dutch and Swedes, of whom the Swedes are the best known, to settle there but the population of the region when Penn arrived was mainly composed of English who had moved in under the regime of the Duke of York.

In 1633, an English nobleman, Lord Baltimore, who had for years been seeking favor with the Stuart monarchy, announced that he had become a convert to the papacy, and, with the zeal of a new convert, desired to establish a colony in the New World where Catholics, then laboring under heavy disabilities in Great Britain, could enjoy religious freedom. He applied for, and Charles I granted, a charter for the foundation of a semi-feudal proprietorship, with the stipulation that freedom of worship should prevail.

If one stops to consider what a howl of outraged virtue would have been raised by the people of Great Britain, and what a hurricane would have descended upon the head of the monarch, had he granted the Catholics a charter without stipulating for freedom of worship, it will be realized that the much-vaunted "toleration" of Lord Baltimore's colony was not entirely an evidence of his own broad-mindedness. However, this toleration had its limits. Disbelief in the doctrine of the Trinity was a capital offense.

In 1634, the little town of St. Mary as established as the center for the new colony. Few Catholics of the home country seem to have been anxious to take advantage of the opportunities offered, and Lord Baltimore began to seek tenants elsewhere. As early as 1634, he was writing to Boston and urging Massachusetts people to emigrate, but the first great invasion of Puritans came in 1649.

Inspired by enthusiasm for the cause of the King, after he had lost his head, the Virginians under the leadership of Governor Berkeley passed ordinances expelling non-conformists from their colony, and a thousand of these who had previously gone from

New England to Virginia were driven out and took refuge in Maryland, establishing the settlement which later became Annapolis.

During the next generation most of the arrivals in Maryland were either Puritans or Quakers. The policy of tolerance was not held to apply to Quakers, who, by a law of 1659, were to be whipped out of any town which they entered, but this measure does not seem to have been enforced very long, and English Quakers from other colonies soon formed an important part of the population.

In 1689, word reached the New World of the expulsion of James II, and the occupation of the British throne by the uncompromisingly Protestant House of Orange. While James II was on the throne a general alarm had arisen throughout the colonies over the prospects of Catholic aggression.

Many of the colonies contained a sprinkling of the Huguenot refugees who had been driven out of France only a few years before because of their Protestantism, and there were thus in every colony men who knew the Revocation of the Edict of Nantes and the terrible persecution which followed. The tragedy of the Thirty Years War was also still fresh in the minds of many.

There was no disposition in America, therefore, to look upon the Catholics as a group who, if in power, would distinguish themselves by a policy of broad toleration, and the one colony in which there was any appreciable number of Catholics, namely, Maryland, naturally felt the situation most keenly.

The number of Catholics in the colony at that time, however, even including Negroes, was only a few thousand, and their capital of St. Mary was a hamlet of scarcely sixty houses. Probably eleven-twelfths of the population of Maryland were Protestants, and of them a majority were Puritans. These lost no time in taking steps to protect their freedom which they knew the Catholic church would never tolerate if able to do otherwise, and by a homemade revolution turned out the proprietary government and set up a staunch Protestant regime. Under this new rule, however, the few Catholic residents were subjected to no harm, but were placed under approximately the same disabilities as they had long lived under in Great Britain. Thereupon the little Roman Catholic principality in the United States was at an end, and the then Lord Baltimore, fourth of that title, shortly conformed by returning to his ancestral Protestant faith.

The Revolution of 1689 cost St. Mary its existence, for the Puritans transferred the capital to their own town of Providence (rebaptized Annapolis), and the headquarters of the Roman Catholics soon relapsed into the wilderness.

Maryland continued to be almost wholly an English colony, with more than its share of Negroes and transported convicts, and with a very slight sprinkling of aliens, much as all the colonies had. When the Acadians were transported from Nova Scotia in 1755, a considerable number of them were landed in Maryland.

Baltimore, founded in 1729, languished for a quarter of a century, but in the decade before the Revolution it began to grow with such rapidity that in a few years it was one of the half dozen most considerable towns of the continent.

The back country of Maryland was settled independently from Pennsylvania, to a considerable extent by Ulster Scots and Palatines, though there was also a steady encroachment on this cheap land by men from the tidewater who could not get possession of farms in the more expensive and fashionable as well as prosperous region.

By the Revolution, Maryland had reached a population of 250,000. Perhaps one-seventh of this was in Frederick County, where Palatines had begun to settle as early as 1710, and into which they began to enter in large numbers after about 1730. Despite this back-country element, Maryland must be recognized as being, at the time of the first census, an Anglo-Saxon colony in culture, in traditions, in language, and in population.

VII

VIRGINIA AND HER NEIGHBORS

THE settlement of Virginia, beginning with Jamestown in 1607, was of a different character from that of the northern and middle colonies. It was not a colonization project undertaken by families, but an exploitation by adventurers. In a sense it may be compared with the Klondike Gold Rush at the end of the nineteenth century. Men went forth seeking fortune and expecting to return in a few years with newly acquired wealth. The motley array of colonists sent to Jamestown by the Company during the first decade of activity seems to have been drawn from every part of the British Isles and every stratum of society.

After ten or a dozen years, the proprietors recognized that the wealth of their plantations would not consist in gold and pearls but that they were facing an actual colonization project, which could only be built upon the foundations of family life. An early recognition of this fact has been one of the principal sources of strength in all British colonization, and the proprietors of the Virginia colony, while continuing to encourage men of all sorts to go to their settlement on the James River, undertook one of the famous eugenic enterprises of history by sending over several shiploads of young women to make homes for their settlers. The undertaking seems to have been carried out in good faith and with good judgment and the result was notably successful. A little later, however, the continuing demand for wives led to a sort of traffic that probably produced a less carefully selected feminine population for the plantations. On the whole, it would probably be fair to say that the "First Families of Virginia" represented a higher social standard in the male than in the female lines.

The year 1619 was racially eventful. It saw the arrival at Jamestown both of the first shipload of "uncorrupt maydes for wives," and the landing of the first cargo of Negroes. The next half-century brought the development of the plantation system and the spread of Negro slavery and the problem of miscegenation between Negro women and the lowest and most unintelligent type of white servant came into prominence. In this way originated the mulatto group which has ever since been a characteristic feature of the Negroes in the United States. Those admirers of the Mulatto who boast that he carries in his veins the blue blood of the aristocratic families of the South, would do well to read the actual records of Virginia and other colonies during the seventeenth century and see what sort of white stock actually formed the foundation of that half of this hybrid group.

The colony continued to grow for the first quarter of a century by attracting voluntary adventurers from whom the rule of the survival of the fittest exacted so heavy a toll that probably the survivors were a fairly fit lot. The abandonment of the original proprietary company in 1624 led to a marked change in the manner of populating the colony, and for the next generation the bulk of the immigrants were assisted in one way or another to get to Virginia and allowed to work out the money advanced them by their labor after their arrival.

At its best, there was little difference in the colonization plans that British colonies have always used to get desirable settlers from "home." In the case of Virginia it brought a vigorous population of all sorts, and the name of "indentured servant" covers not merely the domestic in the kitchen and the laborer in the tobacco field but artisans' apprentices and medical students. Under the extremely trying conditions many of these immigrants were unable to survive. Governor Berkeley asserted that four out of five died during the first year of residence, while Evelyn, the diarist, declared that five out of six succumbed. Such statements at least point to an excessively high mortality which must have spared most frequently those who were physically and mentally superior and well adapted to be among the founders of a new colony. Hence it seems clear that the importance of these indentured servants in the later development of Virginia, as of other colonies, is not to be reckoned in proportion to the number who arrived, but to be estimated upon the much smaller number who survived and founded families.

Another type of assisted immigrant of which a

great deal has been heard was the deported convict. Some of these were evidently men who had cheated the gallows, for the Virginians continually protested against their arrival. Apparently much the larger number, however, were men of superior quality in many respects. When nearly three hundred offenses were punishable by the death penalty in England, many of those convicted were not persons marked by great moral turpitude, and the so-called "transported convict" might have been equally well a pirate, or a preacher who persisted in expounding the gospel without proper license from the ecclesiastical authorities so to do.

Large numbers were political prisoners who found themselves temporarily on the losing side; still more were mere prisoners of war. During the Protectorate, victories like Dunbar and Worcester and the suppression of the Irish Rebellion by Cromwell in 1652 were followed by deportations of prisoners of war to the colonies, and the government felt fully justified in recovering part of the expense of transportation by selling the services of these able-bodied and intelligent men for seven years to the highest bidder. Unquestionably most of the foundation stock of this kind that survived to perpetuate itself would be entirely fit for colonization. During the same period many cavaliers took refuge in Virginia.

When the royalists were again in power after 1660, a similar stream of Commonwealth soldiers and non-conformists began to come into the colonies. The Scotch Rebellion of 1670 brought another accession to Virginia, and in 1685 many of the captives at the Battle of Sedgmoor were exiled here. Such labor was welcomed by the Virginians in marked distinction to the real criminals, of whom there were apparently only a few thousand in all. After about 1700 the spread of Negro slavery reduced the demand for white indentured labor and less of it arrived.

In the great diversity of men and women brought over in these and other ways, there are some who figure in the ancestry of the best families of Virginia at the present time, and others who, from the beginning, were misfits in the colony. Such of the latter as survived the trying ordeal of the tobacco fields either ran away, or, when their term of service expired, drifted out to the borders of the settlement.

The Virginia holdings were large and far beyond the reach of an ordinary man without capital, in marked contrast to conditions in New England, where the great majority of the settlers were small landowners. The freed bondsmen therefore had to go to the frontier or drift down into North Carolina or some other region where they were not handicapped by their lack of funds. The most shiftless and least intelligent of them tended to collect in the less valuable lands at the fringe of civilization, or to drift along to other similar settlements farther west and south. In this way originated one of the peculiar elements of the Southern population, the "poor white trash." Their numbers were recruited generation after generation by others of the same sort while the able, enterprising, and imaginative members were continually drained off to the cities or sought better land elsewhere. These "poor whites" in the Alleghanies and through the swamp lands of North and South Carolina have been an interesting feature of the population for three centuries. Largely of pure Nordic stock, they are a striking example to the eugenist of the results of isolation and undesirable selection.

During the Stuart period Virginia was the refuge of many Puritans. They were, however, looked upon with disfavor by the prevailing royalist sentiment and the activities of Sir William Berkeley as Governor were such that not less than a thousand left the colony. Their place was taken by Royalists, invited by the Governor to find a refuge in Virginia as soon as news arrived of the execution of Charles I. Within the next twelve months probably a thousand Royalists appeared bringing many of the family names which have been conspicuous in the Old Dominion ever since. Richard Lee came a little earlier, in 1642, but it is after the death of Charles I that one begins to meet in Virginia such names as Randolph, Cary, Parke, Robinson, Marshall, Washington, and Ludwell.

The place of origin in Great Britain of most of the Royalists is not so easily traced as is that of the Massachusetts Puritans who came to America in groups, sometimes as entire congregations, but random samples of families which afterwards furnished distinguished leadership show that they came from practically all over England and Scotland: Washingtons from Northamptonshire, Marshalls and Jeffersons from Wales, Lees from the part of Shropshire adjoining Wales, and Randolphs from Warwickshire. James Monroe's ancestors were Scotch and Patrick Henry's father was born in Aberdeen. They had at least one thing in common, that they were of English and Nordic stock. Examination of lists in the land office at Richmond indicates that fully 95 per cent of the names of landowners during the seventeenth century were unmistakably Anglo-Saxon.

The tidewater population was fecund and spread steadily up to the fall-line of the rivers, by its own multiplication. Men and women married early. Colonel Byrd described his daughter, Evelyn, as an "antique virgin" when she was twenty. "Either our young fellows are not smart enough for her or she seems too smart for them," he moaned. With a high death rate second marriages were common. It has been the custom of late for sentimental feminists to refer to the large families of the Colonial period as having been produced by husbands who thus killed off one wife after another. Such nonsense is easily refuted by an examination of genealogies and of tombstones. Many a husband had to marry several wives because of the high death rate, but equally many wives had to marry several husbands apiece for the same reason.

The toll taken by hard work, unhygienic conditions, and childbirth without proper care among pioneer women, was no greater than the toll taken by hard work, unhygienic conditions, and Indian warfare among the men. If Colonel John Carter married five wives successively, in an age when divorce was unknown, Elizabeth Mann married six husbands.

While a purely Nordic population was thus occupying tidewater Virginia east of the Blue Ridge, another Nordic invasion from a wholly different source was entering upland Virginia on the other side of the mountains. The Shenandoah Valley is virtually an extension of the interior valleys of Pennsylvania; and while an occasional pioneer pushed his way to it through the mountains from the eastern front, the real settlement came through the side door beginning about 1725 and reaching the proportions of an invasion about 1732.

Ulster Scots coming down through Pennsylvania began that penetration of the Piedmont from north to south which is such a striking feature of the history of the South Atlantic coast during the next century. With them were some Alpines, mostly Germans from the Palatine, representative of the so-called Pennsylvania Dutch stock.

When General Braddock, whose army was nearly wiped out by the French and Indians in 1755, sighed, "Who would have thought it?" and expired, he nevertheless had cleared a road for the rapid spread of this immigration along the mountain valleys, not merely into Virginia but on through the Carolinas and to Georgia. His road was followed a few years later by General Forbes' road through the same country, and the way was open.

The upland and mountain sections of Virginia therefore came to be represented by a group with a very different outlook from those of the tidewater, dominated as it was by large landholders. This diversity of original settlement, which was of sufficient importance to effect in the Civil War a cleavage of the State and establish West Virginia as free soil, is still apparent and makes itself felt in the twentieth century.

North Carolina represents an overflowing from Virginia to the South. It was a frontier for the Old Dominion where landless men could find new homes more easily than to the westward, where they encountered the Blue Ridge. In 1653 a settlement was begun at Albemarle by Virginians who were not in accord either with the established religion or else with the political control of their colony. Most of these were Quakers.

By adopting a remarkably liberal code of laws, which welcomed insolvent debtors by cancelling their indebtedness, this colony attracted an element which the more conservative Virginians regarded with suspicion. A continual infiltration of landseekers led to steady colonization, and gradually the tidewater section of North Carolina developed as a separate region, not very thickly settled, not very prosperous, not very distinguished in any way. A few French

VIRGINIA AND HER NEIGHBORS 139

Huguenots drifted in after the Revocation of the Edict of Nantes. In 1710 a group of Palatines, who had left their German homes because of religious persecution, and had sought refuge in England, was passed on to North Carolina through the enterprise of a couple of Swiss promoters who were looking for colonists. As a courtesy to the promoters the settlement was given the name of New Bern, which has led to a general supposition that the population were Swiss. In fact, they were nearly all German Alpines.

Another immigration, this time of Nordics, began a few years later when Scotch Highlanders, disappointed at the results of the 1715 uprising on behalf of the Old Pretender, fled the country and came to North Carolina, starting a settlement on the Cape Fear River. Later, following the collapse of the Young Pretender in 1745, the Highlanders again found themselves in a bad situation at home. Shipload after shipload landed at Wilmington in 1746 and 1747. This emigration of Scotch Highlanders continued until the Revolution, during which time they showed themselves, strangely enough, loyal to the Hanoverian dynasty and mostly fought as Loyalists against the Continentals.

The general breakup of the clan system with the accompanying distress in the Highlands caused most of this emigration, although some of the Scots were deported as prisoners of war. Campbelltown was the centre of their settlement, and it is unfortunate that its present name of Fayetteville conceals its interesting history. Some of the Highlanders are said to have brought cattle with them, and they pushed on into the interior of the State because of the great areas of succulent grass and peavine stretching toward the mountains which provided excellent fodder for their herds.

The sympathetic patronage of Gabriel Johnston, the Governor of the Province from 1734 to 1752, was largely responsible for the welcome extended to these Highlanders. Himself a Scotchman, he was under strong suspicion of not being too loyal to the Crown. At any rate, his hospitality to the Highlanders brought to North Carolina the largest group of Highland Scotch that came to the colonies. These men of the purest Nordic blood form a selected group anthropologically. It is no mere coincidence that the tallest average height of a population in the United States at the present time is in these North Carolina counties that were settled by the Scotch Highlanders after "Bonnie Prince Charlie" ceased to be a political possibility.

While the back country of North Carolina was thus being penetrated from the seacoast by the Highland Scots, the Lowland Scots were drifting into it along the foot of the mountains from Pennsylvania and Maryland through Virginia. This was the principal source of increase of the population during the eighteenth century, and still gives to the State its characteristic complexion. Along with the Ulster Scots came, as said above, some of the German settlers, thus bringing a small Alpine element to the

State. The southern tidewater region also developed at the same time as a northern extension of settlement from South Carolina.

South Carolina was settled only a little later than North Carolina by the establishment of Old Charles Town in 1665. This settlement, shortly moved across and up the river to a better location, prospered and expanded until it became South Carolina.

Originally a sort of offshoot from the West Indies, this region caught the attention of the Huguenot refugees a few years later, perhaps because Coligny had marked it out a century before as a desirable home for them. It attracted a larger proportion of the French refugees than any other colony; and although they were unwelcome at first to the English who were in possession, they soon assimilated themselves to the Anglo-Saxon population with which they were racially identical and became an important element in the upbuilding of the State. In Colonial and Revolutionary times, Gendron, Huger, LeSerrurier, deSaussure, Laurens, Lanier, Sevier, and Ravenel were all Huguenots who distinguished themselves in the service of the State.

The establishment of large-scale agriculture with plantations devoted to rice or indigo sharply limited the possibilities of settlement in the tidewater region of South Carolina, and it became a country of large holdings worked by Negro slaves in charge of overseers. Meanwhile the owners largely made their homes in or near Charleston, and brought it to the position of the fourth city of the colonies in importance.

The growth of the colony would have been slow had it not been for the influx of the Ulster Scots coming along the foot of the mountains from the north after the middle of the eighteenth century. The upcountry thus became quite different from the tidewater, so different, that in South Carolina as in North Carolina and Virginia it was a question whether the State might not split on slavery a few years before the Civil War, and the Upland population was only whipped into line for secession by sharp practice on the part of the political leaders in the slaveholding regions.

Other small elements were incorporated easily in the Nordic population of the State, but the loss to the colony was heavy when the Loyalists left after the Revolution. On the 13th and 14th of December, 1782, 300 ships set sail from Charleston carrying not merely the soldiery but more than 9000 civilians and slaves. Half of these went to the West Indies, and most of the others to Florida where such of them as had not subsequently removed were presumably reincorporated into the United States a generation later. On the other hand, hundreds of Hessian deserters stayed in the community, as also occurred in others of the colonies, thus introducing the first noticeable immigration of Nordic Germans into the State. As previously noted, most of the so-called Palatine immigration of Germans in the eighteenth century was Alpine, in sharp contrast to the

North German Nordics, who came to this country in large numbers in the middle of the nineteenth century after the futile revolutions of 1848.

Georgia was the last of the thirteen colonies to be settled. Even at the Revolution it was so weak that it was regarded by many of the Colonial leaders as more of a liability than an asset to the confederation. Its establishment in 1732 by Oglethorpe was on a basis appealing more to sentiment than to practical views. As in the case of some other similar schemes in contemporary times, Parliament was persuaded to appropriate nearly a hundred thousand pounds to aid the oppressed of all countries. Most of the few thousand persons who were settled by the original trustees were English, and were selected with as much care as possible from among those who were apparently "down on their luck," and who might prosper if relieved of their debts and put back on land. Many of these insolvent debtors were doubtless victims of political and economic changes, but it soon transpired that in too many cases the man who did not have sufficient capacity to make a living in England, likewise lacked sufficient capacity to make a living in the newer and more difficult conditions of Georgia.

In addition to these English debtors, Oglethorpe enlisted on the Continent small bodies of oppressed Protestants and established several other little settlements. Waldenses from Piedmont in Italy were settled in one place, a colony of Scots in another,

German Moravians at still a third point, and a few French families elsewhere, as well as a colony from Salzburg, made up of a predominantly Alpine stock that had suffered for its religious principles enough to deserve all the sympathy it received. The hardy Nordics (Scotch Presbyterian Highlanders) who had been settled on the southern frontier, to afford protection for Georgia from the Spaniards and Indians, were almost exterminated by the Spaniards and of all these various undertakings Savannah was the only one that prospered.

It was necessary to abandon the attempt to create a prosperous colony by means of establishing a refuge for the oppressed. Unfortunately the change was accompanied by the introduction of Negro slavery. Nevertheless, when Georgia became open to outside settlers, there was a valuable accession from colonies to the north, one of the most interesting of the groups being the Dorchester Society, which came in 1752. This Protestant congregation had left England in 1630 and founded Dorchester in Massachusetts. In 1695 a part of them had moved to South Carolina and, two generations later, some of these went still farther south to midland Georgia.

Their example was followed, or perhaps indeed preceded, by many other Carolina planters, so that the influx from this source became a real element of strength to the more southerly colony. Shortly thereafter the flood of Ulster Scots, rolling along the Piedmont, began to reach the uplands of Georgia and assured its future.

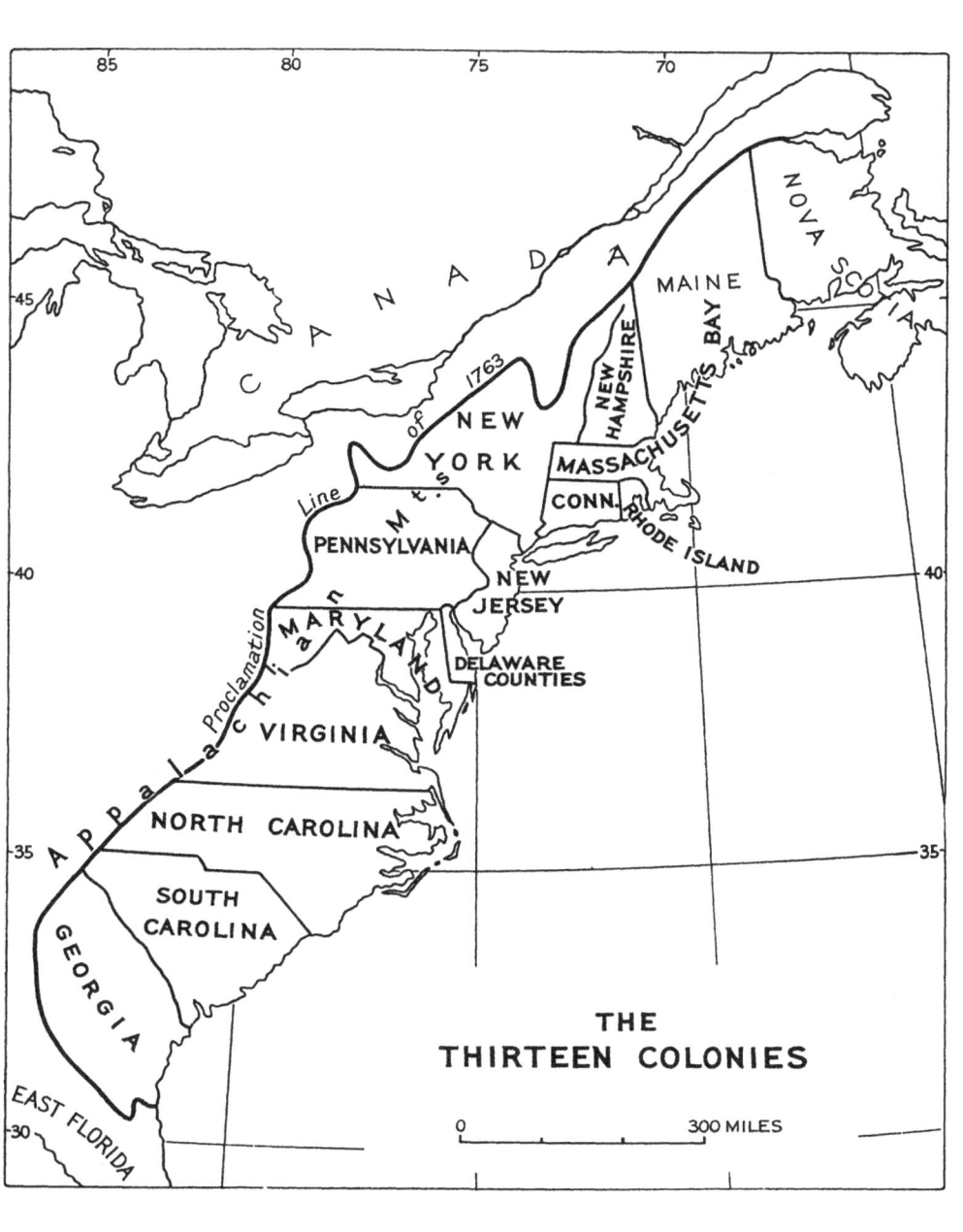

The Georgians of the present day are descendants of the Oglethorpe colonists in only insignificant proportions. The Nordic settlers who came in through North Carolina, English from the tidewater region, and Ulster Scots from the Uplands, are the real founders of the State.

After the Revolution, Georgia benefited by the prevalent unrest and the tide of migration that flowed in all directions. It received settlers from all of the Southern States and some of the Northern ones, as well as new arrivals direct from Europe.

Kentucky for a generation prior to the Revolution had become known through hunters of game bringing back glowing accounts of the beauty and fertility of the level lands of central Kentucky. Access in the one case was down the Ohio River by boat, and in the other by a long and hazardous trip through the mountains, entering by the Cumberland Gap, the most practicable of several difficult passes. The danger from Indians was so great on the Ohio River that most of the invaders preferred those dangers of a different type to be encountered by the Cumberland Gap entry. It was the route which Daniel Boone, acting for a land company, had blazed: the narrow trail, six hundred miles long, that has become famous as the Wilderness Road.

By the time of the Revolution several hundred people were in Kentucky, and more were coming each year from the inland portion of Virginia, and, to a less extent, from Pennsylvania. During the

Revolution the population rose and fell in accordance with local conditions on the frontier and the ravages of the Indians. With the end of the Revolution a great tide of immigration set in, composed in part of soldiers who were given land grants by the Virginia Government. With them was an element of Loyalists, as well as many families from Maryland, both seeking to get away from unpleasant associations in the East.

From 1780 onward the route down the Ohio began to be more used. The Indians were driven back or the boatmen learned how to cope with their ruses, and the annual migration began to be counted in thousands. In the year 1786 as many as 3000 went down the river, in 1788, 10,000, and in 1789, 20,000. Meanwhile, the immigration through the Cumberland Gap continued steadily. The growth of Kentucky was on a scale unparalleled in North America up to that time. Within a few decades from the day when the first cabins were erected in the region, a population of 70,000 people had entered the State, and it had half as many inhabitants as Massachusetts.

Compared with the Scotch tone of Tennessee, Kentucky was overwhelmingly English in aspect. Virginia was definitely its progenitor, a large part of its early population having come through the Shenandoah Valley. Next as feeders were Pennsylvania and North Carolina, while other regions contributed but small minorities, those from Maryland being probably the most numerous. The government of Virginia was seriously concerned by its losses of population from this cause. After the Revolution, officers who had served with the Virginia forces were compensated by allotments of land in the Kentucky region. The State attracted other settlers of a superior social and economic status. These gave a tone to its society and laid the foundation of a local aristocracy. Kentucky long remained distinctive because of its conspicuously English atmosphere and the social refinements which it showed in contrast to some of its neighbors. Kentucky remained part of Virginia until 1792 when it was admitted as a State.

Tennessee was, in fact, only the western part of North Carolina which originally stretched beyond the Appalachians as far as the Mississippi. The French had established a trading post on the site of Nashville as early as 1714. But the State was actually settled from the East rather than from the West, and, indeed, its western third was not settled until well into the nineteenth century. The first area of settlement was in the river valleys near the North Carolina border, and this remained the principal area during the period here considered. A second and less important point of growth was in the center of the State. In northeastern Tennessee the earlier settlements were from Virginia, and the settlers supposed that they were still within the limits of the Old Dominion.

The settlers from North Carolina soon began to push through the mountain passes and established the groupings that go in history by the name of the Holston and Watauga settlements. Many of the early settlers, of whom some hundreds were present before the Revolution, were, as noted, from the upland portion of Virginia, and were Presbyterians from Scotland, often by way of Ulster, while the principal early influx from North Carolina was connected with the uprising in the Piedmont section of that colony about 1770. An insurgent element known as the Regulators put itself in opposition to the royal governor, and, being beaten, fled over the mountains for safety. A large proportion of these were from Wake County. They brought in an element of Baptists contrasting with the Presbyterianism which, on the whole, characterized the State from the beginning and still does so owing to the predominance of the Scotch in its settlement.

While the eastern community was growing, settlement began in the central portion of the State in what is known as the Cumberland district. This was for years almost isolated from the neighboring settlement to the east, the center of which was Nashville, while the eastern settlement headed in Knoxville, which became the capital.

During the Revolution the settlement of this territory continued steadily until the State had 10,000 or 12,000 inhabitants. North Carolina made liberal allotments of Tennessee lands to its soldiers who had fought in the Revolution, and this continued the stream of immigration. By the time that President Washington was inaugurated the eastern section of the State had some 30,000 inhabitants, the Cumberland district about 7000, and both were growing steadily. Western Tennessee was still Indian territory.

The population of Tennessee in 1790 was typical of the upland population of the South in its racial make-up. It is definitely a mere extension of the western part of North Carolina, though its inhabitants were often born in Virginia, and to a less extent in other States, as was true of the inhabitants of North Carolina itself.

In the Mississippi Valley at this period there were a few settlements established under the French and Spanish regimes, which had attracted a miscellaneous crowd of adventurers and traders. Since this territory did not become part of the United States until the Louisiana Purchase of 1803, it will be dealt with more fully in the next section. In this period we are dealing with comparatively small numbers for this entire region.

Of nearly 4,000,000 people, both white and black, in the United States in 1790, at the time of the first census, 95 per cent were living east of the Appalachians.

In territories of the present United States other than the settlements already covered, there were three little islands of population. One lay along the Mississippi in southwest Illinois, a remnant of the old French settlements with some English and American additions. A second was around Vincennes, Indiana, with a population like that of the Illinois settlements but more strongly American. A third was in Ohio, where settlement was just beginning, the first serious colonization being that made in 1788 at Marietta by New Englanders.

Although the Revolution grew out of economic and political causes, it represents primarily one of those costly and unfortunate internecine wars in which the Nordics have been prone to indulge at intervals for two or three thousand years, and which have done so much to weaken them as a race.

Had there been no complications the effects of the Revolutionary War might have been less permanent. Winner and loser would have lived on terms of peace with each other, as they did in England after the Civil War and in the United States after the Rebellion. But the hard feeling that goes with any conflict was intensified by several factors. The Ulster Scots, in particular, had reason to feel themselves badly treated by England, and they carried into, and through, the Revolution, an unusual animosity. This feeling of resentment was shared and kept alive by many other Americans through the injudicious behavior in Canada of a number of the English governments after the Revolution.

The tradition of one hundred and fifty years of common action of the colonies and the mother country in opposing France was forgotten overnight and a sentimental attitude for which there was astonishingly little actual basis led to a glorification of France and everything French for a generation or more—an attitude that has not entirely disappeared to this day. The antagonism toward Great Britain was maintained for political reasons during the next century mostly by Irish agitators. This ill feeling prevented the close co-operation between the two greatest sections of the English-speaking races, which would have meant so much for world peace and harmony, and which would have laid the basis for a closer co-operation of all the nations of predominant Nordic stock, in the interest of the progressive evolution of mankind. A first object of statesmanship should now be to regain that solidarity of the Nordics, in the interests not merely of world progress, but of the very survival of civilization.

Denominational questions in the United States were scarcely an issue after the Revolution, for the bitter sectarian feeling that had existed earlier was rapidly disappearing, and the Roman Catholics had not yet been able to raise the issue of bigotry, for the country was overwhelmingly Protestant. Of approximately 4,000,000 persons in the United States in 1790, Catholic writers make varying claims running as high as 35,000 or 45,000 persons of their faith. Without stopping to inquire how many of those claimed for Rome were merely nominal adherents, and how many were Negroes, one may remark that at the most, about one American in each one hundred might have had some affiliation with the Roman Church. When the Catholic hierarchy was established for the first time in the United States by the appointment of the Jesuit John Carroll as bishop of Baltimore in 1789, he reported to his superiors that there were about 16,000 Catholics in Maryland, including children and Negroes; something over 7000 in Pennsylvania, some 3000 French around Detroit, and about 4000 scattered through the rest of the country. To this total of 30,000 might be added the unknown but small number of nominal Catholics on the frontier, in the Mississippi Valley, and in other regions where there were no priests to minister to them, and where their children, at least, were fairly sure to grow up outside the church. It is probably accurate to say that there never has been a nation which was so completely and definitely Protestant as well as Nordic as was the United States just after the American Revolution.

The total white population found in the United States by the first census (1790) was 3,172,444. To this should be added, for the present purpose, the population of parts of the continent that are now, but were not then, in the United States, that is Louisiana and Florida. The latter had but a few thousand inhabitants. The Louisiana Purchase territory may be credited with 36,000, of whom nearly one-half were Negroes. The French are estimated at about 12,000. Professor Hansen gives the figure of Whites only for the Louisiana Purchase area in 1790 as 20,000. The addition of Negroes would probably increase these population figures considerably. Texas may be allotted 5000 (Spanish) Whites, New Mexico and Arizona 15,000, and California 1000 at this period. But it will be shown later that the use of the word "White" in these Spanish-American lands is frequently largely a "courtesy title." Finally, the census enumerators did not reach the Old Northwest Territory, where there were already some 11,000 residents, about equally divided between American and French. The total white population of the territory now comprised in the continental United States may therefore be put at approximately 3,250,000 in 1790.

Disregarding the French and Spanish in the outlying regions, the only race, aside from the Nordic, that was important enough to be counted at this period was the Alpine, represented by the Germans. In Maine one in a hundred of the population might have been German, but in the other New England states the Alpines were negligible.[1] In the middle colonies they were an important element, perhaps one in every ten or twelve in such States as New York, New Jersey, and Maryland, and one-third of the whole population in Pennsylvania. Through the Southern States they formed perhaps one in twenty of the population, confined mainly to the upland regions and, having spread over from these uplands and from Pennsylvania into the west, they amounted to about one in seven in Kentucky and Tennessee.

Nine-tenths of the whole white population of 1790

[1] Studying the percentage of various nationalities in Colonial times, and later, one is guided partly by records of immigration, partly by the names of the inhabitants, as recorded in census and other returns. There was always a tendency, in an Anglo-Saxon region, to corrupt names of other nationalities, occasionally in such a way as to make them appear English. This fact must be allowed for in all calculations in this field.

was therefore Nordic in race, and ninety-nine hundredths of it Protestant in religion. It was all English-speaking, save for the little island of Pennsylvania Dutch, and for the French and Spanish on the frontiers. It was all living under a political and cultural tradition that was characteristically British.

At the time of the Revolution there were about 6,000,000 people in England and about half that number in the colonies.

The preceding pages have been devoted to describing the conditions in the English colonies at the end of the Colonial Period. Let us now consider the situation of the continent as a whole.

Never before in the history of the Nordic race had there been an event comparable in importance to this occupation of North America, north of the Rio Grande, by the English and Scotch. The Canadian French were too few to be a serious obstacle to the development of the country and, as will be seen in the following pages, the rest of Canada was in race, language, religion, and cultural traditions identical with the original British colonies.

Thus we have the most vigorous race in existence, with a few outside elements which were entirely in sympathy with the dominant type, in possession of the richest and most salubrious continent in the world. That this country was healthy and well fitted to breed a highly selected race is shown by the comparison of the fate of the colonists who went to the West Indies with those who went to New England.

These Puritan migrations were in their general nature identical, but the enervating climate of the Caribbean Sea proved fatal to the Nordics who went there, while the vigor of the New Englanders as a body was increased by the elimination of weaklings through a harsh but beneficent climate.

To appreciate how highly selected a race the Americans were at that time, one has only to consider the extraordinary group of men of talent and ability, some fifty-five in number, who represented the colonies at the Convention of 1787 at Philadelphia. Those men framed the Constitution of the United States, which after a hundred and fifty years of stress and strain still remains the model for such documents throughout the world.

Let the reader consider whether our 110,000,000 whites of today could produce the same number of men with corresponding ability and equally high motive, in spite of the fact that our population is more than thirty times as large as in 1787.

So we find in 1790 a practically empty continent, its eastern half buried under a mantle of forest, with a coast line broken by ports and short navigable rivers. Across low mountain ranges we first find a vast central valley traversed for hundreds of miles by wide rivers; then a belt of treeless plains covered with succulent buffalo grass; next a region long called the "Great American Desert"; then a range of mountains dimly known to the Colonials as the "Stony Mountains"; beyond them a great alkaline desert, next the Sierra range, and lastly the genial

Pacific Coast. The western half of the continent abounded in mineral wealth, while in the central valley the virgin soil awaited the plow. These conditions had their counterpart in Canada. Wild game abounded, inviting the fur traders to explore the remoter places and enabling the settler to find ready food, while he built his log cabin and planted his crop.

Such was the continent and such the opportunity. In the following pages we shall see what has been done with these opportunities by the British race.

Before leaving the Colonial Period, it is well to call attention, once more, to the history of the frontier. For a hundred years and more the frontier was beset by savages often instigated by the French in Canada. The Indians killed and tortured the lonely settlers and burned their log cabins. This desultory warfare cost the English many hundreds, if not thousands of lives along the frontiers of New England as well as of Pennsylvania and Virginia.

The Indians found by English settlers on their arrival in America were probably, as to many of their tribes, the most formidable fighting men of any native race encountered by the Whites. Not only were they redoubtable warriors in their own surroundings, but they were beyond question the cruelest of mankind. The Assyrians, of all ancient peoples, were reputed to be the most fiendishly cruel, but bad as they were, they did not compare with the American Indian. The details of the torture of prisoners taken in open warfare are too revolting to describe. These tortures were carried out by the squaws while the bucks sat around and laughed at the agony of their victims. There is nothing like it in history in any part of the world and the result was that the aboriginal Indians were regarded as ravening wolves or worse and deprived of all sympathy, while the Whites stole their lands and killed their game. No one who knew the true nature of the Indian felt any regret that they were driven off their hunting grounds. This attitude was found wherever the Whites came in conflict with them and explains why they were scarcely regarded as human beings.

The effect of the existence of the Indians on the frontier was to slow down the advance westward of the settlements and to compel the backwoodsman to keep in touch with his countrymen in the rear. If there had been no hostile Indians, the settlers would have scattered widely and would have established independent communities, such as were attempted in Kentucky and Tennessee after the Revolution. In this respect the Indians were a benefit to the Whites.

At the close of the period ending in 1790, despite the loss of many valuable elements at the time of the Revolution, the American race was homogeneous and Scotch and English to the core. It was bursting the bonds of the old frontier and ready to pour a human deluge over the mountains and inundate the West.

VIII

THE OLD NORTHWEST TERRITORY

THE second period to be dealt with covers the years from the first census, 1790, to the eve of the Civil War, 1860, and deals with the organization of our government and the extension of settlement westward to the Pacific. Free land and a very high birthrate among native Americans led to a great increase of the population, so that the white inhabitants of the United States, about three millions and a quarter in 1790, became twenty-seven millions and a half, in 1860, though immigration during the seventy-year period was not over four and a quarter million.

From 1790 to 1820, no official record of immigrant arrivals was kept. Thousands certainly arrived during those thirty years, but it seems probable that they were nearly all English and Scotch.

Just as the termination in 1790 of the preceding period was marked by a racial loss, caused by the expulsion of the Loyalists, so this later period was terminated by an internecine Civil War, costing the country three-fourths of a million Nordic lives, counting killed and died of wounds only. The descendants of those men who gave their lives for their country on both sides would have filled up the West,

THE OLD NORTHWEST TERRITORY 159

instead of its being largely populated by the immigrants we recklessly invited to our shores.

During the period referred to (1790-1860), there was, as said, no heavy immigration except from two sources, Ireland and Germany, and both of these occurred in the later portion of the period.

The displacement of agriculture by sheep in Scotland at the beginning of the nineteenth century dispossessed thousands of farmers who moved to America, sometimes with the active assistance of their landlords. The population of some districts, as Perthshire, Argyllshire, and Inverness-shire, fell sharply, because the people, no longer able to make a living, moved away. North America was the favorite destination.

Southern England experienced a similar movement. The price of agricultural products, which had been forced up during the Napoleonic wars, fell steadily for a long time. Farmers could not make a living. The counties of Kent, Hampshire, Somerset, and Surrey were the chief centers of emigration. These people also turned their faces toward North America.

Ireland, too, was in perpetual ferment and the emigration from that island was increased as the result of the abortive revolutionary attempts of the United Irishmen in 1798 and 1803. After the leader of the latter, Robert Emmet, was executed, his elder brother, Thomas A. Emmet, came to New York, practised law, and within a decade became the attorney-general of the state. The Emmets, like most others of these Irish refugees, were Protestants in religion.

Later, in 1845, the potato crop failed in Ireland, and soon after the starving peasantry, many of them from the lower types of western Ireland, swarmed over here. The women became domestic servants and the men day laborers, doing the heavy work of ditch digging and railroad building. They were Roman Catholic and that fact excited animosity in many sections of the country. They were not welcome in the West when they drifted there. It was not unusual to see on the frontier railroad stations and in advertisements in New York newspapers, "No Irish need apply." There was some violence and an American party was organized to check their entrance into local politics, for which they showed great aptitude.

Since then, these Irish have been forced upward in the social scale by later arriving immigrants over whom they had the advantage of speaking English. They became the nucleus in America of the present Roman Catholic Church, which has spread rapidly in this country. The Irish did not take to agriculture and have never shown much liking for the larger industries.

The total number of Irish immigrants during the forties and fifties amounted to more than a million and a half, and that first migration has been followed by a continuous stream of southern Irish down to the last few years when the quota restrictions went into effect.

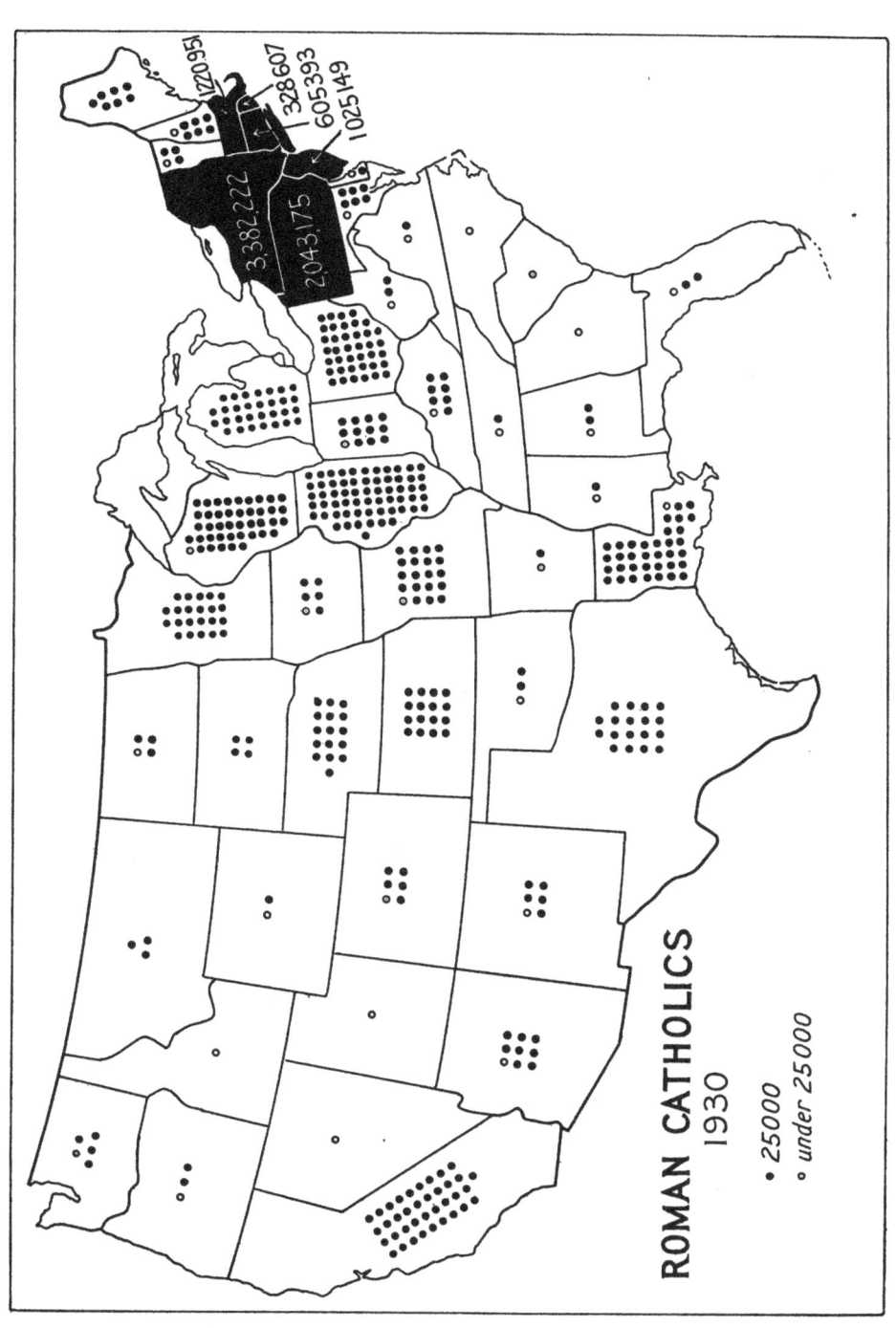

As soon as they secured a certain amount of wealth and rose in the social scale, they established schools and colleges of their own, the teachings and, indeed, the existence of which conflict with those of the public-school system of the United States, and to that extent they have impaired the unity of the nation. Some regiments of Irish fought on the Northern side in the Civil War, but the draft riots of New York were caused by the Irish who did not want to fight for the Union. In addition to the shanty Irish there came over some middle-class families of importance.

The second immigration of importance occurred a few years later when a large number of Germans were forced over here by the failure of the Revolution in Germany in 1848. These Germans were very different from those who migrated to Pennsylvania in the eighteenth century. Many of them were from northern Germany and were Nordics, including individuals of some culture and distinction. They settled in certain cities of the West, notably in Cincinnati, Milwaukee, and Saint Louis. For the most part, however, they took up public land and became hard-working farmers. They did not in the mass improve the population already here intellectually, racially, or physically, and they impaired our national unity, at least for the time being, by the introduction of their own language.

At the end of the period here considered there were in the United States more than one and a quarter millions of German-born, of whom about one-fourth were Roman Catholics. This church, which in 1790 controlled not one in a hundred of the population, could in 1860 count upon one in every nine of the Whites.

Outside of the Irish and Germans, who were preponderantly Nordic, there was not much immigration of importance. The census of 1860 enumerated 4,138,697 foreign-born persons out of a total of nearly 27,000,000 Whites. England, Scotland, and Canada accounted for most of those who were neither Irish nor German. Thus at the end of this period the racial unity of the United States was still virtually unimpaired.

The French in the old Northwest Territory were negligible in number, amounting to but a few thousands. The number of Mexicans in Texas, Arizona, and New Mexico when we took over those countries was but a few thousand more. These Mexicans considered themselves Spanish; but as a matter of fact, the veneer of religion, language, and culture was very thin, and racially most of them were at least seven-eighths Indian. The same condition prevailed in California in 1846; the number of Mexicans being even smaller than in Texas.

Many of the original Colonial charters granted by the English kings provided for a north and south boundary by latitude, but the western boundary was often defined as the "South Sea," and not unnaturally many of these boundaries overlapped. After the Revolution, the original colonies were induced to

THE OLD NORTHWEST TERRITORY 163

cede to the Federal Government their indefinite and conflicting claims to the western lands. This general and important cession of territory had two results: it gave the impoverished Federal Government lands which could be sold for its own benefit, and it led to the establishment of communities which looked to the Federal Government for everything they needed, which in itself was a long step toward unity of government.

In 1787 the western boundaries of New York and Pennsylvania were fixed as they are at present, and out of the country south of the Great Lakes, north of the Ohio River, and east of the Mississippi was erected the Northwest Territory under the special guardianship of the Federal Government.

This "Northwest Territory" had been seized during the Revolution by an extraordinary group of adventurers and frontiersmen under General George Rogers Clark. Thereby the Thirteen Colonies were in physical possession of these districts south of the Great Lakes when the Treaty of Paris was signed in 1783. Without such actual possession of the Old Northwest, it would have remained part of Canada, an outcome which would have limited the growth of the United States westward or, more probably, have led to another war. The reluctance of the British authorities in charge of the outposts in this territory to surrender their forts in accordance with the terms of the treaty, and their alleged backing of the Indians, were among the causes underlying the War of 1812.

As population increased, new States were created in succession out of this territory—Ohio (1803), Indiana (1816), Illinois (1818), Michigan (1837), and Wisconsin (1848).

Ohio's first straggling settlers had pushed northwesterly across the Ohio River during the Revolution, but the first real, permanant settlement was by the New England Company which established Marietta in 1788. This New England immigration, though soon swamped by that from other States, played an important part in the organization of the territory and in the shaping of its future policies.

Scarcely had the Massachusetts group, led by General Rufus Putnam, taken possession of its vast grant around Marietta, when a new group led by Judge J. C. Symmes of Kentucky occupied a grant of a million acres between the Great and Little Miami Rivers, including the sites of Cincinnati, Dayton, and many of the most important of the early settlements of the territory.

Virginia had reserved a military district of more than four million acres to reward its soldiers of the Revolution, and this quickly began to be settled largely by veterans from Kentucky which was at that time, it will be remembered, still a part of Virginia.

Connecticut on the other hand had stipulated for its own Western Reserve of nearly 3,000,000 acres, extending in an oblong, 120 miles, from the boundary of Pennsylvania along Lake Erie, and the settlement of Cleveland marked its nucleus.

Thus Ohio, within a few years after the Revolution, started with four different growing points. The Virginia element increased the most rapidly, partly because of its proximity to Kentucky, partly because of its easy access by the Ohio River, so that the English and Ulster Scots of the southern part of the State soon dominated the whole.

A similar element was continually coming across the Pennsylvania border from the Monongahela country, and before long the Pennsylvania emigration to Ohio became the greatest from any one State, filling up the central part which comprised the great wheat belt. Even as late as the Mexican War, one-fourth of the members of the Ohio Legislature were natives of Pennsylvania, exceeding the members born in any other State, or in all the New England States combined, or in Ohio itself.

Through Kentucky came not merely Virginians but a steady stream of Ulster Scots from North Carolina, many of whom, however, had previously been Virginians. The southern parts of the State, therefore, took on some of the complexion of the slave-holding States, while the northern part was tinged by the culture of New England and the Central States, many coming in from western New York, which from the present point of view is to be regarded as merely an extension of New England.

Thus for a score of years the population of the States to the south and east of Ohio, which, dammed back by hostile Indians, had been ready to overflow for some time, poured into the new territory. Then the flood slackened until after the close of the War of 1812, when it was renewed with vigor. Men from all parts of the United States who had served with the western and northern forces in the War of 1812 had seen the beauties of the new country and determined to settle there as soon as peace was declared and they could dispose of their holdings at home. So far as New England was concerned this tendency was accentuated by two remarkably cold winters in 1816 and 1817, which surpassed the memories of the oldest inhabitants. General economic and social conditions were favorable for a widespread movement of population. The northwestern part of Ohio had been cleared of Indians and was then thrown open to settlement.

This second great flood of immigration into Ohio was in general of the same character as the first, bringing into the State from all sides an almost purely Nordic population of British ancestry, except for the small element of Pennsylvania Dutch who for a while kept much to themselves, maintained their own customs and their own language, and thus cut themselves off largely from the march of progress. Their Alemannish dialect was rapidly becoming almost as far out of line with the literary language of Germany as it was with the English language of their adopted home.

Later Ohio received a quarter of a million of German and Irish immigrants. But of the 2,339,511 inhabitants whom the State contained in 1860, a million and a half were born in the State itself.

Indiana, a typical American State, owes nothing worth mentioning to the original French population. In early days it must be considered little more than an extension of Kentucky. Virginia had set aside a large tract for rewarding the men of George Rogers Clark's expedition and these were the original land agents, so to speak, for the territory. But all along the border a frontier population drifted there across the Ohio River. As late as 1850 there were twice as many Southern people in Indiana as there were from the Middle States and New England put together. A good share of these were from Kentucky, which means that they or their parents were previously from Virginia or North Carolina.

That Indiana was in sympathy a Northern State bears testimony to the fact that these migrants had little in common except original racial stock with the older slave-holding population. The Ulster Scots were the largest element, although there were also many Quakers from North and South Carolina, some of whom were of Huguenot descent. It was this element which made of Indiana a principal route of the "Underground Railroad," as the system of smuggling runaway slaves out of the slave States was called. But in the southern part of the State there was much sympathy with the slaveholders.

The settlement of Indiana falls almost entirely in the nineteenth century, the number of people there prior to 1800 being negligible and confined for the most part to lands under the protection of the little post of Vincennes. On the northerly side of the Ohio River, at the Falls, the settlement of the tract of 149,000 acres, which Virginia had conveyed in 1786 to General Clark and his soldiers, was well under way.

The rapid settlement of Indiana was a part of the great westward movement beginning with the panic of 1819, and the hard times that followed. The price of cotton was steadily declining in the South and it was easy for the poorer farmer heavily in debt to sell out or simply pack up and quit, moving on to free and richer land in a new country. Many of the Ulster Scots in the South were hostile to slavery, while others of them, strongly Jacksonian in politics, were opposed to nullification and shared the reputed death-bed regret of the hero of New Orleans that he had not hanged John C. Calhoun. South Carolina therefore sent a large contingent of Ulster Scots to the new territory, in addition to the general immigration which has already been mentioned.

The Southern stream was met in the old Northwest Territory by the stream of New Englanders coming over the line of the Erie Canal after crossing the Hudson at the great break in the highlands near Albany. Many of the settlers of northern Indiana had tarried for a season in Ohio and moved westward as they had a chance to harvest the unearned increment by selling their farms at a profit and migrating to take up cheaper land and start again.

THE OLD NORTHWEST TERRITORY 169

Indiana missed the main flood of foreign immigration in the generation before the Civil War. The Germans were going elsewhere because of clannishness, while the Irish avoided Indiana because of its lack of great cities. By the time the Scandinavian flood began to come in, land values in Indiana were already high and the new settlers went farther west and north.

Indiana, therefore, of the States in the Northwest Territory is the most nearly Nordic in population and the most nearly American, and, at the end of the period under consideration, it represented an overwhelmingly native-born population originating, in not very unequal parts, from the Northern and Southern States, respectively Though the foreign element was rapidly gaining ground, it had not begun to make itself felt even as late as 1833 when northern Indiana was a wilderness, while southern Indiana was already well peopled from Kentucky, Tennessee and the Carolinas.

The development of internal improvements together with the general migration from Northern States to all points west brought a complete change in the political complexion of the State. In 1836, alone, land sales in Indiana amounted to 3,000,000 acres and in the decade from 1840 to 1850 the population of counties bordering the new Ohio canal increased 400 per cent, while the State began to look to New York as an outlet for its products rather than to New Orleans.

From 1820, the date of the founding of Indianapolis, to 1860, Indiana had twice quadrupled her population and from almost purely American stock. During these forty years, it is calculated that a million people came to the Northwest from the slave States of the South. At the outbreak of the Civil War, Indiana had a population of 1,350,000 of which only about one in eleven was foreign-born. More than half of the aliens were from Germany, and Indiana seems to have attracted particularly the Nordic element, since Prussia contributed the largest quota. Ireland was represented by only 24,000 persons at that time and like the smaller French and English groups, they were scattered through the State and soon became lost in the general mass.

This distinctive character of Indiana, almost purely American, Protestant, and Nordic in 1860, gives the key to much of its history since then. As elsewhere the immediate surrounding States had contributed the bulk of the population. The census returns showed that the ten States constituting the birthplace of the largest number of Hoosiers in that year were, in order of importance: Ohio, Kentucky, Pennsylvania, Virginia, New York, North Carolina, Tennessee, Maryland, New Jersey, and Illinois. So far as the New England element was represented, it had come almost wholly through other States.

Illinois, like Ohio, had attracted a few settlers before the Revolution, mainly to the neighborhood of the half-dozen little French trading posts. The French population of this district had never been large, and when it was taken over by Great Britain in 1763, most of the French inhabitants who could get away hastened to do so, either returning to Canada or going down the river to Saint Louis or New Orleans.

With the withdrawal of the little French garrisons only a few hundred persons of French ancestry were left in the territory. These were of two different origins. Part had come down from Canada and represented the "Habitant" French, who were largely Alpine. The remainder had come up the river from New Orleans and represented a more heterogeneous and probably inferior group. Some of the Canadians brought their families; but for the most part the French element was made up of single men who formed loose alliances with Indian squaws. For these various reasons the French influence on the subsequent population of the region is too negligible to justify consideration.

The raid made by the Kentuckians under George Rogers Clark during the Revolution had given the Americans a more detailed knowledge of this region, and by 1800 several thousand of them had already drifted across the border and started settlements. This immigration increased up to the outbreak of Indian hostilities in 1811 followed by the War of 1812 which almost completely checked settlement along the old western frontier.

After the declaration of peace and the opening up of land sales in 1814 and 1816, Illinois began to have a real boom. By this time the choicest locations in

Ohio, Indiana, and Kentucky had either been taken by settlers or bought by speculators, so that the new arrival looking for a bonanza turned to Illinois or Missouri.

Following the general rule of migration in the United States, which was not broken until the gold rush to California in 1849 introduced new conditions, the settlement of Illinois was mostly from the States closest to it, and at the beginning was almost wholly from the South, particularly from Kentucky, Tennessee, and Virginia. Insignificant little Shawneetown, on the Ohio River just below the mouth of the Wabash, gave easy access to the lower end of Illinois—that "Egypt" which is still a Southern Democratic stronghold. For a short time it was even the seat of government.

In this population the presence of a sprinkling of Northerners from Pennsylvania was resented and an occasional stray Yankee was scarcely tolerated. The settlement of the northern part of the State by New Englanders was made to a marked extent by colonies or organized groups, and from the early thirties one reads continually of the movement of caravans from all the New England States and western New York. Here again the opening of the Erie Canal gave easy access to northern Illinois by water. Prior to that time the lead mines in the northwestern part of Illinois and the southwestern part of Wisconsin had been the main attraction, and had been developed almost entirely by the Southerners.

THE OLD NORTHWEST TERRITORY 173

In general, it may be said that up to that time three-fourths of the population of Illinois came from south of the Mason and Dixon line, with Kentucky making the largest single contribution, although a small foreign element was already arriving, mainly from the British Isles.

At the date of Statehood in 1818, Illinois may be said to have been dominated by the Ulster Scots who had come in from the southern Piedmont. These represented, on the whole, a class which for lack of wealth and other reasons had not been slaveholders, and had no particular sympathy with slavery, having found by personal experience that the presence of slave labor was disadvantageous to a large part of the white population. As a matter of fact, probably not more than one Southern family in four ever owned a slave.

The population required of a new State for admission to the Union in 1818 was 40,000. By the beginning of the Civil War the population of Illinois had increased to a million and three quarters. Obviously this change in little more than a generation represented only in small part the natural increase of the original settlers from Kentucky and Virginia. So rapidly, indeed, did the forces of progress act in Illinois that many of the old-timers packed up and moved on, as had happened during the previous generation among their parents, and Illinois in the following generation will be found strongly represented in the early migration to California, Kansas, Nebraska, and Colorado. To show how little slave-holding sentiment there was in the early Illinois population, in spite of its Southern origin, it is interesting to note that most of the Illinois contingent in Kansas were Free-State men whom the South regarded as enemies to its cause.

For every one of the old-timers who moved farther west, a dozen Yankees arrived along with many Pennsylvanians, while the Southern immigration almost entirely stopped, having been diverted to Texas or to territories beyond the Mississippi.

The people who left the slave-holding States in the decade prior to the Civil War were largely seeking free soil themselves. This movement of some of the best Nordic stock out of the South just before and at the beginning of the Civil War has not been given as much importance as it deserves. It was a factor in the weakening of the South and the strengthening of the North. While slavery was a curse in the opinion of many an owner of a great plantation, he was caught in the system and felt that he could not get away. The poor man, on the other hand, found conditions less and less to his liking and many of the more intelligent decided to get out of a country where they were obliged to compete with Negro slaves and were looked down upon by their white neighbors. In this way the lands along the Illinois Central Railway became a lode-stone for ambitious and dissatisfied farmers from Tennessee, Alabama, and even from Georgia. With the outbreak of hostilities this trickle became temporarily a torrent as political refugees who did not care to remain in a slave-holding republic at war with the American Union began to seek freer air.

The railroads developed a new specialty in transporting whole families with their furniture and agricultural implements to points in Illinois, Iowa, and Wisconsin, while steamers made their way up the Mississippi crowded with refugees and great numbers of Missourians crossed the river to Illinois with all their worldly goods. Many of the latter returned home after Missouri was cleared of secession, but their place was taken by new streams of Southerners released by the victories of Union armies and coming to join friends and relatives in southern and central Illinois.

The decline of leadership in the South after the war was not due entirely to the loss of its men on the battle-field. Although this was by far the principal factor, another important one was the flight from the South of many of those who were not in sympathy with the fire-eating politicians who had forced secession upon often unwilling communities.

Before this time, however, the streams of foreign-born which poured into the Mississippi Valley had already begun to influence the composition of the population of Illinois, so that even in 1850 one in four was of alien birth. The largest element was German, who formed farming communities, mainly in the northern and central part of the State. By 1860 there were 130,000 of them in Illinois, together with others who had also come from Pennsylvania.

Ireland sent the group of second importance, and

the great internal improvements in this period were largely the product of their labor. As elsewhere the Irish showed little inclination for farming, which had proved so ruinous to them in Ireland, and they made a restless floating population in the large cities. In 1860 they represented four times as large a proportion of the population of Chicago as they did of the State as a whole.

The State attracted a large English immigration. The Illinois Central Railroad had been built to a considerable extent with English capital, and the stockholders saw a chance to increase the value of their shares by promoting emigration to the lands owned by the company, so that by 1860 there were 41,000 English-born in the State.

Another large element of English descent, which had come into the State in an extraordinary way, had already left. This was the group of Mormon converts who were brought over from 1840 onward. By 1844 it was estimated that of the 16,000 Mormon arrivals, 10,000 were English. Most of these went west to Utah later, or were scattered within a few years.

The last important Nordic element in the State was that of the Scandinavians who had only begun to come before the Civil War, at which time there were little more than 10,000 of them in the State as against 87,000 Irish.

Michigan, owing to its proximity to Canada, and the importance of Detroit as a headquarters, had a distinct French atmosphere in its early days. Unlike those in some of the more distant settlements, the French inhabitants at Detroit did not intermarry frequently with the Indians, and they represent therefore a relatively pure French Canadian stock. American immigration was slow, and not until 1805 did the inhabitants become numerous enough to warrant a separate territory. As late as the beginning of the War of 1812 four-fifths of the 5000 people in Michigan were French. In 1817 the first steamboat appeared on the waters of Lake Erie and the Erie Canal was begun, and from that time the Americanization of the territory was rapid.

By 1830 a hundred ships, both steam and sail, were on the Lakes, and a daily line ran between Buffalo and Detroit. In 1836 when the State Constitution was adopted the population was nearly 100,000, mainly from New England and its extension in western New York. The Empire State can very definitely be called the parent of Michigan.

Many of the New England farmers who had bought farms from the great land companies in western New York found themselves unable or unwilling to complete their payments and sold their equities for enough to buy government land in Michigan and move their families, while from the rocky hills of Vermont a steady stream came without any intervening stop. By this time many of the French Canadians had moved out, and of eighty-nine names signed to the Constitution of 1835, not more than three can be identified as French.

178 THE CONQUEST OF A CONTINENT

The tide of alien immigration at this period was late in reaching Michigan. A group not found elsewhere was that of Dutchmen who came like some of the earlier settlers, seeking religious tolerance and freedom. The town of Holland has been a centre for them since 1847. Of the 749,113 inhabitants of the State in 1860, one-fifth were foreign-born, divided not unequally between English, Irish, Germans, and mixed Canadians.

Wisconsin's first settlement was at the lead mines of the southwestern part and attracted largely Ulster Scots from Virginia, Kentucky, and Tennessee. A little later these were reinforced by another Nordic group of Englishmen from Cornwall who formed an important element in that region.

The second migration scattered agricultural communities throughout the southeastern part of Wisconsin along the lake shore. This immigration was almost wholly 'from the New England States and the New England part of New York State, and was accomplished roughly in the years 1835 to 1850. By 1847 when Statehood was achieved the territory had a population of nearly 250,000 and was virtually a New England colony.

Of the seventy-six men who composed the second Constitutional Convention, one-third came from New York, one-third from New England, and the rest were scattering.

During the decade which ended with the Federal Census of 1850, the growth of the State had been

THE OLD NORTHWEST TERRITORY 179

nearly 900 per cent, a record rarely exceeded in America. This extraordinary surge was due largely to the sudden arrival of a foreign element which has ever since made Wisconsin a State apart from all the others. Even as early as 1850 one-third of the population was actually foreign-born. Of the foreign-born who came to the State during the territorial period, the British Isles contributed about one-half and foreign-language groups the other half. The English-speaking immigrants soon blended with the native population, with the exception of the Roman Catholic Irish who were less easily assimilated. In the decade before the Civil War there was a stream of Belgian immigrants amounting to at least 15,000. Some hundreds of Russians also came in and the Scandinavians had begun to arrive, although they did not play an important part until after the Civil War. Danes and Norwegians were beginning to come in some numbers but few Swedes as yet.

The great immigration of this period was the German, which introduced another partly Alpine element into the overwhelmingly Nordic population of the United States. These had begun to come after 1830, when the Revolution in France had stirred up similar, but less successful, political upheavals in the parts of South Germany adjoining France. Many of the politically discontented decided to leave the country or were obliged to do so, and they found in Wisconsin conditions particularly to their liking. In the first place the State offered a variety of climate and soil that was not dissimilar to that in which they were brought up. In the second place land was cheap and good and there was much forest land for which the Germans showed a notable preference. Not only was the possession of timber an asset, but it was to the German immigrant a mark of social status. Forests had largely disappeared in Germany, except on the great estates of the nobility. Hence, to own a piece of forest land was a mark of superiority. Only the few could afford the forest land in Germany but in Wisconsin every small farmer could feel himself as good as the Duke or Prince whose yoke he had renounced. A third important attraction after Statehood was a provision that the alien could vote after only one year's residence. This gave the Germans a political importance without delay which they lost no time in using.

German settlement in the United States follows a belt beginning with Pennsylvania and running due west through Ohio, Indiana, Wisconsin, Iowa, and Missouri. This was partly due to an avoidance of the Southern States with whose products they were not familiar and with whose land system and slave labor they were not sympathetic. Being in this belt Wisconsin immediately took and retained such a prominence that patriots from the "Fatherland" seriously urged that it become a genuine German colony.

The Pennsylvania Dutch had already shown how little disposed the German-speaking peoples were to become citizens of a new country with a whole heart, and the new tide of immigration followed this ex-

THE OLD NORTHWEST TERRITORY 181

ample. They attacked the public-school system from the beginning and insisted on having their own schools and on having their children taught German in the American schools. They kept their own social organization and even went so far as to get the State laws published in the German language in Indiana in 1858. This tendency toward hyphenation has made the Germans a less valuable element in the American population up to the present time than they should have been.

The early German immigration to Wisconsin was on the whole from southern and central Germany, and was predominantly Alpine in race and Roman Catholic in religion. Statehood in Wisconsin coincided with the unsuccessful Revolution of 1848 in Germany which started the real flood of German immigration that reached its maximum numbers in 1854, and continued with noticeable strength for more than a generation longer.

The principal Nordic emigration in the '40s was from Pomerania and Brandenburg, and many of the South Germans, while largely Alpine, were Protestants rather than Catholics. In 1863, just after the end of the period here considered, the church authorities reported that Wisconsin contained 225,000 German Lutherans as against 105,000 German Catholics. After that the Germans pressed more and more into the northern and central regions of the State.

Wisconsin then at the end of the period here considered (1860) had probably the largest non-Nordic population of any of the American States, although even here the Nordics were in a great majority. With one-third of its population foreign-born, it was surpassed in this respect only by California.

IX

THE MOUNTAINEERS CONQUER THE SOUTHWEST

MEANWHILE the States of the lower Mississippi Valley were coming into existence at a rapid rate.

Alabama had no American settlement until after the Revolution, save for the sporadic appearance of adventurers or traders. But in 1798, when the Mississippi territory was formed, including the present State of Alabama, there was already a movement of settlers from the adjoining States on the east and north, and this continued rapidly until checked by the war with the Creek Indians in 1813 and 1814. This war advertised the territory. Its termination threw the land open to settlement, and more than 100,000 people located in Alabama within five years. The slight French and Spanish element in Mobile and two or three other places was soon reduced to insignificant proportions.

The State was settled either by those who came down some of the rivers of that region, particularly from Tennessee, or by those who came through Georgia, stopping long enough at the land office in Milledgeville (then the State capital) to make the necessary arrangements for acquiring title to real estate. An unimproved but passable trail ran thence through Montgomery to Natchez, and over this

"Three Notch Road" (so-called from the blaze which marked it) a stream of settlers from the Atlantic seaboard States passed into the broad belt of rich blackland which quickly made Alabama and Mississippi the heart of the Cotton Kingdom. Alabama is, for the most part, the offspring of Virginia, North and South Carolina, Georgia, and Tennessee, and therefore represents almost entirely Scotch and English blood. Its foreign-born population was negligible in 1860, amounting to little more than 12,000, almost half of whom were Irish, in a total of virtually a million.

Mississippi: As in most others of this group of States, the supposed influence of the earlier French and Spanish settlements is more sentimental than real. American settlers began to filter in after 1763, some coming even from New Jersey, Pennsylvania, and New England. A few Loyalists drifted down to the Mississippi country during the Revolution, joining the British who were attached to the district at that time in military or administrative capacities. One of the elements of this Loyalist immigration consisted of Scotch Highlanders from North Carolina.

The census of 1850 furnished the first opportunity to ascertain the origin of the population. The main immigration naturally was from other Southern States which contributed 145,000 against 5000 from the Northern States. In the same year 18,000 natives of Mississippi were residing in other Southern

States, principally in Louisiana, Texas, Arkansas, Alabama, and Tennessee.

At the census ten years later the Mississippi natives, then located in other Southern States, had almost doubled in number. The enumeration gives an interesting picture of the way in which population was flowing backward and forward between adjoining States at that time as it has in almost every other period in American history.

Since the population of Mississippi before the Civil War was almost identical in composition with the population of the other Mississippi Valley slave States, most of which owed their inhabitants originally to Virginia and subsequently to the States which Virginia had colonized, it was not surprising that these people found it easy to move from one part of this region to another. Of nearly 800,000 population at the outbreak of the Civil War, the foreign-born, still mainly Irish, constituted only one in a hundred. But nearly half of the population of the State was colored, and thus no element of racial strength. In this respect Mississippi's record was surpassed only by Georgia and South Carolina. This latter State was the only one in which Negroes actually outnumbered Whites at that time. Other Southern States later reached the same unenviable situation, and it continued in South Carolina until after the shift of Negro population which followed the World War.

Louisiana at the time of the Purchase in 1803

presented among its 50,000 residents a more varied group than could be found in any other American State. The foundation of this population was French, the Spanish element never having been important. These French seem to have represented a much more heterogeneous lot than did the early French-Canadians. One colonization scheme after another had been launched in Paris, and settlers had been recruited by all sorts of means, many of them of more than doubtful merit.

Here, however, as in other colonies, it must be remembered that the final population represented not those who arrived, but those who both survived and left posterity. This fact has too often been disregarded in the accounts of the origins of the American population. If France shipped prostitutes to New Orleans to provide wives for its soldiers, nevertheless this is now of importance only in so far as such persons left descendants. In one case, of which the details exist, forty-four girls were sent out from France in 1722. They all married, but only one left offspring.

Another element in the population was the Acadian refugees, who, uprooted by the New England militia in 1758, were driven to almost every part of the colonies. Some made their way to Louisiana, as Longfellow has described, though drawing a very erroneous picture, in *Evangeline*. Others were scattered through Maryland, Virginia, and the Carolinas, in fact on almost every part of the Atlantic coast. The total number of persons expelled from Nova

Scotia at this time probably did not exceed 6000, and many of these certainly died from hardships. In any case only a minority was directed to Louisiana, so that the original settlement of Acadians must represent a very small part of the population. The so-called "Cajan" population of some of the southern parishes of Louisiana is, at the present time, largely of other origins, chiefly Negro.

Another group of French refugees came from Haiti by way of Cuba after 1800, when the Negro uprising there drove out the Whites. Many of these were persons of good quality but as many as could do so went elsewhere after peace returned.

Still another source of population was the notorious Mississippi Bubble sponsored by the Scotchman John Law about 1717. This was the period at which the Germans from the Palatine and adjacent regions were emigrating in large numbers, as has been previously set forth in detail, and 10,000 or more of them were persuaded to go to Louisiana. According to accepted accounts, not more than 2000 of these Alpines actually arrived, and when the bubble burst, they settled along the Mississippi above Baton Rouge in a region which is still known as the German Coast.

An ill-natured English traveller, John Davis, visiting Louisiana in the year before the Purchase of 1803, has left the following picture of these two elements as they appeared to him:

"The Acadians are the descendants of French colonists, transported from the province of Nova

Scotia. The character of their fore-fathers is strongly marked in them; they are rude and sluggish, without ambition, living miserable on their sorry plantations, where they cultivate Indian corn, raise pigs, and get children. Around their houses one sees nothing but hogs, and before their doors great rustic boys, and big strapping girls, stiff as bars of iron, gaping for want of thought, or something to do, at the stranger who is passing.

"The Germans are somewhat numerous, and are easy to be distinguished by their accent, fair and fresh complexion, their inhospitality, brutal manners and proneness to intoxication. They are, however, industrious and frugal."

A small Spanish settlement, New Iberia, was made in 1779 of colonists largely from Andalusia and the Canary Islands. At least the former element doubtless contained Moorish blood.

Finally, there was an immigration from the American colonies which had been coming in for a generation previous to the Purchase. One of the first groups was from North Carolina. From time to time other small bodies of settlers crossed the mountains to the Tennessee River, where they constructed flat boats and floated down to the Ohio and thence to the Mississippi. A few years later a group of Scotch Highlanders from North Carolina arrived, settling near Natchez. The early American immigration to Louisiana came on the whole from the upland parts of the Southern States, and was therefore Scotch and English. After the Purchase a similar immigration increased greatly in numbers.

The census of 1860, which credited the State with 708,002 people, revealed that only 81,000 of these were foreign-born, the Germans and Irish being in about equal numbers. Nearly all of the remainder who were not natives of the State were born in adjacent States of the Mississippi Valley, the Whites being made up in about equal proportions of native-born and those born in nearby States. The former contained much of the old French and mixed stock; the latter was almost entirely of British antecedents.

Arkansas, at the time of the Louisiana Purchase, did not contain 500 white people. The current of immigration down the Mississippi had gone past the Post at the mouth of the Arkansas River without taking the trouble to turn aside. Settlement can scarcely be said to have begun before 1807, and at the census three years later there were only 1000 people in the territory.

It was not until after the passage by Congress in 1818 of the Land Act that the pioneers, each carrying in a leather wallet a certificate which entitled him to a homestead, began to work their boats up the current of the Arkansas River. There was a steady though not rapid arrival of settlers from Virginia, the Carolinas, Kentucky, and particularly Tennessee—which has often been regarded as the original parent of Arkansas.

Attempts have been made to trace a line of migration from the first settlement in North Carolina, the undesirable character of which was mentioned earlier, through Tennessee and down into Arkansas, and to attribute to this element of the population the backwardness of some parts of the last-named State. A few settlers came from Georgia or Alabama up the Mississippi River but this involved a long struggle with a strong current and it was easier for them to settle in the blacklands of Mississippi or Louisiana.

There were about 14,000 persons in Arkansas in 1817 when it was created a Territory. Thereafter it made a steady growth, derived generally from all the Southern States of the Mississippi Valley, until nearly the time of the Civil War when Indiana and Kentucky began to contribute some settlers. Its population therefore was in general made up almost wholly of British stock. Its 1860 population of 435,350 was one-fourth black, the Whites being almost wholly native-born, a thousand Germans and a thousand Irish being lost in the mass.

Missouri must be considered from a double point of view. As a French outpost, St. Louis had become the refuge of much of the French population of the whole Northwest Territory when that passed under English control, and for many years the city remained a foreign settlement. Scattered settlers began to occupy the river banks after or even during the Revolution. In the westward march of population down the eastern slope of the Mississippi Valley small groups soon began to enter Missouri, until at the census of 1810, they amounted to 20,000 persons occupying a strip of land along the Mississippi with a small isolated settlement at the lead mines.

On the other hand, as a territory where slavery was permitted, Missouri naturally attracted emigrants from Virginia and North Carolina, Kentucky and Tennessee. Within ten years after the Louisiana Purchase it was estimated that four-fifths of the people in Missouri were Americans and they were rapidly moving from the river back into the interior.

The Missouri River was naturally an avenue of access for these people. The interior of the State soon began to have the collective name of "Boone's Lick" because the Boones had made salt in that district in 1807. A real rush into this region began about 1817, and Kentucky showed its loyalty to its adopted son (who it will be remembered was a Pennsylvanian by birth) by contributing 90 per cent of the immigration. The State has been called the daughter of Kentucky and within limits this is not inappropriate. Tennessee, however, was strongly represented. The whole population was in general of the upland element originally from Virginia and North Carolina, largely Ulster Scotch in its more remote origin.

By 1830 the movement of population had reached the western border of the State. Until this time the settlement was purely British in character save for the now negligible remnant of French on the Mississippi. Missouri then began to get a part of the immigration of German Alpines which makes Saint Louis still one of the American cities with a most marked German tinge. At the same time some of the old American stock who objected to slavery and its influences were passing north and west of Missouri into Iowa, Kansas, and Nebraska. On the whole, however, at the close of this period Missouri remained a Nordic community mostly of Virginian stock going back eventually to Great Britain. Its population of well over a million was nine-tenths white and eight-tenths American-born, the Germans outnumbering the Irish two to one among the foreigners. Kentucky had been by far the largest contributor, Tennessee came next, followed by Virginia, while Ohio, Illinois, and Indiana together accounted for only about as many as Kentucky alone, that is, 100,000.

This Missouri population, with its Ulster Scotch tinge, played an important part in the settlement of the trans-Missouri West. It contributed a large percentage of the plainsmen and mountain men of later date, as well as of the cowboys on the cattle ranges, to say nothing of the gun-men and bad men of the frontier.

Florida missed the establishment of one of the earliest and what might have been one of the greatest of Nordic colonies in North America when Coligny's settlement of Huguenots was massacred by the Spanish on September 20, 1565. The latter made no effective use of the territory which was looked upon by the government of Mexico probably in about the same light as the Virgin Islands are now looked upon by the government in Washington. In 1763 Spain ceded Florida to England in return for Havana, which had been captured during the Seven Years' War.

A second Nordic invasion of Florida occurred at the time of the American Revolution when the English Loyalists from the Southern colonies sought refuge there to the number of more than 13,000. If these had remained as permanent settlers the State would have benefited immensely, but most of them left in 1784, when the Spaniards reoccupied the territory and abolished religious freedom. Some went to England and others to the West Indies or Nova Scotia. The development of the peninsula was thereby long delayed.

East and West Florida became part of the United States in 1819. A Florida colonization scheme, of little importance numerically, deserves mention in passing because it represented the first real establishment in American territory of the Mediterranean peoples who have formed such an important element in the immigration of the last half-century. This was a colony established by British promoters to which they brought 1,500 Greeks, Italians, and Minorcans about 1767. Sickness soon greatly reduced their numbers, but a few of the descendants of these people are in the State at the present time.

As late as the Civil War, Florida was one of the weakest of the American States, with but 140,000 population, of which well over a third was colored. Nearly all of the Whites represented a southward thrust of the Atlantic seaboard states, from or through Georgia. Foreigners were a scattered lot, constituting but one in twenty-five of the white population.

X

FROM THE MISSISSIPPI TO THE OREGON

AFTER the Old Northwest Territory was filled up, it began to overflow into the territories across the Mississippi which the Louisiana Purchase had provided.

Minnesota's early settlers were French and half-breeds, who came over the border from Canada, together with a small number of Scots escaping from the breakup of the Red River Colony in Manitoba in the first quarter of the last century. This Red River is, of course, the Red River of the North which forms the present boundary between Minnesota and the Dakotas.

Beginning in 1837 treaties were made with the Indians which gradually opened up the land to settlement; but in 1849, when a territorial organization was effected and the first official census taken, there were less than 5000 persons in the region.

Meanwhile the flood of immigration was reaching the nearby States, and Wisconsin and Iowa were growing with tremendous spurts. The tide soon began to flow up to Minnesota, coming by four principal routes. Some of the invaders came from Milwaukee across Wisconsin by land. Others from Chicago by land through northern Illinois and southwestern Wisconsin. Still others from Chicago to Galena, embarking there on the river steamers. Another group embarked at Saint Louis and came 800 miles up the Mississippi to Fort Snelling, the nucleus around which the Twin Cities began to develop.

When the Rock Island and Pacific Railway was built through to the Mississippi in the early summer of 1854, the gateways really opened. The next season saw 50,000 persons in the territory of Minnesota. That number was doubled in 1856. In 1854 the sales of public land had amounted to 300,000 acres, in 1856 to 2,300,000. Most of this population, which evidently came to stay, was from the Middle States. The States of the Old Northwest and New England were not far behind, but little of the Southern emigration came this far north. The years 1855, 1856, and 1857 marked the high tide of the flood of immigration of territorial days which has not since been duplicated.

The Scandinavian immigration, which has colored Minnesota so strongly, began in this decade, and brought a steady stream of hardy Nordics who avoided the cities, their objective being to acquire land, establish a home, develop a farm, and become American citizens. A substantial part of the German migration also reached Minnesota, so that in the census of 1860 one-third of the foreign-born population was German. By this time the Canadian elements had been completely swamped. The Federal Census of 1860, three years after the territory had been admitted to Statehood, found 170,000 inhabitants, of whom 58,000 were foreign-born. The Germans at this time still somewhat exceeded the Scandinavians in number. The native-born were overwhelmingly of British ancestry and represented a prolongation of the westward movement of population from New England that had been going on for more than two centuries. Minnesota at this time had a Nordic population and was predominantly Anglo-Saxon in character.

Dakota was included in Minnesota in 1860 when a few settlers had already begun to enter the region. Dakota Territory, however, scarcely deserves consideration until the final period is herein reviewed.

Iowa had no real settlement until the spring of 1833, when several companies of Americans from Illinois and elsewhere settled in the vicinity of Burlington, although John Dubuque established a settlement in 1788 on the site of the city which now bears his name, and, with his descendants, carried on a business of mining lead and trading with the Indians for a generation or more. Settlements then began to be made at other points along the Mississippi, and in 1838 the country was cut off from Wisconsin and established as a separate territory.

As in the States of the Old Northwest Territory, the early population of Iowa was made up principally from the Southern States; and when Dubuque was formally declared to be a town in 1834 its 500 citizens were mostly from Tennessee, Kentucky, and North Carolina.

The delay in the settlement of Iowa, as compared with that of the States east of the Mississippi, was due mainly to the fact that it was held by the Indians. The Black Hawk War kept the country disturbed for three years. At the end of that time the chief was utterly routed and ultimately captured, and in September, 1832, a treaty was signed in which the Indians relinquished what was afterward known as the Black Hawk Purchase, comprising about one-third of the present State of Iowa.

At that time there were probably not fifty white men in Iowa, but thenceforward the settlement was extraordinarily rapid. The pioneers from the South came up the Mississippi, while those from the East could go down the Ohio. But since the purpose of most of the settlers was to take up farm land and since the livestock and implements necessary for this purpose could not be transported easily on the small river boats, the great bulk of the immigration was overland in wagons drawn by oxen, horses, or mules.

In 1836 there were 10,000 Southerners in the territory. In the following two years this number had more than doubled and the census of 1840 made it 43,000.

Foreign immigrants began to appear in small numbers, but the new arrivals were still largely of Southern upland stock, mainly of Scottish ancestry. By the Federal Census of 1850 Iowa had nearly 200,000 people and, although the settlement had begun at the most only seventeen years before, one-fourth of the population was Iowa-born.

As in the Old Northwest Territory, the direct contribution of New England was small. Most of the settlers came from adjoining States, and, while many of them went back to New England in pedigree, a still larger number in the early years came from the Southern States. This was true in Iowa nearly up to the time of the Civil War.

The ebb and flow of population in these States was so rapid as to make the task of tracing its details difficult. Thus in 1843 meetings were held in various points in Iowa to form companies of emigrants for Oregon. In 1849 the territory contributed its share to the California gold rush. Whole communities were depopulated almost as fast as they had been populated a few years previously, but many of these travellers probably returned after failing to find fortune ready to hand in the Golden State. Ohio was sending on settlers to the three States beyond her. Indiana and Illinois were attracting large bodies of settlers from Ohio but sending on others to Iowa. Iowa itself was contributing heavily to the population of Utah and Oregon. But these were all of the old native English Nordic stock.

By 1860 Iowa had a population of 674,913. The foreign-born made up nearly one-sixth of the total, two-thirds were German or Irish, and the remainder English or Scandinavian.

Iowa, by the outbreak of the Civil War, had become a Northern State, not so much from the direct

New England immigration (only 25,000 of its people were New England born) as from the general drift of population, and from the fact that, as pointed out previously, many of the Southerners who came into the Northwest Territory had very little sympathy with the slaveholding point of view.

Iowa then entered the Union as a State almost completely Nordic and overwhelmingly Anglo-Saxon, populated by settlers from all parts of the original States who were moving westward in the hope of finding an advantage. What an immigrant of the 1830's said about Iowa pioneers he encountered, holds good of most of the westward movement—that it was made up of three classes: "men with families seeking to ameliorate fortune, men with families seeking to retrieve fortune, and young men attempting fortune." While the first pioneer surge into a new territory often contained a surplus of bachelors, the permanent settlement was made by men who brought their families.

Kansas-Nebraska's settlement in the decade before the Civil War is a familiar episode to every one who remembers his American history.

Daniel Morgan Boone, a son of the Kentucky Pathfinder, is often alleged to have been the first American settler in Kansas, having been sent there by the government in 1819 to aid the Indians in agriculture. But the settlement of the State did not begin seriously until 1854, when treaties were made with the tribes of what was at that time an Indian territory.

Missouri, adjoining Kansas to the east, had then nearly 600,000 inhabitants, and the counties bordering on the Kansas line contained a population of some 80,000 whites, as shown by the census of 1850. These naturally were the most available material for settlement of the new land and in a short time they had staked out the best claims in the river bottoms. While they do not bear a good reputation in the Kansas histories, where they generally go by the name of "border ruffians," they represented, worthily or not, pure Nordic American stock. Most of the Missourians who had moved into Kansas at that time were simply seeking new homes and were not even in favor of slavery. The trouble that was made on the border was due to small organized gangs of quite a different complexion.

Kansas represented a real battleground for the slavery and free-soil elements, and colonies were organized in a number of the Southern States, but particularly in Alabama and Kentucky, to move to the new territory and insure its retention for the cause. Most of the Southern settlers naturally stayed as close to the Missouri border as possible. The Free-State settlers on the other hand tended to get away from the border, to leave the belt of pro-slavery settlers behind, and to stake out their claims well within the interior of the territory.

The New England Emigrant Aid Company was the principal crusader in the campaign to make Kansas free soil, and proclaimed widely that it would send 10,000 men into the region. Its funds, however, were scanty, and beyond advertising the opportunities of the country, it gave little substantial aid to the emigration. Contrary to what is generally supposed, the number of settlers who came directly from New England to Kansas was small. As had been the history elsewhere in this country, most of the settlers came from nearby States such as Illinois; though often of New England ancestry.

In the first census of the territory, in 1855, more than half of the population was found to be from the South, although the Slave States' representatives made strong protests against the manner of taking the census which was sudden and in mid-winter when many of the Missouri settlers had returned to their old homes. The high-water mark of the Southern immigration was in 1856. Thereafter the emigration from the Free States increased until by 1860 it outnumbered the Slave-State natives nearly three to one. That year's census, crediting Kansas with 107,000 population, also revealed that Missouri and Kentucky were the principal sources of the pro-slavery immigration, while the main sources of the free-soil immigration were in the following order: Ohio, Indiana, Illinois, Pennsylvania, and New York, with only 3000 direct from all the New England States together. Indeed, there were almost as many natives of North Carolina in Kansas as there were natives of Massachusetts.

Kansas was at the end of this period a western State, of almost wholly British complexion. The streams of Scandinavians and Germans which afterward entered the State had scarcely begun at this period. Kansas was, to a marked degree, the offspring of New England through the Central States, while not much more than one-fourth of its population, arriving from the border States, had ancestral lines running back to Virginia.

Nebraska, like many other Western States, was first settled by trappers, traders, missionaries, and soldiers. In 1845 the Mormons, driven out of Illinois and Iowa, stopped in the Nebraska country, but most of them afterward moved on to Utah. Meanwhile, the State was being traversed each year by hundreds of emigrant trains on their way to the Pacific Coast, and thus became known to people from all parts of the Union. During the years 1849 and 1850 it was estimated that more than 100,000 people crossed the Nebraska plains in this way. Some of them would stop there for various reasons, while others came into the section to cater to the needs of the emigrants. Thus Nebraska was gradually built up out of the overland traffic. The early migration to Utah and to Oregon was succeeded by the rush to California, and that had scarcely died down when the boom days in Colorado brought new contingents to the region. Before this had disappeared the Transcontinental Railway opened up the territory in real earnest.

The first boom year in the territory was in 1856 when a large number of permanent settlers came in. In 1860 the population numbered 28,841, and even at this time relatively few of the settlers depended upon agriculture, most of them still "living off of the tourists," which became a recognized profession in some States half a century later.

Utah, when Brigham Young led his Saints there in 1847, was a desert as to the region of the Great Salt Lake, with scarcely even a population of Indians. The early population was almost wholly Nordic, made up of people from the New England States, New York, and those States in which the Mormon Church had temporarily settled, or through which it had moved successively to Illinois, Iowa, Missouri, and Nebraska.

The Mormon authorities made a determined effort from the outset to bring converts from Europe, the first one arriving from Liverpool in 1849. At that time the English mission was said to have 30,000 members. In the fall of 1849 the Mormon leaders established the famous Perpetual Emigrating Fund which was used thenceforth to aid the transport of converts.

The Mormon Utah settlement by 1850 had a population of 11,000. The number of converts brought from abroad during the first ten years is put at 17,000, mostly from England. By 1887 the Mormons are said to have brought more than 85,000 of the working classes from England and northern Europe to the Great Basin of the Rocky Mountains.

Brigham Young in 1849 organized his territory as "The Provisional State of Deseret," including what is now Utah and Nevada, and parts of Wyoming, Colorado, New Mexico, Arizona, and California. This had but a short existence even on paper, for in 1850 Congress passed a law organizing the territory of Utah which also included what is now Nevada.

Toward the end of this period the discovery of rich silver mines in the Nevada section began to attract a miscellaneous population from all parts of the West. By 1863 a Mormon census of Utah gave the territory a population of 88,206, of whom probably a majority were foreigners. The great bulk of these were English, particularly from the factory towns, but Brigham Young boasted that fifty nationalities were represented in his territory a few years later. On the whole, however, the population was almost entirely Nordic.

Idaho's first settlement is supposed to have been made by a party of Mormons in 1855 when it was still a part of Washington territory. At the close of the period here considered it was still a part of Washington and was just beginning to get a population of its own because of a gold rush in 1860.

Its early settlers were from Oregon, Washington, and northern California, and included an unusual proportion of men bred in the Southern and Southwestern States.

Montana had scarcely begun to receive settlers at this time.

Meanwhile the tides of colonization were flowing

over the "great plains" to deposit their load on the Pacific Coast.

Oregon's settlement may be conveniently dated from the expedition of Marcus Whitman in 1836. The few trappers and traders who had arrived in early days may be disregarded. Thus began the short-lived race between the United States and Great Britain to colonize the country and to have their claims to possession based on effective occupation. American immigration did not commence in earnest until 1842 or 1843, but continued steadily, until the discovery of gold in California diverted many to that territory.

Most of the early American settlers came from Missouri or Iowa, and represented therefore either the Southern or New England pioneer stock. In general it may be said that Oregon at that time was settled from the Mississippi Valley, and mainly by men who came as genuine settlers with their families, in striking contrast to the adventurers who invaded California.

Meanwhile, the British colonizers were coming from Canada, many of them French-Canadians, while the rest were mostly of Scotch ancestry. But the American population grew so much more rapidly that by 1846, when the Treaty was made defining the parallel of 49° as the boundary between the two nations, there were nearly 8000 American settlers in the Oregon territory as against about 1500 of British allegiance.

In 1860, of the 30,500 native immigrants in the State 40 per cent were of Southern birth. Nearly half of these were from Missouri, and a large part of the others from Kentucky or Tennessee. The remainder represented principally the New England stock which has always been considered to be the foundation of Oregon.

The actual permanent settlement of the Puget Sound country began in 1845, but progress for some years was slow. Scarcely had a start been made here when the gold rush turned everyone's attention to California. Following this came the Indian war of 1855 to 1856, and shortly afterward the Civil War upset all plans, leaving the few scattered inhabitants of the Puget Sound region in the midst of a wilderness, surrounded by hostile savages, and inevitably neglected by the government to which they naturally looked for attention.

Washington was separated from Oregon and established as an independent territory in 1853. The census found there only 3965 white persons, a small number to assume the responsibilities of a separate political existence. Walla Walla Valley was opened up in 1859, when the removal of a military interdict and a survey of public lands allowed a waiting population of some 2000 to rush in and spread over the whole of eastern Washington within a short time.

XI

THE SPOILS OF THE MEXICAN WAR

It has been remarked often that it was a mere accident that gave North America to the Nordics instead of to the King of Spain, when Columbus turned from his course to follow a flock of birds and thus sighted the West Indies instead of the mainland, but several other incidents played an equally important part in giving this empire to the British. The defeat of the Invincible Armada by the captains of Elizabeth stopped the expansion of Spain and thus gave the British an opportunity to begin their colonization, and the Louisiana Purchase by Thomas Jefferson's administration virtually made certain that by far the larger part of the North American continent should belong to British stock, rather than to French or Spanish. Jefferson himself, who believed that the Purchase was illegal, saw its tremendous possibilities, but no one in his day could realize just what this action would mean in extending a Nordic civilization to the Pacific Ocean.

The settlement of the Louisiana Purchase by Americans made certain the conquest of Texas, which was extraordinarily aided by the fact that in the period after the War of 1812 there were not many more than 5000 Mexicans in that vast territory. The great Plains stretched southward as a wide-open domain, inviting settlement by those who were farsighted and aggressive enough to possess themselves of it.

The beginning of the American settlement of Texas is always dated from 1820, when the Connecticut Yankee, Moses Austin, started his colonization scheme. Austin himself had lived for some years in Missouri, but most of his settlers, like most of the other early pioneers of Texas, came from the lower Mississippi Valley or from Tennessee and Kentucky, with a sprinkling of adventurers from the Central and New England States and even from Europe.

By 1835, when the Americans so outnumbered the Mexicans that the throwing off of the Mexican yoke was inevitable, there were 30,000 or 35,000 Nordics settled in the territory. The original background of these can easily be remembered from what has been said before in these pages about the settlement of their respective States. They were overwhelmingly English and Scotch and predominantly from the trans-Appalachian part of the United States.

The idea that most of these settlers went to Texas as a deliberate plan to acquire this region for the extension of the slaveholding States seems to have little basis. Most of them went, just as most of them or their fathers had gone to Tennessee or to Louisiana a few decades previously, in search of better and cheaper land, freer opportunities, and a possible fortune. It was the accident of geographical location that gave to Texas its importance as slaveholding territory, and that led indirectly to the war with Mexico.

On technical grounds there was little justification for a declaration of war in 1846, but from a larger point of view it was one of the most important and most beneficial acts ever taken by the American Government, in spite of the feeling of the Abolitionists, because it formed the final procedure in the spread of American sovereignty to the Pacific Ocean.

The United States was indeed deprived a few years later, at the time of the Gadsden Purchase, of the outlet to the Gulf of California which it should have had. Whether this was due to the climate of that region which made the surveyors shirk their duty, as one story goes, or to the drunkenness of the mapmakers which led them to draw the boundary line crooked, as another story has it, the result is unfortunate and might yet perhaps be rectified by a further purchase. The Southwest should have an outlet on the Gulf in the logic of the case.

This does not involve any desire to take over Lower California which is a peninsula of negligible value for Nordic purposes, and contains a Mexican population which under no circumstances should be incorporated in the United States. From a racial point of view it is indeed fortunate that the desire of James K. Polk's Administration to include the whole peninsula of Lower California in the transfer of sovereignty was not accomplished. Still more disastrous would have been a realization of the wishes of an important element in Congress which desired to annex a large part of northern Mexico.

Similarly, one can scarcely avoid being grateful

nowadays that Cuba did not get its independence in the first quarter of the nineteenth century instead of at the end. Henry Clay and others, encouraging the Cuban patriots, had virtually arranged to have the island taken over by the United States. In this instance abolitionist sentiment in the North, which prevented an extension of slave territory, was more beneficial to the true interests of America than it was a generation later—for the acquisition of Cuba would have brought into the union an indigestible mass of Mediterraneans and blacks.

When the suspicions and jealousies of international relations abate somewhat, it may be possible to make a slight rectification of the Arizona boundary which will give the Southwest its intended outlet on the Gulf of California. Such a step would doubtless promote the prosperity of the adjoining Mexican territory in every way. If Mexico could be persuaded to accept a gift of some of the United States' possessions in the West Indies, in return for this favor, the whole transaction would be most satisfactory.

It is now easy to see that Mexico could not have retained Texas under any circumstances, but the catastrophe (from the Mexican point of view) was made quick and certain by the encouragement of American immigration, in spite of refusals to discuss a sale of the whole territory to the United States, and by an attempt to fasten an objectionable State religion on the immigrants they had invited.

In the days of the Lone Star Republic, immigration increased rapidly. The Mexican War not only gave unlimited advertising to the region but furnished many Northerners with an opportunity to see something of it first-hand, and by the close of that conflict there were some 200,000 Americans in Texas. During the decade from 1850 to 1860 the growth of the State was exceeded by few in the Union.

Unfortunately much of this population was made up of Negroes who have ever since formed one of the real handicaps of this immense American Empire. As we have seen, the great bulk of the population of eastern and southern Texas came from the adjoining slave States, and it was not until the time of the Civil War that the northern counties had begun to attract settlers from Illinois, Missouri, and Arkansas. The war put a stop to this movement, but it was resumed later.

Meanwhile southern and western Texas had been attracting a German emigration made up largely of Alpines from the States along the Upper Rhine. This reached serious proportions as early as 1842, when a group of noblemen with uncertain motives fostered an Emigration Society Land Company. The movement continued in force up to the Civil War and indeed had not ceased altogether until the outbreak of the World War. Though Texas had but 20,000 German-born in 1860, these were so concentrated that half of the entire population of the southern part of the State, in the region surrounding San Antonio, was German. Here, as elsewhere, the Ger-

THE SPOILS OF THE MEXICAN WAR 213

mans greatly diminished their value to their adopted country by an unwise insistence on retaining the customs and the language of the Fatherland.

The history of any country demonstrates that national unity is a necessary condition of national survival. Those who have come to the United States of their own will, to profit by what opportunities they find may well be expected to yield a wholehearted allegiance to the country which thus benefits them, or to move elsewhere.

New Mexico, when it became a part of the territory of the United States, had a population made up of native and Mexican Indians, some of the latter having enough Spanish blood to cause them to consider themselves white men. The self-styled Spanish-American population of the present day is, properly speaking, composed of those whose ancestors were in the territory at the time of the Mexican War. The Spanish part of the description must be considered largely a courtesy title, for the amount of real Spanish blood in this hybrid population was always from a biological point of view nearly negligible, and the American part must be understood to mean native American Indians. The persistence of the Spanish language and culture is of course only a passing phase.

The Federal Census of 1850 credited New Mexico with 61,000 population not counting Indians, but the territory at that time included all of Arizona and Southeastern Colorado. By 1860 the population of the same territory was given at 82,979, plus 55,100 Indians. At this time there were less than 1200 natives of the United States in the whole territory.

Arizona had a fluctuating white population dependent upon the prosperity of the mining industry, but when the Federal troops were withdrawn at the outbreak of the Civil War most of the white men had to leave also. At that time the only real settlement was Tucson, where a few hundred Mexicans lived under mediæval conditions.

California had a population of Indians when the Spaniards coming from Mexico entered it. Most of them were of a very low order of intelligence and social development. The Spanish invaders were largely soldiers, and few of the members of these early expeditions brought their families. Hence, there was undoubtedly some mixing with the Indians from the very first days. In accordance with the custom elsewhere, those who had any white blood called themselves white, and the figures given by early writers for the number of Spanish in the colony must be understood in that light. The amount of real Spanish blood was extremely small and much of it was in the veins of missionaries who left no offspring.

The permanent population was made up of ex-soldiers who had settled down, married Indian women, and taken up land, together with occasional traders, vagabond sailors, and adventurers. The

THE SPOILS OF THE MEXICAN WAR

population of 1820 other than Indian could hardly have represented more than 500 men. The Mexican administration made an effort to supply women of Spanish ancestry to the colony in order to prevent too much matrimonial mixture with the Indians, which, even at that time, was regarded as somewhat disgraceful; but the number of brides who could be sent into a colony of that sort was small.

The population grew mainly by its own natural increase, and the small size of the Mexican population in California was one of the main factors that led to the incorporation of the territory in the United States. It has been computed that the "Spanish" population, most of which was of Indian blood, never exceeded 3000 persons. Prior to the American occupation there were not more than 1200 foreigners in California, three-fourths of whom were American and most of the remainder British. Thus this immense territory, which became a part of the United States in 1848 as a result of the Mexican War, was relatively empty. The amount of Spanish blood in the California population of today must therefore be quite negligible.

The whole trend of migration was changed by the discovery of gold at the end of 1848. In February of that year there were not more than 2000 Americans in all California. By the end of December there were 6000. By July of 1849 this number had grown to 15,000 and six months later it had climbed to 53,-000. The earliest arrivals naturally came from the nearby regions. Oregon alone contributed more than

5000 from its scanty population. But every seaport of the Pacific sent a contingent, and the stream of men that poured into the gold fields was the most cosmopolitan group that had ever been seen in North America. In *The New York Tribune* for December 15, 1849, appears the following item from San Francisco:

"Foreign flags in the harbor: English, French, Portuguese, Italian, Hamburg, Bremen, Belgium, New Granadian, Dutch, Swedish, Oldenburgh, Chilean, Peruvian, Russian, Mexican, Hanoverian, Norwegian, Hawaiian, and Tahitian."

When the territory became a State, on September 9, 1850, its population was at least 150,000, and a year later had probably reached a quarter of a million. Many of the Argonauts stayed but a few months, and, failing to become rich at a stroke, went elsewhere, so that the composition of the population changed markedly from week to week. It was almost exclusively a population of males. Few brought their families; and while prostitutes went to San Francisco from all accessible seaports, they contributed little or nothing to the permanent population.

The first Chinese immigrant found his way into California in 1847, but by the summer of 1852, 20,000 others had followed him. Probably 5000 Mexicans also had come into the territory which they had so recently lost.

By the census of 1860 it appears that most of the

THE SPOILS OF THE MEXICAN WAR 217

riff-raff had drifted out of the State again, and the basis of the permanent population had been laid. The total population was 380,000 of which nearly 40 per cent was foreign-born; the percentage reaching this high mark partly because of the number of Chinese. California had a population more nearly representative of the entire Union than did any other State—about equal numbers were contributed by New England, by the Middle States, by the Northwest, and by the lower Mississippi Valley. This population, it will be remembered, was almost entirely in the northern half of the State. The more homogeneous settlement of the southern half did not get under way until about the middle of the next period.

California differs profoundly from the other frontier regions of the United States in that it was settled from all sections of the country and not mostly from the adjoining States. The vast mineral wealth of the new State supplied it from the very beginning with abundant capital for local enterprises so that it was free from the debtor complex, so characteristic of the other frontier communities.

California faces westward on the Pacific and has developed into a unique and more or less self-sufficient section with a definite self-reliant character of its own.

While the West was thus filling up and the United States was reaching the Pacific Ocean, the States on the Atlantic continued to grow in power and population, largely through their own natural increase, but partly through the immigration of the period. French Canadians began to drift down into New England, as they have continued to do to this day. The single State of New York had by the end of the period a million foreign-born in its population, of whom half were Irish and one-fourth German. New Jersey had become one-fifth foreign-born, Connecticut one-sixth, Pennsylvania one-seventh. The racial character of this immigration was not particularly harmful, as it was mostly Nordic, but the large Roman Catholic element excited widespread alarm.

The arrival of large numbers of ignorant and destitute South Irish Catholics, who occupied the lowest social status here, led directly to the formation of a native American secret political party, nicknamed the "Know Nothings," because of their refusal to discuss or divulge their aims or actions. For the purpose of membership they defined the name Native American to mean a person all four of whose grandparents were born in this country. This party's policy, in the early stage of its career, was to act secretly, supporting the candidate who most nearly represented their views, regardless of his party affiliations. The party at once developed great strength, and in 1854 and 1855 carried State elections in Massachusetts, New York, Kentucky, California, and several other States. It played a large part in national politics in 1856, but its organization was disrupted by the increasing virulence of the slavery issue.

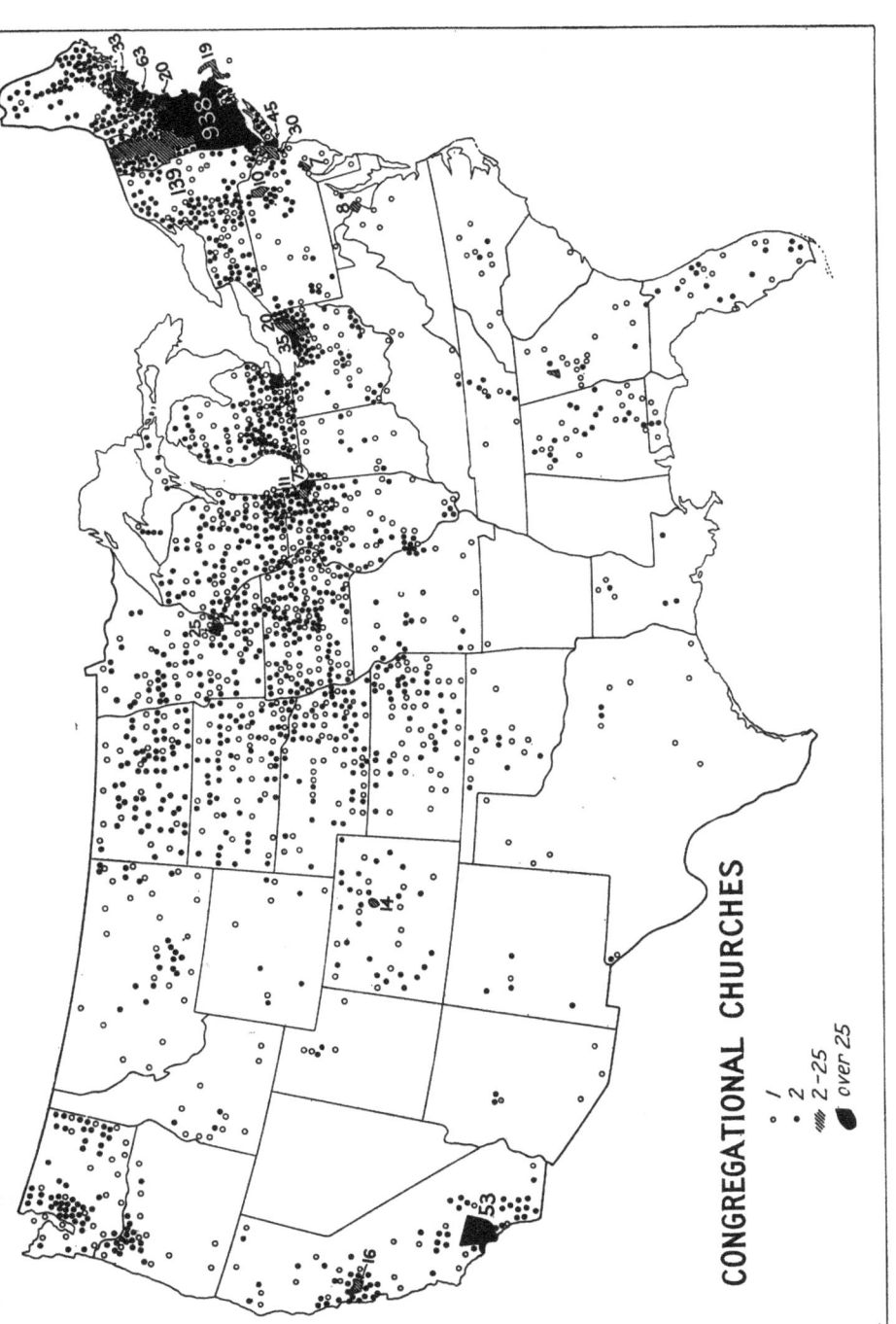

CONGREGATIONAL CHURCHES

○ 1
• 2
▨ 2-25
⬤ over 25

Showing distribution of the 4447 Congregational Churches in the United States. Figures indicate number of churches in shaded areas in which there are too many to be shown by dots and circles. As the Congregational Church is largely identified with New England, the map shows in a general way the westward movement of people of New England origin.

THE SPOILS OF THE MEXICAN WAR 219

The principle of the Know Nothing party was opposition to the political power of the large masses of newly arrived aliens. This was especially directed against the Catholic Church, because it was felt that their establishment of parochial schools was inimical to the public-school system, which the Americans of that time regarded as the palladium of their liberties. This hostility to Catholics was aggravated by the attempted use of public funds derived from general taxation for parochial schools and even more by the exemption claimed and often obtained from taxation of large ecclesiastical institutions as well as churches.

Further opposition to aliens arose from their organization into compact political units which quickly demoralized our municipal governments, a scandal which has existed down to this day.

All this led to the widespread belief that these immigrants, now arriving in large numbers, refused to accept wholeheartedly the customs, principles, and institutions of the country in which they had sought refuge. This belief still persists and has given rise in each generation since the days of the Know Nothing party, to similar powerful and secret anti-foreign organizations. Our alien elements are to this day extremely sensitive to the public discussion of any of these matters. In this respect, Americans probably have less freedom of speech and freedom of press than exist in any of the countries of Europe.

During the colonial period the natural increase of the Anglo-Saxon stock in New England had made it a continual source of population for the rapidly opening West. No one State, however, contributed such a large element of the population of the subsequent United States as did Virginia, the largest and most populous of the thirteen Colonies. One cannot read the history of the movement westward of the American frontier without being impressed by the importance of the Old Dominion in supplying settlers for the West, first to Kentucky, thence to the States of the upper and lower Mississippi Valley, later to the Great Plains, and finally to the Southwest and the Pacific Coast.

But if Virginia has been the most fertile source of settlers, New England has more nearly put its stamp on American civilization; and this was made possible largely because there was an available emigrant stock in Massachusetts and her sister States, to carry this impress in person. Before the Civil War, however, the birth rate of the old white stock in New England had declined to the point where it was probably not replacing its own numbers.

In 1860 the religious unity of the United States had been somewhat impaired. The unity of language was as yet scarcely menaced. The unity of institutions, traditions, and culture was breached only temporarily. The racial unity of the country was little changed from 1790. The United States was still nine-tenths Nordic.

Earlier in these pages a description is given of the

THE SPOILS OF THE MEXICAN WAR 221

empty continent which lay open to settlement by the British stock on both sides of the Canadian border.

Let us see what use was made of this opportunity in the period from the end of Colonial times to the Civil War.

A continent was occupied and the territory of the Union was swept westward to the Pacific. The forests were cut down and the wild life destroyed. The Indians were evicted. The mineral wealth of the western mountains was ransacked. The coal was exploited, and the once fertile soil of the Southern States greatly depleted through the reckless growing of tobacco and cotton. Waste was the order of the day in America.

All this was perhaps inevitable, but never since Cæsar plundered Gaul has so large a territory been sacked in so short a time. Probably no more destructive human being has ever appeared on the world stage than the American pioneer with his axe and his rifle.

In 1860, at the end of this period, we find the essential elements of national unity still unchanged, but we were about to engage in a fratricidal war, which was to destroy the best blood of the nation. We had admitted large numbers of Irish and German immigrants who impaired, in the case of the Irish, our religious system and introduced certain undesirable racial elements. The Germans who came were largely Protestants and only temporarily disturbed our unity by clinging to their foreign language. Both of these elements, however, were predominantly Nordic, and it was not until the next and final period that the unassimilable Alpines and Mediterraneans came here from southern and eastern Europe. The tragedy of the Civil War and the introduction of cheap labor were still to come, so that in 1860 the United States was at its high-water mark of national unity.

The Indians had been ruthlessly swept aside, as was unavoidable because a few hunting tribes could not be allowed to possess a continent, but the Negro question could have been postponed, and the men who died needlessly on Southern battle-fields could have been used to populate the States of the Far West.

In the next chapter we shall study the swamping of this American civilization, which reached its zenith in 1860.

XII

THE ALIEN INVASION

THE period 1860–1930, with which we are now dealing, is characterized by the end of free public land in the West about 1880. It is also marked by the great development of industries in the North and East, which created a demand for cheap labor, and attracted a mass immigration of non-British and non-Nordic workmen from southern and eastern Europe. This immigration for the most part went to the cities and industrial districts.

The Southern States, which had not entered upon an industrial expansion before the Civil War, did not welcome immigrants of the low-grade factory type, hence the South has remained characteristically American. One of the strange results of the Civil War has been that while the victorious North sold its birthright of culture, religion, and racial purity for a mess of industrial pottage, the South, though defeated and impoverished, retained its racial inheritance unimpaired.

Some of the earlier immigrants in this period sought the lands in the West, while they were still to be had. The land hunger having carried most of the energetic, ambitious, and able Nordic immigrants westward, the industrial expansion of New England, Pennsylvania, Ohio, and of some of the adjacent States resulted in an unfilled demand for low-grade

224 THE CONQUEST OF A CONTINENT

factory labor in the East. This demand was quickly recognized by the steamship companies, which began scouring Europe for immigrants to transport to America.

The most fertile recruiting ground for this type of humanity was in South Europe, Italy, the Balkan countries, and the provinces of the then Austrian Empire and Russia. Inducements were offered potential immigrants to come to America. There was no discrimination as to type or quality. Many criminals were rounded up, especially in southern Italy and Sicily, with the connivance if not the actual initiative of their governments.

As to the ratio of criminals to the native American population, some interesting figures have been compiled through a first-hand survey of 242 State and federal prisons in the United States during 1931–32. Most of the criminals referred to were committed for serious offenses. The criminals from northwestern Europe were well under (sometimes only one-quarter) their ratio to the general population. South Europe and eastern Europe were very much higher. The Filipinos were over twice as many as the proper allowance, native-born Negroes were two- and three-quarters above their allowance and the Mexicans were six and one-half times as many as their ratio to the general population would entitle them to be.

It was in this period that the Polish Jews began their tumultuous and frantic invasion, a flood which only recently has been checked, and that with the greatest difficulty. The great mass of immigrants from South Poland, Galicia, and Russia were Ashkanazim Jews, descendants in part of Alpine Khozars, with a Mongol admixture, who entered the eastern Ukraine from Asia in the early centuries of our era. Many of the Khozars and their Khan were converted by Jewish missionaries and they formally accepted Judaism in 740 A.D. It is doubtful whether there is a single drop of the old Palestinian, Semitic-speaking Hebrew blood among these East European Jews. They are essentially a non-European people. The language they speak, Jüdisch, or Yiddish, is a corrupt German of the Franconian dialect mixed with Slavic and Hebrew elements, which fact strengthens the tradition of a large migration of German Jews into Poland in the Middle Ages. It may be that the strain of these German Jews has died out, leaving only their language behind, but in any event the Polish Jews are now distinctly Alpine —a mixture of Slavs and of Asiatic invaders of Russia.

Exact figures of Jewish immigration are not obtainable until 1899, when this group was listed separately. Prior to that year probably 500,000 Jews had arrived; after that date nearly 2,000,000. From the beginning of this century the Jews made up 10 per cent of the total immigration into this country, and there are now more than 4,000,000 of them here, half of the number being in New York City. This is more than one-fifth of the Jews of the world.

Because they speak Yiddish, they are often colloquially referred to as "German Jews." But, in fact, the number who come from Germany is small, and, as said, the great bulk of them are more properly described as "Polish Jews" and are much despised socially by the true German Jews. Many of them are from those parts of Poland which were held by Russia prior to the World War. Immigration figures show the last place of residence of Jewish arrivals, 1899–1924, to be as follows:

Countries	
Russia and Poland	1,243,000
Austria-Hungary	260,000
Rumania	103,000
United Kingdom	73,000
Turkey	20,000
Germany	15,000
British North America	57,000
All other countries	67,000
	1,838,000

Meanwhile the immigration from northern Europe declined, not only relatively but absolutely, and at the same time the native American, whose ancestry was predominantly Nordic, began to be crowded to the wall. In certain sections of New England that progressive change soon became all too evident and has made them no longer American but foreign communities. The French Canadians, Irish, and Poles took over whole districts and occupied the abandoned farms. The Polish Jews, settling almost entirely in the larger cities, built up a

Ghetto population similar in most respects to the congested urbanism of their homeland.

Americans were so obsessed with the idea of a "Refuge for the Oppressed" that they even welcomed the draining into our country of that morass of human misery found in the Polish Ghettos. When the objection arose that there were already 1,000,000 Jews in New York City, an effort was made to divert this migration into Texas, where the wide-open spaces were supposed to provide room for the 7,000,000 Polish Jews.

The German Jews, who also came into this country in smaller numbers at the end of the last century, were of the Alpine type, closely resembling those from Poland, Galicia, and Russia. All of these Jews are in sharp contrast to the Sephardim Jews, a superior group, largely Mediterranean in race, a very few of whom came from Holland to America in Colonial times. These latter had reached Spain by way of North Africa and later fled to Holland to escape the Inquisition.

The immigration from Scandinavia was entirely Nordic. Sweden is purely Nordic, and Norway and Denmark are overwhelmingly so. Lithuania and North Poland are also Nordic lands, as are the German provinces along the Baltic; but South Poland and Galicia are Alpine, as are the majority of the immigrants who come from South Germany. Those from the provinces of the former Austrian Empire are mostly Alpine, although a few Nordics came from the Tyrol.

The Balkans, Greece, Asia Minor, and Armenia sent over practically only Alpine immigrants. French-speaking Switzerland was originally Burgundian territory and contributed some very valuable Nordic racial elements to America. Those from German-speaking Switzerland were largely Alpine.

The period of the great European migration to the United States covered just a century. Prior to that time, since the founding of the Union, most of the immigration had been English and Scotch. Up to 1860, as will be recalled, this British character of the immigration continued, except for the beginning of the great stream of Germans who have been, next to the English, the largest single element in our population.

The early Germans in the United States were, as previously described, mostly Alpines from the upper Rhine—the Palatinate and Swabia. In the '40's the area of the German emigration spread. At first to the western states and provinces, which were much more Nordic in character (Hesse, the Rhineland, Westphalia, Thuringia). All this region had an easy outlet by the Rhine to the seaports; moreover emigration was stimulated by the result of revolutionary activities, which forced many to leave.

After transportation began to be improved by railways, the main currents of emigration began to flow from central and eastern Germany. Emigration reached its first crest in the southwest and west of Germany in the middle of the '50's, its second in Central Germany toward the end of that decade, its third in the eastern part of the empire in the '70's and '80's. This later emigration was, on the whole, more Nordic than the earlier stream.

After the World War, when business conditions in Germany brought about some years of active emigration with the United States as its main objective, the current of emigration shifted again to the northwestern and southwestern districts (the former Nordic, the latter mainly so) and away from the northeast, which was even more Nordic.

The Scandinavian immigration, another main source of the Nordic population of the United States, dates almost entirely from the period since the Civil War. The largest volume was between 1877 and 1898, when more than 1,000,000 arrived. One-fifth of the entire population of Norway and Sweden moved to the New World, nearly all of them seeking farms in the States of the upper Mississippi Valley. There has been also an active immigration from Scandinavia since the end of the World War. In general, the United States was the only destination which a Scandinavian emigrant considered. Of those who left the homeland, not one Swede in fifty directed his course elsewhere than to America. No other emigrant population has shown such a single-minded interest in the United States, though the Norwegians have not been far behind, with 96 per cent of their departures destined to the United States; and the Danes, with 88 per cent.

Arriving at New York or sometimes Quebec, the immigrants made their way to Chicago or Detroit, and thence were distributed to the States west of the Great Lakes. The Norwegian movement was the earlier, beginning with the southern and central counties of that kingdom and gradually working its way north until arrivals were giving as their birthplaces little towns far north of the Arctic Circle.

In a few decades Norwegians owned six times as much farming land in the States of Minnesota, Wisconsin, Iowa, Illinois, Michigan, and the Dakotas (four-fifths of the immigration being found in the States named) as did all the farmers in the "Old Country." No nationality has sent such a small percentage of its people into the cities—one in five of the whole, as compared with a half of the Germans, and a still higher percentage of the Irish and Italians, who seek an urban life.

This tendency to agricultural life and to prompt and whole-hearted Americanism has made the great body of Scandinavian immigrants one of the most valuable that America has received.

Meanwhile there continued a steady immigration of English and Irish. The latter envenomed our political life up to the last few years, by introducing into the United States their old political and religious feuds with Great Britain, and endeavoring to involve this country in their plans for Irish freedom. As a consequence, the friendly relations which should exist between the two great Anglo-Saxon nations have been kept disturbed, and a systematic policy of twisting the lion's tail was pursued, not merely by the Fenian agitators, but by American

THE ALIEN INVASION 231

demagogues anxious to cultivate the "Irish vote."

Prior to 1880 only 5 per cent of the immigration was from southern and eastern Europe. Between 1860 and 1880 less than 250,000 immigrants from eastern and southern Europe came over. Then came the rush, and between 1890 and 1910 more than 8,000,000 immigrants reached our shores from southern and eastern Europe.

A group not homogeneous with the old native American population is the Italian. It began arriving after 1870, but did not reach large proportions until after 1890. Then it soon became a flood. From 1900 until the World War cut down immigration, the Italians far outnumbered all other peoples arriving on our shores.

Northern Italy has furnished us some fine types of immigrants. They are mostly Alpine with a Nordic admixture. Southern Italy, that is, Naples and Sicily, sent us almost exclusively a Mediterranean stock, which formed the great mass of Italian immigration and was of extremely inferior type. They are derived to some extent from the slaves whom the Romans gathered along the coasts of the Mediterranean from Syria to Morocco and employed on their large estates or latifundia. Among them, however, are to be found remnants of the pre-Nordic Mediterranean population of Italy.

In earlier decades the emigration from Italy was mostly of North Italians, commonly spoken of as "Genoese," but mainly from the crowded Italian Riviera west of Genoa. These went to neighboring countries, particularly France, and to South America, few of them reaching the United States. When Italian mass emigration to this country began, it was from central and southern Italy and Sicily, who are of quite different racial stock from those of the more northerly districts.

The northern Italians are well thought of in the countries to which they have gone. The southern Italians seem to be far inferior in quality. While the country of their origin, Magna Græcia, two thousand five hundred years ago was the source of a large part of the world's progress in civilization, it is doubtful whether the reader can name a single man produced in that region during the last two thousand years, whose ability or eminence was such as to give him a worthy place in the world's history.

Add to this that the United States did not receive even the best of the southern Italian population, but in some instances rather the part that the local authorities were most happy to get rid of, and it is easy to understand how the Italian children in the American schools have shown themselves in almost every test to be a group apart, widely separated from every other white racial group and close to the Negro-Mulatto children in their ability.

Of the non-English-speaking peoples who have arrived in the United States during the last century, the 4,500,000 of Italians are outnumbered by only one group, namely, the nearly 6,000,000 Germans.

The Italians have been more inclined to return home than some others. In all the immigration, it has been observed that a considerable proportion of the immigrants stayed only temporarily, sometimes for a season of work, sometimes for a generation or until they had accumulated enough money to return to the "Old Country" and live on their investments. It is usually figured that the arrivals should be diminished by about one-third to give the net of permanent immigration. There are of course exceptions —thus it is relatively rare for a Jew who came to the United States to move out of the country later.

During the sixteen years, 1908–23, the total alien emigration from the United States was 35 per cent of the total alien immigration, and the differences between the racial groups in respect to this tendency were immense.[1]

This ebb and flow of migration is often overlooked. It is impossible to understand the population figures without bearing it in mind.

While the departure of so many unassimilable aliens is highly favorable, the fact that migratory cheap labor thus floats into and out of the country

---

[1] The Chinese stood at the head of the list, emigrants from here exceeding immigrants by 30 per cent—that is, none were coming in as permanent residents, because of legislative restrictions; and some of the earlier arrivals were going home to stay. In a number of groups the outflow was more than half of the inflow—Bulgarians, Serbians, Montenegrins, 89 per cent; Turkish, 86 per cent; Koreans, 73 per cent; Rumanians, 66 per cent; Magyars, 66 per cent; Italians (South), 60 per cent; Cubans, 58 per cent; Slovaks, 57 per cent; Russians, 52 per cent.

The lowest rate of re-migration was that of the Jews, 5 per cent. The Irish showed 11 per cent; Scotch and Welsh, 13 per cent; Armenians, 15 per cent; Dutch and Flemish, 18 per cent; Mexican, 19 per cent; English and French, 21 per cent; Scandinavian, 22 per cent; Syrian, 24 per cent; Lithuanian, 25 per cent; and Finnish, 29 per cent.

to compete with the native white, may of course have most serious effects socially and economically on the older stock. Fortunately, this has now been stopped by suitable restrictions.

Taking a long view over the whole history of immigration into the United States in the century and a half before 1930 one sees that approximately half of the total was from the countries of northern and western Europe, which are largely and some distinctly Nordic in population, and which sent us people who, in most cases, were easily assimilated by the Native Americans. Most of these came in during the first century of the Republic's life, as pointed out above.

After 1890 the tide turned strongly to southern and eastern Europe, the countries of which in 1913 (the last year of unrestricted immigration) sent 85 per cent of the total as against 15 per cent from northern and western Europe. The main contributors to this later stream, often called the "new immigration" as distinct from the "old immigration" were, in order of importance, Italy, Austria-Hungary, and the Russian Empire.

XIII

THE TRANSFORMATION OF AMERICA

UNDER the impact of the "new immigration," most of it dating from the beginning of the present century, the complexion of the States which, as repeatedly shown, was almost wholly Nordic and Protestant, began to change rapidly. As concerned their native-born population, most of the States followed the rule, often mentioned in these pages, that a State is populated, in the first instance by its own increase, and secondly by movements from the States directly adjacent to it.

Maine, according to the 1930 census, with about one-tenth of the population of New England, is only five-eighths native stock, *i.e.,* native white of native parents. These were mostly people born in Maine, with a few from surrounding States. Of its foreign stock, three-fourths were French Canadians.

New Hampshire presents a similar picture, with a slightly higher percentage of native Americans from nearby States.

Vermont's native population, aside from that portion born in the State itself, came from New Hampshire or Massachusetts and even more from New York. As in the two States previously mentioned, most of the foreign stock is from French Canada, and that which was not from Quebec is mostly Irish.

The Slavs and Italians have made little inroad in these three States.

Massachusetts in 1930 was more cosmopolitan, with 300,000 residents from other New England States and nearly 100,000 from New York. The old white stock, however, now makes up but one-third of the population of the Bay State. French Canadians, Irish, Italians, Poles, Russians, and Scandinavians, in the order named, have completely overwhelmed the native stock—even such a small country as Lithuania is represented in Massachusetts by more than 50,000 people.

Rhode Island's population, similarly, is now only one-third from the old stock. Its complexion is similar to that of Massachusetts. French Canadian Catholics control the government in many communities.

Connecticut, like Rhode Island, has about one-third old American stock. Here the Italians are the dominant element in number, with Irish, Slavs, and French Canadians almost equally numerous.

Thus New England, with its more than 8,000,000 population, has been virtually lost to the native Americans. Their birthrate in that area has long been far below the level necessary to prevent its dying out, and migration to the west is not now caused by the region's increase, as in Colonial times, but by an actual uprooting of families whose place is taken by others who in race, language, religion,

THE TRANSFORMATION OF AMERICA 237

culture, and institutions are quite out of harmony with American traditions.

A similar picture is observed when one turns to the 26,000,000 inhabitants of the Middle Atlantic States—the most populous, the wealthiest, and in many ways the most powerful section of the country.

The old stock makes up but one-third of New York's population. For its composition every State in the Union has been drawn on, with Pennsylvania and New Jersey furnishing the largest contingents. The State has well on to half a million Negroes— mostly in Manhattan, though the ratio of increase of Negroes in some of the other cities of the State vastly outstripped the ratio of increase of Whites between 1920 and 1930. Thus while the Whites of Buffalo increased 11 per cent in the decade, the Negroes increased 200 per cent; in Syracuse they increased twice, in Utica four times, in Rochester seven times, in Albany eight times, as fast as the whites—due, of course, to the migration of great numbers of mulattoes from the Southern States northward.

With its two million Jews, its million and a half Italians, its million Germans, and its three-quarters of a million each of Poles and Irish, together with substantial contingents from almost every other country on the map, the Empire State is scarcely able to meet the requirements of the Founders of the Republic, who, like Thomas Jefferson, feared above everything else the formation of an alien, urban proletariat as creating a condition under which a democratic form of government could not function successfully.

Three-eighths of New Jersey's population were still of the old native stock in 1930, though half of these were born in other States, particularly New York and Pennsylvania. The rest of the population was a heterogeneous mixture of half a million British (largely Irish), half a million southern Italians, a quarter of a million Poles, a somewhat larger number of Germans, and so on down the list.

Pennsylvania makes a somewhat better showing, with more than half of its population still old native Americans. Of the later arrivals the largest number, well on to a million, was of British (including Irish) extraction. Italy and Poland each sent more than half a million, Germany not much less, Russia and Czechoslovakia each more than 200,000.

In both these divisions, then, the New England and the Middle Atlantic States, containing as they do more than a third of the entire population of the United States, the old American stock is now reduced to a minority. Fortunately, this cannot be said of any of the other major divisions of the country, though it is true of a few other individual States —Wisconsin, Minnesota, and North Dakota—where the foreign-born or their offspring are in a slight majority, but of good Nordic stock. On the whole, it is the northern and central parts of the Atlantic Coast that have become the worst un-American parts of the Union. The South Atlantic States play a much less important part nowadays than they did a cen-

THE TRANSFORMATION OF AMERICA 239

tury ago, in furnishing population to the rest of the country; but they are still American. In the following discussion their Negro population is ignored, and consideration is limited to the Whites, unless otherwise stated.

Delaware, with more than three-fifths of its people belonging to the old stock, has drawn no great additions in late years except from its neighbors on the west and south, Pennsylvania and Maryland. Its alien element is a cosmopolitan one in which no single group particularly preponderates.

Maryland is three-fourths native. Its industrial and commercial life, centered in Baltimore, has drawn a population from an unusually wide area, and this tendency has been greatly accentuated because many of the cosmopolitan group in Washington, D. C., actually reside in Maryland. Thus in addition to the heavy contingents from Pennsylvania and Virginia, it has groups of a thousand or more each from half the States in the Union. The bulk of its foreign population is made up of Germans, Poles, Russians (including Jews), and Italians, in addition to the British.

The District of Columbia, as the seat of the Federal Government, naturally draws its residents from every part of the United States, the largest element of what may be called its permanent population being from Virginia and Maryland. There is no large foreign element, but the Negroes, more than one-fourth of the whole, are nowhere more aggressive. It is generally understood that the reason Congress has never been willing to grant the residents of the district the right to vote, even in local affairs, is that it would be likely to put the political control in the hands of this Negro block, which would always find unscrupulous white politicians ready to forget their own birthright and truckle to it.

Virginia is almost purely of old native stock, Virginian born. Its seaports and its proximity to the District of Columbia account for some residents from other States. After dealing in quarter millions and half millions to describe the foreign-born of the North Atlantic States, it is with something like incredulity that one notes only 23,000 foreign-born Whites of all sorts in the Old Dominion. The number who are native-born of foreign or mixed parentage, and therefore classified as "foreign stock," is twice as large; but many thereof are British. With Virginia, one reaches the region where the old native American holds his ground.

North Carolina makes a still more striking picture. In its population of more than three million, the 1930 census enumerators found scarcely 25,000 foreign-born or of foreign parentage. North Carolina is an active industrial State, yet it has been able to attain to its modern development from its own resources. Its neighbors on the North and South, together, have supplied a hundred thousand citizens; other regions have contributed a few; but the old white American stock in this State, as in many others of the South, has been largely self-sufficing.

South Carolina is not only of the American stock,

but has had few outsiders, even from adjacent States. In addition to natives, a very few British and Germans, a very few Northerners, and moderate contingents from the nearby States make up its white population, which is still but slightly larger than the Negro element in the State.

Georgia fits into the same pattern, though it has attracted a few more of the "new immigration"—Slavs and Italians; and a few more Yankees, so that its population, on the whole, is somewhat more cosmopolitan.

Florida, on the other hand, has had an influx both of Northerners, who have almost changed the political complexion of the State; and of the foreign stock, largely Nordic, it is true, but with a West Indian element that is less assimilable. Of its million Whites, a sixth are of foreign stock, including almost every one of the nationalities found anywhere in the United States. But despite this somewhat cosmopolitan nature of its population, the State is overwhelmingly Nordic, like the other Southern commonwealths.

West Virginia, cut off from the Old Dominion by a technically questionable move at the beginning of the Civil War, showed by this very "secession" of its own that its population differed widely from that of the Tidewater. As pointed out earlier, the latter region was English and the mountains were Ulster Scotch, with a widely different outlook on life. The western part of the State had never been a great slave-holding region, partly because of the sentiment of the people, partly because there was little for a slave to do there that a free white could not do much better. To this day only one in sixteen of the population of West Virginia is colored, and it is still largely native white, despite the coal mines, which in other regions have come to depend largely on the labor of Slavs. In the 10 per cent of its foreign-stock population West Virginia has a scattering of Slavs, as also of almost every other people, but the largest element is British, the next German.

Kentucky offers no exception to the rule that the Southern States are still almost wholly native white. The only important foreign element is a small German one. It still retains a little of the tendency which made it, a century or more ago, one of the chief colonizing States, for it has more of its native sons scattered throughout the Union, than has almost any other Southern State.

Virginia still sends out a surplus population, and Georgia notably has done so, though mainly to the States nearest at hand. Kentucky and Tennessee have sent out pioneers to more distant regions. At present, for instance, they have as many representatives on the Pacific Coast as have all the South Atlantic States together.

Tennessee's racial make-up is very similar to that of Kentucky, although there is still the marked contrast in the "atmosphere" of the two States, which has existed from the beginning.

Alabama's composition is not very dissimilar to the two just mentioned, save that the Italian element

THE TRANSFORMATION OF AMERICA 243

is a little larger. Its main foreign stocks, however, are British and German.

What has been said of these States applies almost literally to Mississippi. The Whites, forming a little less than half of the total population, are almost all of the old native stock. The emigration of Whites (and of Negroes, too, for that matter) from the cotton States during the last fifteen or twenty years has been largely due to the ravages of the boll weevil, which made cotton less profitable and prevented many small farmers from making even their expenses.

Georgia has been hit harder than any other State, probably, by this movement out of the State and thousands of acres of good farming land are now lying idle there, for lack of hands to work them. The same holds good to some extent in other States of the region. Many of the small farmers have moved westward, first perhaps to Texas or Oklahoma, and then on to the Pacific Coast, the automobile now taking the place of the covered wagon of their forebears.

Arkansas differs in no important respect from Mississippi, save in having a much smaller proportion of Negroes. Its old white population has likewise begun to move, though more often northward, as to Missouri or Kansas. But Oklahoma and, also, Texas have been the great outlets for the Arkansas farmers.

The climate and resources of Louisiana have attracted some 50,000 Italians—a small element compared with those in the Northeastern States, but large for the South. Louisiana has always been more cosmopolitan than any of the other Southern States, and this is still the case, yet 85 per cent of its Whites are of the old native stock. Most of those not born in the State have come from States directly adjoining. While to a certain extent there has been the usual interchange, Louisianians going to other nearby States, mainly Texas, nevertheless Louisiana has been relatively unimportant in settling other States since the Civil War.

Its population is less homogeneous than most of the Southern States. The northern part of the State, with a majority of the inhabitants and with political control, is made up largely of Nordic Protestants who have come in from Arkansas, Mississippi, Tennessee, or elsewhere, and who differ little from the inhabitants of those States. The southern part of Louisiana, on the contrary, is largely Roman Catholic in religion, and to a large extent French-speaking. In some towns there are no public schools. The parochial schools teach the children in French, and the Catholic Church has made particular efforts to perpetuate the use of that language. The State Convention which revised the constitution in 1921 made the literacy qualification for the exercise of the electoral franchise, the ability of a citizen to write his application for registration "in the English language *or his mother tongue.*"

The State has the highest rate of illiteracy of any in the Union, whether one considers the total population including Negroes, or limits the figures to the native Whites. It has been part of the United States for one hundred and thirty years, but United States officials, when going into many parts of it, still have to be accompanied by an interpreter. With only two or three exceptions, every bishop who has been in charge of Catholic interests in Louisiana since Thomas Jefferson's day has been foreign-born and foreign-trained.

For such reasons the feeling of separate interests and lack of unity and national identity have tended to continue; and when the "Cajan" representatives attend the State legislature at Baton Rouge, they address the House in eloquent English, but among themselves, discuss their program in a French patois.

Oklahoma, due to its peculiar history, is one of the cosmopolitan States. When the territory was thrown open to settlement in the great land rush of April 22, 1889, speculators from all parts of the United States were attracted to the scene. But most of the settlers in the northern part came from Kansas or Missouri and in the southern, from Texas or Arkansas. In the next year, when the territory was formally organized, one-third of its population was Indian or Negro. Subsequent land allotments and colonization tended to perpetuate this dual origin of the settlers, but after the State became a famous oil field, in the early years of the present century, the population became so mixed that this distinction was partly lost. Meanwhile the Indian population was not only swamped by the Whites, but largely intermarried with them, partly because Indian women had titles to valuable oil land. At present Oklahoma is still credited with nearly 30 per cent of all the Indians in the United States, though it is supposed that not more than one-fourth of these are fullblood, and many of those who are legally counted as Indians have but a negligible amount of Indian heredity. The Creeks and a few others have mixed to some extent with Negroes, but this has not been general.

Texas, Missouri, Arkansas, and Kansas are still the principal sources of Oklahomans, in the order named; but there is not a State in the Union which is not represented here, many of them with large contingents. The foreign stock is of equally cosmopolitan background, but makes up only one-sixteenth of the whole. Considering the geographical location, it includes a surprisingly large number of Canadians.

Texas contains nearly half a million people of foreign stock, the German element being by far the largest. Second in importance among the foreign stocks is a Czechoslovakian population which has settled largely in the southeastern part. The Germans are mainly to the west of them. The State began to attract Italians just before the World War. The British element is important, while Galveston has long been largely dominated by Jews.

North Texas enjoyed a boom in 1875 and 1876 when a flood of homeseekers poured in with their emigrant wagons. Many of these were farmers from

THE TRANSFORMATION OF AMERICA 247

the Middle West who had been impoverished by the great grasshopper plague.

Western Texas was settled late, and periods of drought, such as that at the time of the World War, largely depopulated some sections, farmers packing up what they could carry and abandoning everything else to move into a region where nature was less reluctant to aid them.

Texas is still the offspring of the lower Mississippi Valley States, but commercial development and the oil industry have brought in many Northerners, particularly from the Central States. On the other hand, the State's contribution to Oklahoma dwarfs all the other streams that have gone out from it; but it has also contributed liberally to New Mexico and Arizona and in recent years to California.

Turning back now to the East North Central States, which comprise those originally carved out of the Northwest Territory of 1787, one again encounters the full tide of the so-called "new immigration." Here the old native stock is scarcely more than a numerical majority—fourteen million out of twenty-five, to be more exact; a striking contrast to the Southern States, which we have just been considering, where it still forms nine-tenths or more of the total white population.

Five millions of the later arrivals in the North Central States are Nordics, but a number almost equally large are Alpines. Half a million Mediterraneans are present in the Italian immigration, while the area from which the congress of the Confederation, as one of its last acts, declared that Negro slaves should be forever excluded, has acquired nearly a million free Negroes.

Ohio is still two-thirds native, and its great industrial development has drawn population from all sides, though four out of five of its citizens still find their names on the birth records of the State itself. Besides giving population to all its neighbors it has, like the other States of this region, sent a stream westward, not merely to such places as Kansas and Colorado, but particularly to the Pacific Coast.

While the German element in Ohio which, half a century ago, made such cities as Cincinnati centers of Teutonic kultur, is still the most important numerically, it is outnumbered by the Poles, Czechoslovaks, Hungarians, Yugoslavs, Lithuanians, and the like, if they are taken together. The easy access across the Great Lakes has given Ohio, like her sister States, an important Canadian element.

Indiana, most American of States in its early period, still makes an excellent showing, with nearly 85 per cent of its population native white of native parentage. In the interchange of inhabitants it still continues, as it did in the days of its founding, to draw an important Southern element from across the Ohio River. The State of Ohio does the same. The population still tends to move westward, not eastward, from Indiana, taking with it some of the best of American family lines and the purest of American traditions.

The half million of foreign stock within the borders of the State are at least half Nordic. No single group of the Slavs or Mediterraneans is represented heavily, although there are a few of all those national elements.

The people of Indiana deserve recognition for the way they have preserved their heritage. It is no accident that the "Indiana school" of writers has long sounded the authentic American note in literature, in striking contrast to the decadent tone of the output in some of the Atlantic Coast centers where the dominant element is quite un-American.

Illinois, by contrast, is barely more than half native, and the scandals of its politics in regions where the alien vote is self-conscious, have long been manifest to every newspaper reader. With 329,000 Negroes, according to the 1930 census, Illinois ranks in this respect only after Pennsylvania and New York, among the Northern States; but corrupt political rings have made of the Negro an important factor in the government of Chicago, as he has not been in New York or Philadelphia.

Of its foreign-born stock, Nordics are far below a million, as compared with a million and a half of Alpines and a quarter of a million of Mediterraneans. Under the pressure of this competition, the old native stock has shown a strong tendency to move West and South. Texas and Arkansas, for example, have drawn more heavily from Illinois than they have from any other Northern State, and Illinois has also been the greatest single contributor to the development of the Pacific Coast.

Michigan is now just half native. Its geographical location has attracted more than half a million Canadians, many of them belonging to the French Alpine stock there. In the foreign stock as a whole, Alpines outnumber Nordics not far from two to one. Among the 100,000 Italians are many Northerners in the copper mines—big fellows so unlike the Sicilian and Neapolitan to whom the American on the Atlantic Coast is accustomed, that he does not recognize them as Italians. These northern Italians, as previously noted, are not Mediterraneans, but mostly Alpine with remnants of Nordic blood from the days of the Lombards and Goths.

Wisconsin has almost escaped the Negro invasion of the North, so its three million inhabitants are at least white; but the native stock is in a minority, due largely to the great German inrush of the last century. With this came many Scandinavians.

From 1860 to 1880 the immigrant nationalities ranked in the order—German, Norwegian, Dane, and Swede. The only difference since then is that they rank in the order—German, Norwegian, Swede, and Dane. The great Swedish tide of immigration in the last half of the nineteenth century did not acquire full force until the Norwegian had passed its crest.

As late as 1900, three-fourths of the people of Wisconsin were of foreign parentage, and the Germans made up half of these. Milwaukee, with its Socialist administration, had long been conspicuously the center of German influence in the United States.

THE TRANSFORMATION OF AMERICA 251

Up to 1843, it was a Yankee village, earnestly trying to supplant Chicago as the center of the Midwest. By 1856 a third of its population was German. By 1890 one-half of its population was of German parentage and one-fourth actually of German birth. That census year, however, saw the high tide of Germanism in Milwaukee. Poles, Russians, Slovaks, and Italians have modified since then the racial character of the city, which is only one-third German at the present time. In the characteristic political color of the State some students profess to see evidence of the fact that many of the German immigrants were revolutionists fleeing from the Fatherland.

In Minnesota, the Germans outnumber any single group, although less numerous than the three Scandinavian groups put together, so the State is correctly thought of as Scandinavian. Considerably less than half of its population is of the old American stock, but the State is overwhelmingly Nordic, the 150,000 Slavs who have invaded it in recent decades being of little account in its 2,500,000 population. Since the days of its founding, Minnesota has drawn from Canada a desirable element, and has given freely in exchange.

Due partly to its relatively late settlement, the State has not been one of those which have contributed heavily to its neighbors. Its greatest outflow has been to the Pacific Coast, as its inhabitants became prosperous enough to move to a milder climate in their old age.

Iowa, of about the same population as Minnesota,

is two-thirds native and equally Nordic. It has contributed heavily to the prairie and mountain States, and also to the Pacific Coast, but the standing joke which ascribes to Iowa the parentage of all Southern Californians seems to be not quite exact—at least California as a whole has received more of its population during the past generation from Illinois, Missouri, New York, and Ohio, than from Iowa, which stands only fifth in the list.

Iowa, being predominantly agricultural, has felt particularly the unfavorable status of agriculture since the World War. During the decade 1920–30, three out of every five of the villages in the State actually lost in population, the people having either moved into the cities or "gone West." Here as elsewhere, the small village seems unable to meet the needs of the inhabitants. One of the real problems of statesmanship in the near future is to work out a social and economic system under which a larger part of the old native stock, and particularly the most intelligent portion of it, can live under the favorable biological conditions of the small village.

Missouri has nearly a quarter of a million Negroes, in contrast with such States as the three last discussed, in which the colored population is negligible. But of its white population, three-fourths is native, the rest mostly German. Slavs and Italians have only begun to get a footing. On the whole, the State is strongly Nordic and sends out large contingents of Nordics to Illinois on the East, to Kansas and Oklahoma, and to the mountain and coast States

THE TRANSFORMATION OF AMERICA

westward. The importance of the Missouri stock, coming to a large extent from that of Virginia, has been much greater than is generally recognized, in the settlement of the whole West.

The great rush into Dakota took place in the decade after 1875. The Red River country was opened up by the Northern Pacific Railway, and the model farms which were established were advertised far and wide, so that the population of 6000 in this district in 1875 increased more than 2000 per cent in the following ten years.

In 1889 the territory of Dakota was divided on the 45° 55′ parallel, and North Dakota was admitted as a State with approximately 170,000 population. Its subsequent growth has kept it fairly homogeneous from a racial point of view, the State being almost wholly Nordic. Apart from the old native Americans the main elements have been British from Canada, Germans, and Scandinavians. The Norwegian immigration which began in the early '90's was particularly noteworthy. Norwegians now form about one-fourth of the total population of the State. An interesting small group is that of the Icelanders, representatives of one of the oldest, most highly cultured, and most stringently selected of all Nordic peoples.

The Russians in the State, approaching a hundred thousand in number, are mostly German-speaking. They are farmers whose ancestors were invited to South Russia several centuries ago, but who retained their speech and culture to a marked degree.

After the discovery of gold in the Black Hills, the country which is now South Dakota had a rush in 1876 and for some years following, much like that of Nevada and Montana during the Civil War and of California in 1849. This frequently does not result in a well-balanced permanent population, and the real settlement of South Dakota dates from the succeeding period when its prairie lands were taken up by wheat growers from the States of the upper Mississippi Valley. The wheat industry in Wisconsin gradually died during the decade of 1870–80, and many who found the ground unprofitable there moved farther west, as did others with similar motives from western New York and the States of the old Northwest Territory.

South Dakota has a slightly higher percentage of old Americans than its sister to the north; otherwise the two differ remarkably little in size, composition, and resources. In 1920, half of the inhabitants of North Dakota claimed South Dakota as a birthplace; while half of the inhabitants of South Dakota claimed North Dakota as theirs. Of all the forty-eight States, these two are unmistakably the Tweedledum and Tweedledee.

Nebraska after the Civil War continued to attract mainly the old American pioneer class, but it also became a haven for several foreign groups. It is said to contain about one-eighth of all the Bohemians in the United States. The serious permanent settlement of the State began in the early '70's. Many discharged soldiers seeking to make a new start went West with their families. It was only a few years later that the foreign tide began to reach these prairies and thereafter the State attracted large fractions of the Bohemian, Scandinavian, and German immigrations. Like some of the other prairie States it also received many settlers who were listed as Russian because of their nationality, but who, in fact, were Germans whose ancestors had gone to Russia and failed to prosper there. Nebraska, therefore, though less than three-fourths native, is overwhelmingly Nordic.

Kansas is still four-fifths native and nine-tenths Nordic. It has received the same foreign contributions as Nebraska, but in much smaller quantities. At the same time it has continued to receive settlers from the Mississippi Valley, and even from Eastern States, such as New York and Pennsylvania.

On the whole, the prairie States have been notably successful in assimilating their immigrants and maintaining an American tradition. The newcomers were not segregated in slums but scattered on farms. It was almost a necessity for them to learn the speech and adopt the customs of their hosts. While some of the Scandinavians, as in Minnesota, have tried to have their children learn the language and preserve the traditions of the "old country," these have at least been Nordic traditions, and any feeling of aloofness or separateness is rapidly disappearing.

The mountain States date largely from the Civil War, when another of the country's waves of migration and settlement broke loose from its moorings and started westward.

The first great migration of the American stock began immediately after the Revolution, and resulted in the creation of Kentucky and Tennessee by the Southerners, the transformation of western New York by the New Englanders, and a mingling of these two streams as they crossed the Ohio River to open up the Northwest Territory.

The second great migration reached its crest with the panic of 1819. It completed the settlement of the Ohio Valley and of the States along the lower Mississippi and the Gulf.

The third great migration reached its height with the feverish land speculation promoted by Andrew Jackson's experiments in banking and broke with the collapse of the prosperity which Martin Van Buren inherited from his predecessor. It witnessed the settlement of the Mississippi Valley throughout almost its entire length; together with the Nordic absorption of Texas.

The fourth wave, slightly more diffuse, washed over the "great plains" and broke on the crests of the Rocky Mountains during the Civil War, though a heavy splash had meanwhile reached the Pacific Coast. It began with the settlement of Kansas, motivated in part by land hunger, but also by definite political calculations. Meanwhile the conquest of California, the discovery of gold there, the settlement of Oregon, and the Mormon appropriation of Utah, brought into existence an active traffic across

THE TRANSFORMATION OF AMERICA 257

the plains, which was the beginning of Nebraska's existence.

The Rocky Mountain States grew up in the first place out of this traffic, then by the mining discoveries within their limits, and the fact that there was a restless population on the Pacific Coast, ready to surge back eastward, together with a footloose population to the East ready to move into any part of the West.

This Eastern contingent received its impetus from the panic of 1857, when many men, bankrupt or dislocated, were prepared to make a new start. The mining activities in the Far West encouraged adventurers to try their hand at the gold pan, and the country was full of prospectors, some of them professional but mostly amateur. Men who had no jobs at home thought they might as well seek a fortune in this way; it would not cost them much to live, and they could at least see the country. A similar renaissance of prospecting and small-scale mining took place all over the mountains of the West when the depression of 1929 was well under way.

To this element was shortly added another composed of people getting away from the Civil War. Some of these were actual deserters from military service; others went West to escape the pressure of public opinion toward enlistment; others in the border States, ruined by the conflict or unwilling to cast their lot with either combatant, simply started in motion as their fathers and grandfathers had done before them.

The population of the mountain States varied remarkably from month to month, as the crowd moved from one reputed bonanza to another. The government at Washington showed itself unusually ready to set up new governments in that region, because it was on the whole of unquestioned Union loyalty and, if the South, at the close of the war, should be brought back into the Union on the old terms, as President Lincoln evidently planned, a dozen new senators from half as many new Western States could easily be secured, leaving the South in the minority and breaking that deadlock of almost half a century which had been the source of so many compromises and the occasion of so many conflicts.

Colorado, at that time a part of Kansas, was an almost unknown "Indian territory" when prospectors struck gold in the neighborhood of Denver in 1858 and 1859. The rush from Kansas and Nebraska, when the legend "Pike's Peak or Bust," lettered on the sides of emigrant wagons, became traditional, disclosed how little was known of the country. Pike's Peak, though not near the gold diggings, was the only place in Colorado of which most Americans had ever heard.

In 1861 there was enough population to justify territorial government. Statehood was not attained until 1876. From then on until the agricultural period, the history of Colorado was the history of its fluctuating mining camps. But by 1930 the State had reached a permanent basis and a population of more than a million, of which two-thirds was native

THE TRANSFORMATION OF AMERICA 259

and the other third a heterogeneous lot, partly Nordic but containing strong Slav, Italian, and Mexican elements. So far as the native American population was concerned, its geographical origin still represented a fan spreading out from Pike's Peak until it reached the Atlantic Ocean. In large or small proportions, emigrants from most of the older States had converged on the Rockies.

Wyoming, first explored by trappers and fur traders, became important because it was traversed by the Oregon Trail; but it was merely a place to pass through, until the arrival of the Union Pacific Railway and the discovery of gold in the same year (1867) gave it a life of its own. Nearly 6000 persons spent the following winter in Cheyenne—a cosmopolitan crowd of adventurers and speculators. After its organization as a territory in 1859, agriculture had begun, stock raising became important, there were local gold rushes, and the region slowly developed until admitted to the Union in 1890.

Wyoming's population, smaller than that of any other State with the single exception of Nevada, is less than two-thirds native stock, and this represents a blend from all parts of the United States. Iowa, Missouri, Illinois, have all contributed more inhabitants than either of its neighbors, Colorado and Utah. In these mountain States the general rule that a State is settled by its neighbors, quite breaks down. Its foreign stock is equally mixed; while much is Nordic the State has also attracted its quota of Slavs and Italians, and even of Mexicans.

Idaho, after small Mormon settlements of farmers, owed most of its early population to its mines. During the Civil War it grew remarkably, but the fact that it could be reached more easily from the West than from the East, due to access by the Columbia River, made its settlement somewhat anomalous in American history, for it was settled largely by Westerners moving east from Oregon, Washington, and northern California.

In Idaho the development of Mormon colonies has given Utah a strong influence in the State. Apart from this, its population is made up nowadays more from the Mississippi Valley than from the mountain and Pacific Coast States. It is only three-fourths native, but most of the remainder is Nordic, British and Scandinavians both having sought its opportunities. A territory in 1863 and a State in 1890, Idaho now has a population of nearly half a million.

Montana, in the winter of 1862 and 1863 had a total population of 670 inhabitants of whom *The Chronicle* complacently says: "Fifty-nine were evidently respectable women." Like Idaho, it attracted an element of Southern men escaping from the draft into the Confederate Army, but from then on a large part of its population was from the Northern States. Its growth of population was closely linked up with the fortunes of the mining industry.

Territorial status was given Montana at the time of the great gold discoveries in 1864, and the character of its population fluctuated a good deal, both as to quantity and quality, between that date and

THE TRANSFORMATION OF AMERICA 261

1889 when it was admitted to Statehood. It has now more than half a million inhabitants, nearly half of whom are of foreign stock and largely Roman Catholics. Most of the natives are from the Central States; most of the foreigners are Irish, Germans, or Canadians, though Montana has also attracted more than 50,000 Scandinavians.

Utah's population is now about the size of that of Montana, and but slightly more native in character (three-fifths). These natives are to a large extent born in the State, the descendants of the Mormon pioneers. The "Gentiles" are of widely scattered origin. The foreign stock is mostly English or Scandinavian, the Mormon missionaries having worked diligently in those kingdoms. Utah, therefore, represents a Nordic population, and one with a high birth-rate, whence it is evidently destined to continue spreading steadily in the Great Basin.

Nevada sprang almost full grown from the desert, as Venus did from the waves. It scarcely existed, though on the maps as a transmontane part of California, until the gold rush of 1849 brought settlements into existence to take care of the travellers. Then it was attached administratively to Utah, which was also inconveniently distant. The discovery of silver in the fabulously rich Comstock Lode (1859) led to the establishment of Virginia City, and to the inrush of a torrent of miners, particularly from California, where the gold deposits were becoming exhausted.

In 1861 Nevada was established as a separate territory, and Lincoln's administration pushed it through to Statehood in 1864 to get the advantage of two more friendly senators. With the exhausting of the silver deposits in a quarter of a century, Nevada had a severe decline, many of her inhabitants moving away. There was another mining boom in the first ten or fifteen years of this century, but the State has never made a steady and substantial growth, and the 1930 census credited it with no more than 91,058 inhabitants. Not much more than half of these were of the native stock. The foreigners were a scattered lot, with an unexpectedly large Italian contingent.

Arizona was cut loose from New Mexico in 1863, and, after the Civil War, became a typical Western mining community, with a fluctuating frontier population. A district might be active one year and a few years later abandoned.

The Mormons made some of the early settlements in the State and still form a significant part of its population. Like Colorado, Arizona has more than its share of Mexicans, while some of the other Western States, Utah and Nevada for instance, have only negligible numbers of them. The presence of more than 100,000 Mexicans in 1930 gave Arizona, with less than half a million inhabitants all told, a bad position as to its proportion of native stock. If one takes account only of the Whites, 80 per cent are natives of native parentage, the others mostly British or German, with again a surprisingly large Canadian contingent, considering how far removed the two regions are. The American population is of notably cosmopolitan origin, people having gone there from every State in the Union, in connection with mining, or for reasons of health. But Texas is by far the largest single contributor, with California a poor second.

New Mexico stands in the anomalous position of having an almost unparalleled percentage of its population born not merely in the United States, but within its own borders; and yet of having an unparalleled proportion of its population speaking an alien language. An official interpreter is still required in its State legislature, so that the local statesmen who boast of their Americanism but cannot speak English, can make their views known to the Americans. Since the "Spanish-Americans" are classified by the census as white, three-fourths of the population are listed as native white of native parentage. There were also, in 1930, about 60,000 Mexicans born south of the line, hence aliens. The other residents of foreign stock are scattering, with no one nationality greatly predominating.

California, which in 1860 had the highest percentage of foreigners, had not changed this situation strikingly in 1930, despite the great influx of old American stock from the Central States. Of its 5,677,251 residents, just over a half were native Whites of native parentage. The general character of the migration to California since the beginning of this century is too well known to require extended comment. Every part of the Union has contributed;

even Florida is credited with a couple of thousand converts. On the whole, this influx has been of the purest Nordic stock, but if a constitutional convention were now to be called, its makeup would perhaps not differ greatly from that of 1849, which was attended by delegates born in thirty different States of the Union.

The foreign element in California is equally heterogeneous, though largely Nordic, so far as it is white at all. Canada has sent a quarter of a million, nearly all of English ancestry. Italy has contributed nearly a quarter of a million, who make an important part of the population in the northern half of the State. Unlike their fellow nationals in the Atlantic States, these California Italians are mostly from the northern part of that kingdom. Between North and South Italians there is not great sympathy—representatives of the two groups avoid intermarriage. They also avoid migrating to the same territories and, if the Neapolitan occupies the Atlantic States, the Genoese will push on to the other side of the continent. These northern Italians have played a much more prominent rôle around San Francisco than one would anticipate who knows only the southern Italian in New York or Boston.

The State has also attracted 150,000 Russians, partly refugees since the Bolshevik revolution, but mostly agriculturists of an earlier period; more than half a million British, including Irish, more than 300,000 Germans, more than 200,000 Scandinavians.

THE TRANSFORMATION OF AMERICA 265

It is the non-white element that has attracted attention most continuously from the outside world. California had nearly half a million Mexicans, until the exodus which began after the depression of 1929 had made their manual labor less valuable.

It had 45,000 Filipinos, who created serious problems in some regions, both by competing with native labor, and by paying attention to white girls, which is resented by the Americans.

The State's population of 37,000 Chinese is declining steadily. The memorable agitation of the '70's for Chinese exclusion is now only a historical event, but it was important as helping to lay the foundation for a wise immigration policy in the United States. Mining, war times, and the building of the transcontinental railway had kept up inflated conditions for years. Chinese were pouring in, partly to the mines, and partly to the railway, which used them in construction work. Some 15,000 of these Oriental laborers, turned out of work by the completion of the Central Pacific Railway, principally in 1869–70, poured into San Francisco and made their presence unmistakable. A decade of dissatisfaction followed, particularly among American workingmen. The most conspicuous agitator was the Irish drayman, Dennis Kearney. In 1879 the State voted against the further immigration of Chinese by a majority of 154,638 to 883. There have been few issues in American history carried by a more nearly unanimous vote. In the same year the Federal Congress passed an exclusion act which established the principle that an unassimilable people may be shut out entirely, if necessary to protect American standards.

Agitation along similar lines sprang up about 1906-7, due to the rapid increase of Japanese in the State. It was settled, first by a "gentlemen's agreement" between the United States and Japan, by which the latter undertook to prevent the emigration of its laboring class to the Pacific Coast States; second, by a law later adopted in California, which prevented alien Japanese from owning land; third, by a final exclusion of all Orientals through national legislation.

The hundred thousand Japanese shown in the 1930 census are no longer increasing rapidly, in spite of a fairly high birth-rate. The existence of these second-generation Japanese (and the same is true, in proportion, of the Chinese) has, however, created a serious problem all its own, since they are not accepted by either race. They usually do not speak the Japanese language. They are inclined to look down upon its institutions, and admire those of America. Hence the real Japanese element both dislikes them, and does not employ them because of the language barrier. On the other hand, the American does not accept them as Americans, and they cannot be employed easily alongside of and in competition with white natives of the United States. The second-generation Oriental is practically a man without a country. Because of these special racial problems, California has had difficulties that some of the other

States have not fully or sympathetically understood.

Oregon's million inhabitants are two-thirds native Whites of the old stock. Canada, the British Isles, Germany, and Scandinavia, have been the other large contributors. The American population is largely from the Central States.

Washington now has more than a million and a half inhabitants, 56 per cent of whom are of old native stock. Eastern Washington felt a boom in 1862 when it began to accumulate population attracted partly by mines and partly by farming possibilities, until it reached an equilibrium with the Puget Sound end of the State which has always been an important political factor. Many settlers at this time were immigrants from the "border States" of the Civil War, who became disgusted with the guerrilla warfare to which they were subjected, and who were not enthusiastically for either side. During the '80's, the rapid construction of railway lines brought the population of Washington up to a respectable figure in a very few years.

The present Whites are mainly from the States of the upper Mississippi Valley. Canada has furnished 100,000 more of British ancestry, and a slightly larger number has come direct from the British Isles. Germany has contributed 100,000, Scandinavia 175,000. As against this, Italy is represented by less than 25,000, and the Slav countries altogether by not much more than 60,000. Hence Washington is entitled to claim that it is one of the most Nordic of the States.

XIV

CHECKING THE ALIEN INVASION

DURING the earlier part of the immigration period, the tradition of an "Asylum for the Oppressed" of all nations was the ruling principle in the national attitude towards aliens, though even then there was occasional objection to the undesirable character of some of the immigrants.

Various States adopted their own restrictions. Massachusetts, Maryland, Pennsylvania, and others tried to control the flow of new arrivals by head taxes and administrative regulations, while foreign governments sometimes opposed these measures, as in the case of Wurtemberg in 1855. The United States having sent back some paupers who had been dumped on its shores, public resolutions are said to have been passed by the Wurtembergers, protesting at this lack of hospitality. If the paupers were returned, they complained bitterly, "we shall have defrayed the expense of their journey in vain." But the right to deport undesirable aliens had been set forth by the famous Alien and Sedition Acts of 1798, and the Federal Government has never wavered in its assertion of this right.

For a generation before the Civil War, the undesirability of unrestricted immigration was debated, but without definite action. The first federal restriction was the law of 1875, excluding foreign convicts and prostitutes. President Roosevelt in 1907 appointed an Immigration Commission which made a long investigation and a voluminous report that served as a base for future measures and by 1914 most of the undesirable classes, except illiterates, were formally excluded.

The opposition to restriction was from the steamship companies, whose interest was obvious, and from the large employers of cheap labor, who were likewise not at all disinterested. It also arose among alien groups in the United States, that wished to get more of their own people into this country.

The most active forces in its favor were, primarily, organized labor, which wished no more competition from floating aliens with a wholly un-American standard of living and, most of all, the native American groups, eugenists and others who were far-sighted and unwilling to see the racial character and national unity of America destroyed and republican ideals endangered and undermined.

The first attempt at a general restriction to improve the quality of immigration was the adoption by Congress of the literacy test, which provided that those who could not read and write some language should be excluded. This was vetoed by President Wilson.

Meanwhile the outbreak of the World War had, for the time, put a virtual stop to international movements of population, and the nation had a breathing space to consider its future policies. In 1917 the Burnett Act consolidated the existing provisions for excluding undesirables, and included the literacy test. President Wilson vetoed it also, but it was passed over his veto.

At the close of the war, there was widespread apprehension that the unsettled and impoverished peoples of Europe would begin a new mass migration westward. Before the war we had been receiving a million immigrants a year; travellers and consular agents predicted that we might look forward to receiving two million or more annually. It was felt that the literacy test, and the provisions against mental and physical defectives, would not be enough to stop this flood. Congress met the emergency by the Quota Act of 1921, which provided that the number of aliens of any nationality admitted in any one year should be no more than 3 per cent of the number of foreign-born persons of such nationality residing in the United States in 1910. This law was intended to preserve the *status quo*. What the nation was in 1910, that it should be forever.

Such a solution could not satisfy the native Americans, whose people had made the country great. Fortunately, the demand for a more scientific approach to regulation found an adequate representative in the Hon. Albert Johnson, a member of Congress from the State of Washington, under whose leadership the whole system was revised in the famous act of 1924.

Administratively, the proceedings were made more

CHECKING THE ALIEN INVASION 271

workable and more intelligent by placing on the United States consuls abroad the duty of approving passports, without which no immigrant could enter. When the quota was exhausted, the consul was required to refuse his visa on passports until the next year. There was no longer any possibility of hardship and apparent injustice.

Restrictively, the quota was reduced from 3 per cent to 2 per cent, and based not on the 1910 census, but on the 1890 census. The purpose of this was, frankly, to encourage new arrivals from the countries of the "old immigration,"—the countries of northern and western Europe who had contributed most to the American population and whose people were, therefore, most easily assimilable in the United States; and, conversely, to discourage immigration from the countries of southern and eastern Europe, most of whose nationals had come here since 1890.

This law reduced the total possible immigration under quota to 167,750 as against 357,800 permitted by the act it supplanted, and favored the European Nordic whose people made the United States what it is, as against the European Alpine and the Mediterranean who were late comers and intrusive elements. Unfortunately it did not apply to the western hemisphere, hence offered no obstacle to the Indian peon from Mexico nor to the Negro from the West Indies, nor were the Filipinos barred.

The most interesting provision of the law of 1924 and, in one sense, the reason for the existence of this present book, was a provision that the quotas should be based only temporarily on the 1890 census. That basis had been justly criticized on the ground that it made the immigrants of recent times, rather than the old native stock, the determinants of the future composition of the United States. The quotas, it was argued, should be based not on the number of aliens here in 1890, or in any other year; but on the ratio of these aliens to the whole population. The law therefore embodied the National Origins provision—one of the decisive events in the racial history of America.

An investigation was ordered to find the proportions of the various national (not *racial*) groups in the United States at the time of the 1920 census. The general quota to apply from July 1, 1927 (later delayed one year), was fixed at a total of 150,000. Each nationality was to be assigned such proportion of this 150,000 as the number of its people here in 1920 bore to the total population. Thus, if it should transpire that 10 per cent of the total population in 1920 was of Swedish ancestry, Sweden would receive a quota of 10 per cent of 150,000 or 15,000. Or if it were found, for example, that 2 per cent of the total population in 1920 derived from France, the French quota would become 3000.

While a committee of experts went to work on the necessary research for this purpose, an amusing competition began among the alien groups and hyphenates, to exaggerate as much as possible their claims so that their relatives and compatriots might benefit by an increase in their nation's quota. The Irish were perhaps the most industrious in this occupation, for they could take advantage of the confusion, due to the fact, pointed out in these pages time and again, that the territory now composing the Irish Free State had long taken credit for every one who has passed through Ireland. Actually the "Irish" immigration in Colonial times was, as already shown, not Irish at all, but for the most part Scotch, though taking shipping from Ulster; and the Free State Catholics had few representatives in America at the time of the Revolution. Such facts were conveniently ignored by the Irish patriots, who wrote books to demonstrate that the "Irish" not only fought and won the Revolution, but that they made up the predominant element at the present time. "It has been estimated by good authorities," affirmed one such enthusiast, "that at least 25,000,000 of our present population have more or less Irish blood coursing through their veins. We" (*i.e.*, the population of the United States), he went on, warming up to his job, "are no more Anglo-Saxon than we are Hindu!"

If the Irish Catholics were inclined to claim something like one-fourth of the total population, the Germans were prepared to claim anything up to one-third. The quota based on the 1890 census had, in fact, been extraordinarily favorable for the Germans, since they were the group that had been coming into the country in greatest number just before that date, hence they had the largest number of actual foreign-born here present in that year. Their allotment on that basis was almost one-third of the quota for the entire world. The obvious unfairness of basing future immigration on such conditions, and of ignoring almost entirely the English and Scotch stock which was the overwhelming element in the building of America, but which together received only 20 per cent of the quota, was generally recognized.

Scarcely had this injustice been removed and the National Origins measure gone into effect, however, when business depression began to throw men out of work, and it was universally felt that no new seekers for jobs should be brought into the country to displace the workers already here. Administrative restrictions, therefore, cut down the incoming flow of aliens to almost nothing. At the same time, many recent arrivals went back home, thinking they could weather the storm better among their own people.

A direct benefit from the depression, then, was that it practically stopped foreign immigration. When the time comes for consideration of the renewal of present administrative restrictions, the National Origins Act will be on the statute books as a protection. Meanwhile Americans can consider what further measures they need to take to extend the quota provision to the western hemisphere.

The actual contribution of the alien groups to the population of the United States is based not merely on their net immigration, but also on their fecundity after they settle here. Many familiar studies show that, in general, the immigrant women are more fecund than the old stock. They marry earlier, show a lower percentage of sterility, and have larger families.

The fact that women are in a minority among most of the recent immigrant groups has, however, tended to cut down their contribution. Of the whole foreign-born group, men and women have in late decades been in the ratio of about five to three. This means that the group, as a group, will make a smaller contribution than it would, had each man brought a wife with him. On the other hand, the surplus males usually marry women of other groups, their descendants being thus assimilated into the population more quickly, whether for good or for ill.

Again, the increase of the foreign-born groups is cut down by the fact that for the most part they have a higher rate of infant mortality. Variations among the races are striking. Thus while the native white has an infant mortality rate of 94 per 1000 births, that of the American Negro is 154, that of the Poles about the same, that of the French Canadians 171, that of the Portuguese 200, as shown in some extensive studies made by the Federal Children's Bureau.

In the second generation, the fecundity of the alien groups begins to decline. It is generally said that the immigrant's daughter bears one less child than did her mother. Hence if immigrants are let in slowly, they are not likely to swamp the native stock; and as to those already here, although some of them, particularly the Italians, have remarkably high birthrates, they will probably lose this advantage within the next couple of generations.

The question is often raised, whether the population of the United States would not be just as large today, if immigration had been permanently excluded in 1790. In other words, if no alien had arrived since the founding of the United States, would the descendants of the Colonial population have produced as many citizens as there are now here? This hypothesis, often known as Walker's Law, assumes that the fecundity of a group is cut down by the competition of immigrants, and that the latter do no more than fill the places which would otherwise have been filled by natural increase.

No one would claim that such a generalization is exact, but as a general tendency it seems to be near the truth. The United States would have grown large and strong, had immigration been shut off a century ago. It will continue to grow large and strong, with immigration shut off at the present time. That does not mean that the rate of growth which has been maintained during the last century will continue for another century. The Nordic civilization is at present near the end of a cycle of growth, and its rate of multiplication is slowing in every civilized country. In most of the Nordic nations, the population does not now replace itself. When the women now of child-bearing age pass from the scene, they will not leave enough daughters to take their places.

The influence of the "newer immigration" and its offspring is great enough to carry forward the United States population expansion a little longer, but all signs indicate that, assuming *all* immigration ceased, the numerical growth of the United States would come to a standstill at the end of two or three generations, probably at a figure not higher than 150,000,000 of population, and no more are needed.

All the greater is the need, then, that this stock should be sound in quality. A memorable step toward this goal was taken by the Federal Supreme Court in 1923, when it held that only white persons and persons of African descent are eligible to citizenship.

In 1790 Congress enacted the first naturalization statute, the terms of which confined its benefits to "free white citizens." The restriction remained in force until extended in 1870 by statute giving the right of citizenship to persons of African descent. At present, then, only Whites and Negroes are eligible for naturalization. Interpreting the statute of 1790, the Supreme Court held that the term "free white" must be understood in its common meaning as used by the framers, and could not include a Hindu (Sikh) or, in another case, a Japanese.

Meanwhile the immigration act of 1924 provides that "no alien ineligible to citizenship shall be admitted to the United States." The Supreme Court decisions in the cases mentioned mean that this law excludes all colored and Oriental races—all, in short, save "free Whites" and Negroes. Another safeguard is thus thrown around the American stock.

The three millions of Whites of 1790 have increased to 109 millions in 1930. Of this number, one-third are either foreign-born or the children of such. One wonders how many of the 109 millions are the undiluted descendants of Colonial stock. While mathematical exactitude cannot be expected in such calculations, the census experts have figured that about one-third of the population is of such ancestry.

There are many others who have one parent Colonial and the other going back perhaps to an immigrant of 1850. Such latter, these experts claim, is the equivalent of half of a Colonial descendant. Two of them together they count as equivalent to one Colonial descendant. By this device the experts calculated that the "numerical equivalent" of the Colonial stock amounts to nearly one-half of the entire white population.

The investigations necessary to put the National Origins provision into effect, and to defend it from partisan criticism, brought out the salient facts concerning the composition of the population today—again, of course, subject to such margin of error as is inevitable. The white population of 1920 was apportioned as follows:

England, Scotland, Wales, and North Ireland	39,242,733
Germany	14,833,588
Irish Free State	10,378,634

Poland[1]	3,626,692
Italy	3,566,396
Russia	2,108,283
Sweden	2,024,434
France	1,970,189
Netherlands	1,835,959
Czechoslovakia	1,623,438
Norway	1,431,292
Austria	976,248
Switzerland	961,406
Belgium	790,928
Denmark	735,083
Hungary	703,409
Yugoslavia	440,518
Finland	338,036
Lithuania	293,100
Portugal	272,104
Greece	185,836
Rumania	185,423
Spain	181,658
Latvia	144,844
Turkey	138,389
Danzig	81,522
All other quota countries	262,216
Non-quota countries[2]	5,488,757
	94,820,915

The United States is no longer 99 per cent Protestant, as it was in 1790; but it is still 80 per cent Protestant. Its white inhabitants are no longer 90 per cent Nordic, as after the Revolution; but they

[1] It must be remembered that these figures show national origins, not *racial*. The numbers credited to such countries as Poland, Russia, and Austria-Hungary therefore include very large proportions of Jews.

[2] These are the countries of the Western Hemisphere, of which Canada and Mexico have been the largest contributors.

are still 70 per cent Nordic.⁴ Its future course must be guided in the light of a consideration of these facts.

³ This would, of course, include all Germany.
⁴ The Hoover Committee on Social Trends, in re National Origins, says that "about 85 per cent of the Whites in the United States in 1920 were from strains originating in northwestern Europe where Nordics predominate."

XV

THE LEGACY OF SLAVERY

THE most essential element in nationality is unity. This unity can be based on race, on language, on religion, on a long tradition held in common, or on several or all of these.

In the past century the United States has to some extent lost its unity of religion, of race, and of language. In the same period it has acquired a number of unassimilable elements brought in as cheap and docile labor to develop its industries or else allowed to enter through the false humanitarianism of the so-called Victorian Era. It had been forgotten that a cheap man makes a cheap job.

In the South manual labor was performed by the Negroes, but in the North, where there were no slaves, manual labor was chiefly performed by Americans, and it still is in the districts where there are no aliens. The moment that cheap alien labor was introduced to build railroads or dig canals, such labor became distasteful to the native American, because it was done by lowly foreigners whom they despised.

Among the various outland elements now in the United States which threaten in different degrees our national unity, the most important is the Negro. Unlike the other alien elements the blacks were brought into the country against their will. They brought with them no persisting language, religion, or other cultural attribute, but accepted these elements from their masters.

At the time of the first census (1790) the Negroes numbered 757,208, being 19.3 per cent of the total population. They were naturally mostly in the Southern States. In 1860 the Negroes numbered 4,441,830 and constituted 14.1 per cent of the population. They were still in the South. In 1930 the Negroes numbered 11,891,143 and constituted 9.69 per cent of the population, but there had been a distinct migration from the agricultural districts of the South to the large cities of the North.

When, after the Civil War, the Negroes were granted the franchise the Negro problem was greatly complicated. This ill-advised measure was forced on the country by a wave of feeling aroused by the wanton murder of Lincoln. The North feared to entrust the government of the country to those who had lately been in armed rebellion, so they conferred the voting power on the Negroes and thereby greatly increased the electoral vote of the South. If the franchise had been confined to the Whites only, the influence of the "Solid South" after the Civil War would have been much less than it now is. The purpose of the measure was to make the South Republican, its actual effect was to enhance the power of the South in Congress and in the Electoral College and make that section definitely Democratic. In the words of the late Chancellor Von Bismarck this was worse than a crime—it was a blunder.

The Southerners understand how to treat the

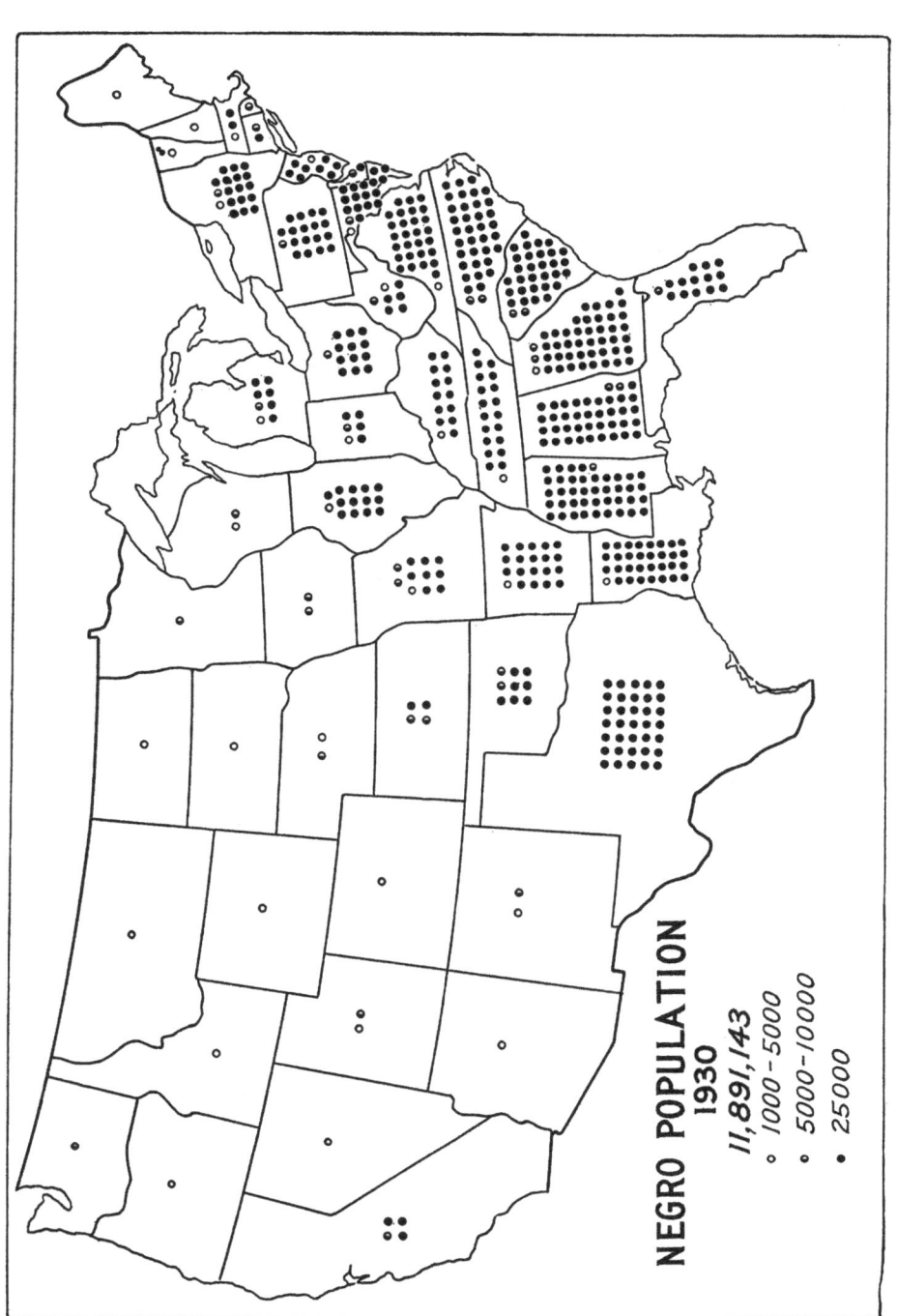

THE LEGACY OF SLAVERY 283

Negro—with firmness and with kindness—and the Negroes are liked below the Mason and Dixon line so so long as they keep to their proper relation to the Whites, but in the North the blocks of Negroes in the large cities, migrating from the South, have introduced new complications, which are certain to produce trouble in the future, especially if Communist propaganda makes headway among them.

In the Negro section of Harlem a further problem is arising from crosses between Negroes and Jews and Italians. These and other Mulattoes are showing a tendency toward Communism. During the World War a Communistic and racial movement was started there and a situation developed which was controlled with some difficulty, though without publicity.

The increase in the relative number of Mulattoes to Blacks is growing greater in the Northern States, as is obvious to any observer in the Negro districts of the larger cities. There can be seen many yellow and light-colored individuals, who are Negro in every other respect. Many of our dark immigrant Whites are themselves darker in color than the yellow Negroes and this enables some of these light Negroes to "pass" as Whites. This problem is one which will increase in gravity.

Evidence does not exist to show whether the number of Mulattoes being produced by primary union of Whites and Negroes is now larger than it was fifty or one hundred years ago. But evidence does exist to show that the intelligence and ability of a colored person are in pretty direct proportion to the amount of white blood he has, and that most of the positions of leadership, influence, and prominence in the Negro race are held not by real Negroes but by Mulattoes, many of whom have very little Negro blood. This is so true that to find a black Negro in a conspicuous position is a matter of comment. E. B. Reuter has calculated that a Mulatto child has a better chance than a black child to achieve prominence in the ratio of thirty-four to one.

Such a situation naturally puts a premium on white blood in the minds of Negroes, and therefore puts a prize on bastardy, discouraging any tendency to cultivate pure racial values on the part of the Blacks themselves. The black man who acquires wealth, at once wishes to show visible evidences of his affluence by acquiring a light yellow or "pink" wife, and the black girl is at a heavy discount matrimonially.

Even in adoption the same tendency is found. Child-placing societies may seek in vain to find a home for the pickaninny with black skin and curly hair, but the light-colored baby, despite other disqualifications, is eagerly adopted by darker Negro parents.

The religious world, the political world, and the educational world alike seem to have conspired to give all the rewards to the Negro with white blood and to make the bulk of the race feel that white blood is the greatest possible good for a Negro. Such a condonation of race mixture is an insidious

THE LEGACY OF SLAVERY

and far-reaching menace to the racial and ethical standards of both races.

How much white blood now circulates in the veins of our Negroes cannot be told. It is generally considered, however, that at least one-third of all those classed as Negroes in the United States have, in fact, some white blood and the proportion is probably larger.

The "pass-for-white" does so purely by virtue of his physical characters which approximate those of his white ancestors. His intellectual and emotional traits may insidiously go back to his black ancestry, and may be brought into the White race in this way.

Mentally and emotionally the Negro is the product of thousands of years of evolution under the most stringent natural selection in the hot lands of Africa. He is notably lacking in just those qualities necessary for success in a modern Nordic industrial civilization, as for instance in self-control and in capacity for co-operation. Physically he is the product of the same circumstances. His tough skin gives him an advantage over the White in resisting some diseases. His lower vital capacity puts him at a disadvantage in others. Thus the Negro is liable to succumb to tuberculosis or pneumonia, and is less prone to cancer and skin affections. With the aid of white sanitation and hygiene, the Negro is holding his own, even gaining ground in the Northern cities where it was formerly supposed he would die out.

Natural selection, therefore, in view of the present vital statistics of the two races, can no longer be relied upon to solve the problem by a gradual elimination of the Negro in America. Comfort has been found in the fall of the ratio of the Negroes to the total population; but their absolute increase goes on just the same.

No satisfactory solution of the problem has been suggested. At present, from a study of past history, there appear to be but three possible solutions.

First, slow amalgamation with the Whites and an ever-increasing number of Mulattoes, who little by little will "pass" for Whites. This amalgamation might easily assume serious proportions in the near future, with an increase of mixed breeds all over the United States. But if the sentimental views about Negroes engendered by the Civil War can be lived down, it may be that the oncoming generation will resolutely face this Mulatto menace. Otherwise the absorption of 10 per cent Negroes and Mulattoes, to say nothing of East and South Europeans, in addition to Mexicans, Filipinos, and Japanese will produce a racial chaos such as ruined the Roman Empire.

A second solution would be deportation, which was seriously suggested a hundred years ago. At that time it might have been possible to re-transport the then slaves to Africa, and such action would have involved only a fraction of the cost of the Civil War. This was considered as a possible remedy by some of the wisest statesmen in the years immediately preceding the Civil War. Today it is not possible, because Africa, with the exception of Liberia,

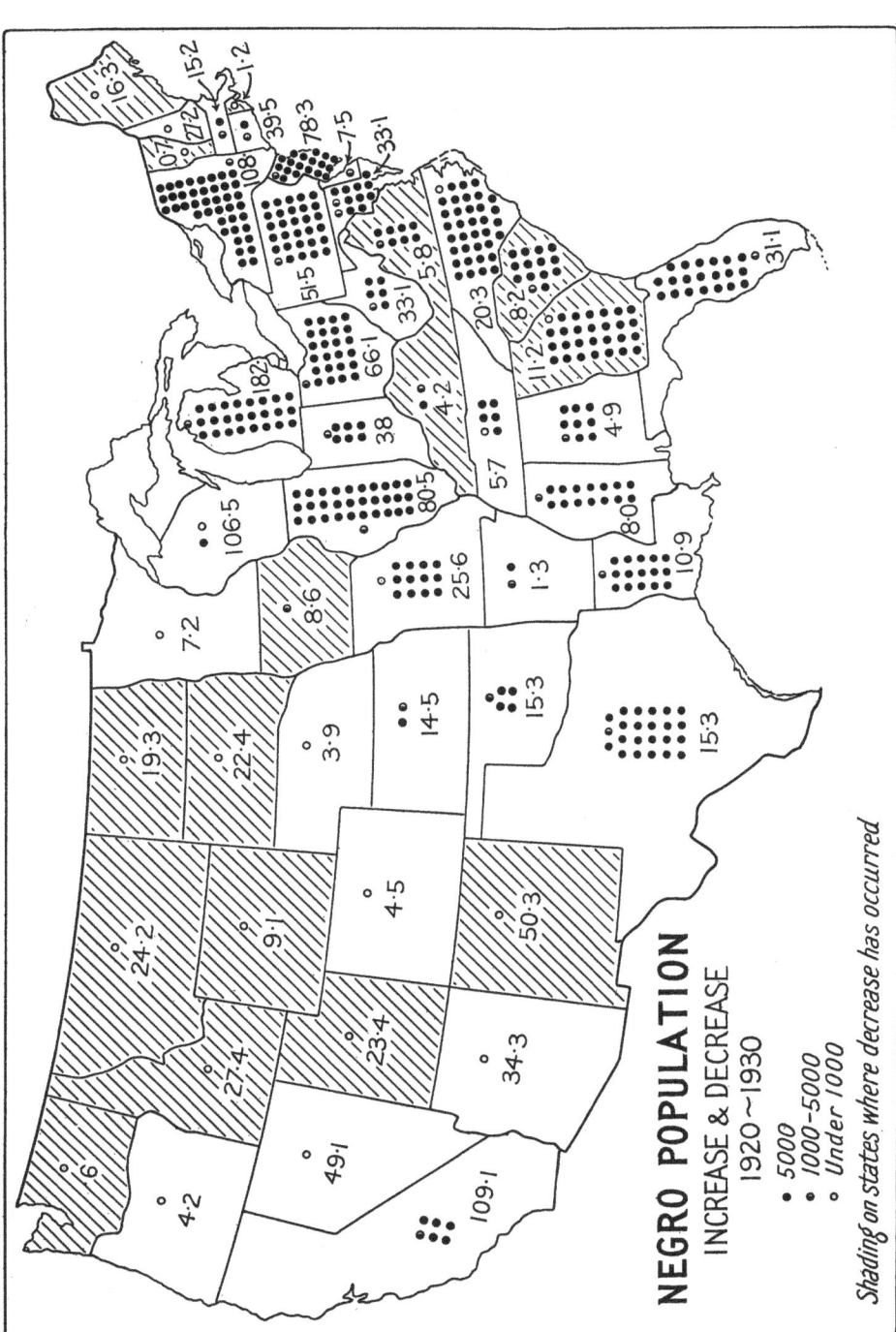

Figures in each State show the percentage of increase and decrease.

THE LEGACY OF SLAVERY 287

is under the control of white states, which certainly would not welcome such an enormous addition to their own color problem, aside from all other practical considerations.

Present-day advocates of repatriation argue that lack of native population is the principal factor likely to hold back the development of some of the healthiest and most fertile parts of interior Africa. The American Negro, they say, might well carry there the education he has received in the United States, and do better for himself than he could expect to do here, especially if, through a rising race consciousness among the Whites, they show themselves less hospitable to his claims for equality.

The substantial following, gained by the Negro Garvey, who started a "Back to Africa" movement a few years ago, is cited as evidence that the Negroes in this country are not necessarily adverse to leaving it. But much more evidence will be needed before the repatriation of the Negro can be considered seriously.

As a third possibility, segregation has been suggested. This would mean the abandonment by the Whites of whole sections of the country along the Gulf of Mexico. This has actually happened in some places along the lower Mississippi River, where the numbers of the Negroes have become so overwhelming that the few remaining Whites have simply moved out and abandoned the district to them. It has happened and is happening in the West Indies. Haiti and Santo Domingo have been entirely turned over to Negroes and other examples of West Indian Islands almost abandoned to Negroes can be found.

Whatever be the final outcome, the Negro problem must be taken vigorously in hand by the Whites, without delay. States which have no laws preventing the intermarriage of white and black should adopt them. During the last quarter-century, many such bills, introduced in Northern legislatures, have been defeated by an organized pro-Negro lobby. The Christian churches in some parts of the North have also taken an unwise stand, in trying to break down the social barriers between Negro and White. This attitude goes back to the days of the abolitionists, who persuaded themselves that the Negro slave had all possible virtues and the Southern White man all possible vices. It was a primary factor in creating the tragedy of "reconstruction" after the Civil War.

Senator Roscoe Conkling hit this attitude off neatly when some one asked him what had happened in the Senate that day. He replied: "We have been discussing Senator Sumner's annual bill entitled 'An act to amend the act of God whereby there is a difference between white and black.'"

More necessary than legislation is a more vigorous and alert public opinion among the Whites, which will put a stop to social mixing of the two races. Social separation is the key to minimizing the evils of race mixture at the present time. Public opinion might well stop exalting the Mulatto and thereby putting its stamp of approval on miscegena-

THE LEGACY OF SLAVERY 289

tion. Negroes should be encouraged to respect their own racial integrity. Finally, knowledge of methods of Birth Control now widespread among the Whites, should be made universally available to the Blacks.

Compared with the Negro, the American Indian offers no serious problem to American unity. On the entire continent north of Mexico there are only about 432,000. The 1930 census gives the Indian population of the United States as 332,397.

The distribution of these Indians is remarkably irregular. The West has the largest number; then comes the South, because of Oklahoma's 92,000, for the Gulf States have few. North Carolina, on the other hand, stands seventh in the list of States arranged according to Indian population. As against 137,000 in the West and 116,000 in the South, the North has but 78,000. These are widely scattered and often little known to the general public. New York State still has 7000 Indians, Michigan about the same number and North Dakota somewhat more; Wisconsin and Minnesota have 11,000 each, while South Dakota stands fourth on the list of all the States with its 22,000. In the West the Indian population is concentrated mainly in Arizona, New Mexico, California, Montana, and Washington, in the order named.

These Indians now represent 371 tribes, or remnants of tribes. How large their numbers were at the time of the first white settlement in North America has been a matter of interesting conjecture.

Most estimates are not much above a million, but the population may have been considerably greater a few hundred years earlier. Since white occupation a few tribes have increased in numbers. Most have diminished, and some have become extinct, more frequently from the white man's diseases and from whiskey than from the results of fighting.

The densest Indian population at the time of the conquest was on the Pacific Coast, which did not come into close contact with the Whites until the last century. This Pacific Coast Indian population was also of a low scale of intelligence and culture, and remarkably broken up into distinct groups which could not understand each other. As many separate languages were spoken by the Indians of this region as by all the other Indians of the United States together. When the first mission on the West Coast was founded by the Spaniards, in 1769, the number of California Indians was computed at 220,000. This has decreased more than 90 per cent at this date.

The policy of the Catholic missionaries was to corral the Indians around the missions. The church considered itself the owner of all the land, and the Indians worked it as tenants. When the Mexican Government confiscated the property of the church, it took title to all the land. Hence the Indians, who had always lived on it, found themselves illegal trespassers, and until about 1913 they were landless, starving fugitives. At that time the government began to provide land for the Indians. While their treatment has decimated them nine times, their iso-

THE LEGACY OF SLAVERY 291

lation prevented intermarriage with the Whites, so the California Indians are of relatively pure blood.

The revolt of the Pueblo Indians of Arizona and New Mexico against the Spanish in 1680–92 was the beginning of their decline. The Navajos and Apaches, on the contrary, have increased in numbers, at the same time avoiding white mixture.

The Indians of the Atlantic Coast were destroyed partly by disease, partly by war; and their remnants were pushed westward year after year by the Whites until they are mostly now west of the Mississippi, many of them being in Oklahoma. The Iroquois are an exception, and have perhaps increased in numbers. They got hold of firearms before their tribal neighbors and were able to destroy many of the latter, incorporating the remnants in their own tribe. The Sioux of the great plains are also said to have increased.

In the Gulf States, on the other hand, the Indians were largely exterminated before their remnants were moved to the Indian Territory. The Chickasaws told the French explorer, Iberville, in 1702, that in the preceding twelve years they had killed or captured for slave traders 2300 Choctaws, at a cost to themselves of 800 men.

In the Northwest and Alaska, whiskey and disease have been leading factors in the reduction of the number of the natives. With this, in many regions, went a low fertility, due partly to starvation.

Nearly all of the American Indians lived as hunters. When the Whites invaded the forests and drove off or killed the game, the Indian economic system was broken up, and they had little opportunity to meet the rapidly changing conditions.

There has been, since early times, some intermarriage between Indians and Whites, but it has not been on a sufficiently large scale to be serious. The estimate however is sometimes made that one-half of the census population of Indians has white blood. Naturally, there is no way of proving or disproving such a conjecture. Only in Oklahoma has such mixing been looked on with favor, and even there some tribes held themselves largely aloof from white miscegenation and punished with death any interbreeding of their members with Negroes. The discovery of oil on Indian tribal lands made the claim to Indian blood a lucrative one and oil revenues unfortunately covered a multitude of sins. Throughout the West in general the term "squaw man" is a bitter reproach.

Taking the country over, the Whites who have married Indians have not been of a high class. But the total number of Indians in the United States is so small that their future is probably that of being absorbed in the White race through miscegenation, unless it be for a few tribes cultivating a racial purity of their own and, with favorable economic conditions, perpetuating themselves for a long time to come.

The Mexican population is found mainly in the Southwestern States, but has also assumed relatively large proportions in such States as Colorado, Kan-

THE LEGACY OF SLAVERY 293

sas, Illinois, and Michigan. The character of this immigration has been described elsewhere in these pages. It has given the United States an alien element with a high birthrate and very low standards of living, with which white laborers cannot and will not compete.

The census of 1930 found nearly a million and a half Mexicans in the United States. It was generally supposed that the number who had entered the country illegally was greater than those who came through the recognized routes. To prevent such a nullification of immigration regulations, mere registration of aliens is not sufficient, for that is likely to affect only those who have entered legally. Our entire population should be registered. The advantages of a universal system of proving identity are many, and extension of the system of registering births, on the one hand, and of registering voters, on the other, would take care of this without setting up much new and expensive machinery.

The menace of Chinese and Japanese immigration has for the present been stopped by immigration laws which exclude any one not eligible to citizenship. A proper application of this rule as established by the Supreme Court might shut off much of the immigration of Indians from Mexico.

Since the end of the World War the immigration of Filipino young men has become a disturbing problem on the Pacific Coast. The number of arrivals up to 1930 amounts to nearly 50,000. These, like the Greeks and some other European immigrant groups, bring but few women with them and therefore form a socially undesirable and racially threatening element wherever they are located.

Unlike the Puerto Ricans and Hawaiians, the Filipinos are not citizens of the United States, with rights of entry that cannot be abrogated. They are citizens of the Philippine Islands, and permitted to enter the United States only by courtesy. Congress, therefore, has full right to adopt legislation which will exclude them, and it should make immediate use of its power to protect white America from this reservoir of 10,000,000 Malays and Mongoloids now under the American flag and at present potential immigrants. If this cannot be done effectively, the United States will have no alternative but to admit that its adoption of the islands and its attempt to salvage them after Spanish misrule was a mistake. As a safeguard to its own racial welfare, it may become necessary to give the Filipino his independence, commend him to the benevolence of Providence and the League of Nations, and have nothing more to do with him.

In the same way there should be no thought of further acquisition of territory in the West Indies or in Central America. It is conceivable that the Central American countries might in a not too remote future be able to form a stable confederation and stand on their own feet more successfully than they have done during the last generation. If such a federation could include the West Indian Islands, the United States might well donate its possessions there.

Hindu immigration has so far been nothing more than a threat. The present immigration restrictions will prevent the immigration of these people, except for travel and study. Experience in many parts of the world has shown the folly of allowing white countries to be overrun by Hindus, and Americans should sympathize with the British possessions that are trying to maintain white supremacy in their own borders in this respect.

In Hawaii the United States has another possible source of undesirable immigration. The dominant element among its third of a million inhabitants is the Japanese, who have held themselves aloof from the other residents and shown little tendency to intermarry. Every Japanese child born in the islands is an American citizen, with the full right of entry to the mainland. The greater part of the rest of the population is a mongrel crowd. Chinese and native Hawaiians, until quite recently, have shown a marked tendency to intermarry. Every effort should be made to find some constitutional way by which Hawaii can be prevented from becoming a continuous source of supply of undesirable citizens of the United States.

While the list of unassimilable elements in the United States is a long one, it must be borne in mind that most of them are still small. A wise population policy promptly adopted and maintained henceforth will give the republic an opportunity to grow along sound and fruitful lines.

XVI

OUR NEIGHBORS ON THE NORTH

BEFORE dealing with the countries to the north of us, it may be well to call attention to the fact that there are three major divisions of Canada. First, the Maritime Provinces, which were acquired by Great Britain at a later date than the other Atlantic Colonies, as they were originally claimed by the French. In this division Newfoundland should be considered. These territories lying east of the United States were settled directly from England or at the time of the Revolution by Loyalist refugees from New England. There is a large Scotch element in the population, which was lacking in New England. On the whole, the area is thoroughly Nordic, except on the shores of the Gulf of Saint Lawrence and the Bay of Chaleurs, where the Alpine French Habitants have infiltrated.

The second division of the Dominion is French-speaking, Roman Catholic Quebec, with a fecund population of low cultural status. The French distrust of the New England Protestants, with whom they had been at war for one hundred and fifty years, was the predominant cause of their failure to join with the revolting American Colonies in 1776. Quebec was known as Lower Canada.

Like the territories of the United States, the Dominion of Canada of today represents a part of the Nordic conquest of North America, the sole exception being the French population of Quebec Province.

The country to the west of the Ottawa River constitutes the third major division and was, after the Revolution, known as Upper Canada. Its original population was composed chiefly of American Loyalists who fled there in numbers after the Revolution. The immigration into Upper Canada from Britain was later very largely Scotch, Scotch Irish, and North of England. This is true more or less of all English-speaking Canada, except possibly British Columbia.

In a measure the Dominion is an offshoot of the United States, and its development proceeded along lines parallel to those of the States to the south of the boundary. The character of the population west of Quebec Province is much the same as that of the United States, lacking, fortunately for Canada, some of our immigrant elements. The country was settled without the terrible Indian wars that afflicted our frontier and without the lawless element so conspicuous in the history of our Far West.

The French settlement of Quebec was contemporaneous with the first English settlement in North America at Jamestown. A majority of the emigrants were from northern France. So far as one can judge at the present time by the descendants of this population, the pure Nordic stock must have been rare among them. They are today in general a stocky, short-necked people, rather of the Alpine build, with eyes often rather dark. The blond hair and tall stature of the Nordic are so rare as to attract attention at once. The type suggests the Pre-Norman population of northwestern France, rather than its Nordic conquerors. Some of the seigneurs, the explorers, and the adventurers of the early period apparently were of Nordic stock, but they were probably always in a great minority and have left few descendants.

Very little satisfactory research has been done as to the origin of the Habitants. A recent study of a typical group has given some indication of the general conditions in Quebec. In this group stature was found to be five feet and five inches, which is about the general average of the French. The cephalic index was over 83.0, which is about the mean for Brittany and is higher than that of Normandy. The hair was rather dark brown and straight, this straightness is slightly suggestive of Indian admixture. The eye color was more often brown than mixed blue and brown. Pure blue eyes were present only in 15 per cent. The tall burly build of the Norman peasant was very rare.

The language spoken in Quebec is an archaic Norman patois of the time of Louis XIV. This fact has given rise to the general belief that the Habitants came from Normandy, but the more probable reason is that the Normans were the earliest immigrants and established their patois, which was accepted by later arrivals. The Normans appeared to have been far short of a majority of the total number of immigrants and Brittany supplied still fewer. The balance was divided among the provinces of the northern half of France.

The physical type of the Habitants of today suggestive as it is of the peasants of the interior of Brittany finds confirmative evidence in their subserviency to the church.

Throughout the French period the population consisted to a marked extent of soldiers, traders, administrators, priests, and others who did not bring their families with them. Efforts of the French Government to encourage family life were not always either well directed or successful. Colbert hoped for a large French population in Canada by intermarriage with the Indians. Administrative regulations penalized bachelors, who, for instance, were refused licenses to enter the fur trade, which was the main source of wealth in the country at that time.

Many of these restrictions were directed by the priests, doubtless not so much for eugenic reasons as with the motive of protecting the morals of the young men by giving them wives. At an early date the colony fell under the domination of the Jesuits, and maintained for a long time a religious tone that in its own way was much more stern and uncompromising than that of the Puritan settlements in New England. Much of the wealth and effort that might have gone to strengthen the colony was sunk in sterile monastic foundations. Even today stone churches are a conspicuous feature of the landscape in the midst of poverty-stricken villages.

At one time there was for some years a directed migration of young women from France, sent out to become the wives of the colonists and early in the history of the country a policy of bonuses for marriage, and for large families, which has been repeated at intervals ever since, was introduced. None the less, the colony grew but slowly and to the failure to establish it on a sound biological foundation is due the collapse of French rule.

In 1665 the first census showed a population of 3215. In the next hundred years this had increased to somewhat more than 70,000, with an additional 20,000 in what are now the Maritime Provinces. That the French could maintain the contest for so long against British neighbors who outnumbered them twenty to one is to their credit, but their lack of recognition that their settlement could not be permanent unless based on a real migration of families ultimately cost them the country.

One of the chief causes of the failure of French Canada to expand beyond the narrow limits of the banks of the Saint Lawrence River, during its first century of existence, was an obscure skirmish which occurred on the west side of Lake Champlain in 1609. Champlain was advancing toward the South in company with Canadian Algonquins, when he encountered a war party of the Mohawks. In the fighting that followed, some Mohawks were killed and captured. At that time and in that place began the bitter enmity of the Iroquois Five Nations and the Canadian French. It was a feud that was never

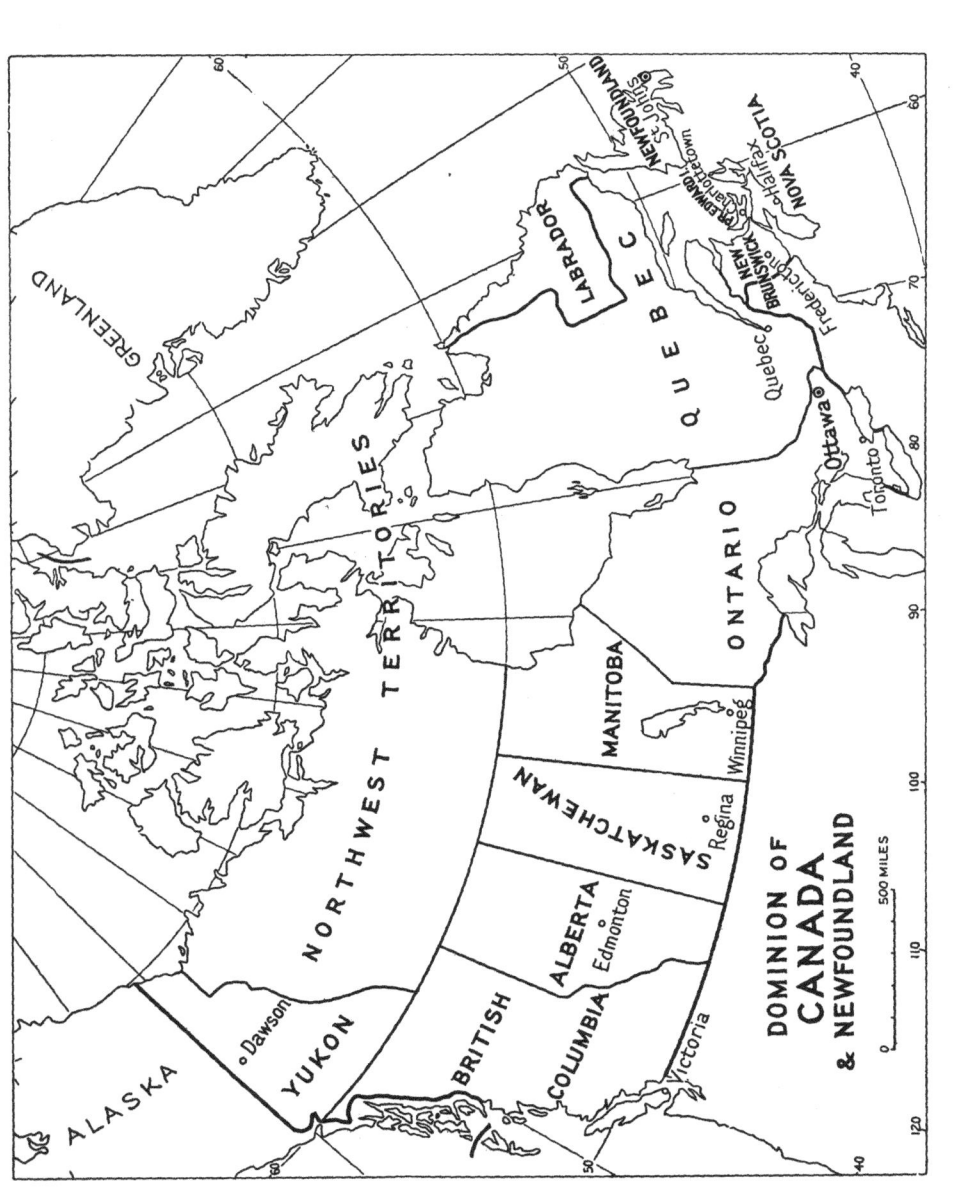

allowed to rest and yearly war parties of Mohawks went north along Lake Champlain and the Richelieu River and devastated the lower portion of Quebec Province. At the same time war parties of the Senecas descended the Saint Lawrence and attacked the French from the West. As long as the power of the Iroquois lasted, which was all through the seventeenth century, they devastated a large part of New France.

In the meantime, the Dutch and English were growing up in security to the South and East. Thus Champlain's skirmish with the Iroquois was the factor that delayed the expansion of France into the region of the Great Lakes and down the Mississippi Valley until relatively late in the eighteenth century.

The French population still centers in Quebec Province, long known as Lower Canada, but it has spread to other parts of the continent both south and west of the Quebec boundary. Their expansion in Canada has been into the neighboring provinces. Emigration to New England began in the eighteenth century but was not considerable until the nineteenth century.

While this French-Canadian population has remained so fecund as to furnish a stock example for every writer, it, too, has felt the trend of the times. For a long time the government of Quebec offered a grant of one hundred acres of land to every man who was the father of twelve living children by one wife. In less than a single year over 3000 heads of families availed themselves of this privilege and in

1907 there was published a list of 7000 families having at least twelve living children.

In spite of this fecundity, the birthrate has been declining for almost the whole of the historical period. Two hundred and fifty years ago the average for all women of child-bearing age in Quebec Province was one child every two and one-half years. By 1850 this ratio had decreased to one in five years. At present it is one in seven and one-half years. Under this method of measurement, the rate of natural increase per head is only one-third of what it was in colonial times. Even the Roman Catholic "Habitant," therefore, has felt the effect of the general decline of birth-rate throughout the western world in the period since the beginning of the industrial revolution.

From the beginning of the nineteenth century there was a small but steady immigration from the British Isles into Upper Canada, though interrupted by the Napoleonic Wars. After the close of that conflict a larger movement of population took place, which brought in an extensive English population. Theretofore most of the arrivals had been Scotch or Americans, so that a visitor in 1810 commented on the fact that he met "scarcely any English and few Irish."

In 1815 the government began to assist immigrants by giving free passage and a grant of one hundred acres of land after arrival with a promise of free rations for the first six or eight months and a like amount of land to each male child on his reaching the age of twenty-one. A wise restriction required a deposit of a little less than one hundred dollars by the immigrant, to be returned to him after two years if he had complied with the terms of the contract on his behalf. These provisions were availed of mainly by Scotchmen going to Ontario. The scheme, however, had the advantage for our present purpose of establishing for the first time records of immigration, which thenceforth can be traced in detail.

In 1819 the emigration from British ports to Canada was in excess of 20,000, and continued for years at about this rate in spite of the booms which Australia and New Zealand were enjoying at the same time. There was a substantial movement of emigration toward Canada in the years 1830–34. In the nine years preceding 1837, more than a quarter of a million emigrants from the British Isles arrived at Quebec on their way westward, more than 50,000 of them in a single year.

Primogeniture in England has been a powerful factor in building up the British Commonwealth. The oldest son of a landed family inherited the estate and the titles, if any, and stayed at home. The younger sons, left to shift for themselves, were ready to emigrate. The colonies have thus received a great many more settlers of first-class ability than would otherwise have been the case. At the same time, the perpetuation of family continuity, through the preservation of the ancestral home intact, has been a strong psychological factor in maintaining a vigorous family life in the upper classes of Great Britain.

By 1840 the population of Canada was approximately a million and a half. During the next generation nearly a million more immigrants arrived from British ports—the great Irish migration changing the racial character of this movement markedly from about 1845. Prior to that time the newcomers were predominantly English, with Wiltshire and Yorkshire largely represented. When the potato famine caused the Irish to seek refuge elsewhere, they naturally turned their steps to England, as the most easily and cheaply accessible of havens. Great Britain could absorb only a limited part of these and began to direct them to Canada, which, indeed, they preferred to the United States because the Catholic Church was strong there.

The emigrants were weak and in 1849 one-sixth of those who started are said to have died on the voyage. The number of Irish who left the United Kingdom in that year was 215,000, of whom nearly half were bound for Quebec. Canada became alarmed at being made the dumping ground of an enfeebled and destitute population so much in excess of its capacity to absorb, and, by increased taxes and other means, slowed down this immigration, which then headed toward the United States. Thereafter many of the Irish who had already gone to Canada moved on down into the Union, so that in the end Canada received a smaller part of the Irish Catholic migration than might be thought.

The census of 1871 furnishes a convenient point

at which to take a review of the population. It then totalled 3,485,761 in the four original provinces (Ontario, Quebec, New Brunswick, and Nova Scotia). British and French together, in the ratio of two to one, made up 92 per cent. The only foreign element which contributed as much as 1 per cent of the whole was the German, numbering more than 200,000 people, or 5.8 per cent.

The French Habitants have always formed a somewhat indigestible mass, but half a century of struggle had resulted in a workable system of government and compromise in the administrative life of the country. The dominant element was the British, and save for the great mass of French there was no large foreign block to menace the country's unity.

In sharp contrast to the settlement of the West of the United States, the occupation of the prairie and mountain provinces of Canada has been marked by law and order. In our West, especially in the mining districts, law was largely disregarded and its place taken by private justice, administered by individuals.

In Canada the Mounted Police have played a most efficient rôle in controlling both the settlers and the Indians. At the time of the Klondike rush in 1898, when hordes of gold seekers scrambled over the passes to the head waters of the Yukon, a handful of Mounted Police maintained a discipline for which the Americans themselves were very grateful. In the same way the administration of the mining laws of the Klondike, which is in Canadian territory, was admired and envied by the Americans there.

The Canadian treatment of the Indians in the western provinces was also marked by an absence of the bloody wars which characterized our westward advance. The only uprising against the Whites was the Riel Rebellion in Manitoba, in 1869, which was by the half-breeds rather than by the Indians and which had special underlying causes. All this has been accomplished without the Whites in any way fraternizing with the Indians.

During the French period, the Canadian Indians always sided with the French against the English, because under the influence of the Catholic priests, the French Indian half-breed was regarded as a Frenchman and, as a result, influenced his mother's people in favor of the ruling race.

There were plenty of offspring of white frontiersmen and Indian squaws all along our frontier, but these half breeds were everywhere kicked out and despised as Indians. This attitude toward the lower race has always characterized our American frontier and while very unpopular with the natives, has served to keep the White race unmixed, in sharp contrast to the French and Spanish colonies.

Canada still has more than 100,000 Indians, four times as many in proportion to the whole population, as in the United States.

Newfoundland, for geographical reasons, even though it has politically no relation to Canada, is the most convenient starting point in reviewing in more detail the subdivisions of the country.

Larger than Ireland, the island claims to be the "senior colony" of the British Commonwealth. John Cabot, a Genoese, sailing from Bristol, discovered it in 1497, according to the traditional account, and took possession of it in the name of Henry VII. Within a few years fishermen, not merely English but French, Spanish, Portuguese, and Basque, were landing there to dry and cure the enormous quantities of cod caught on the Great Banks, which still form the principal wealth of the colony. In fact, some writers believe that the island may have been discovered long before the time of Columbus, by fishermen. At any rate, the effective occupation, though scarcely the continuous settlement of Newfoundland, long antedated the colonization of Virginia and many of the original English residents came from Devonshire.

The aboriginal inhabitants, the Beothics, disappeared half a century ago. They were probably Eskimos, or closely related to them, and are sometimes spoken of as "Red" Indians, in contrast to the "Black" Indians, the Micmacs, who have recently immigrated in small numbers from New Brunswick.

Newfoundland has nearly a quarter of a million inhabitants, but its backward stage of development still makes it little known to the outside world.

On the mainland a long strip of the Atlantic Coast and a large triangle of land behind it are attached to Newfoundland administratively, under the name of

Labrador. Because of its scanty population it may well be disregarded in the present discussion.

Nova Scotia during Colonial days was almost a New England colony. It was known to the French as "Acadie" and was ceded to England in 1713.

Interposed between New England and French Canada, Acadia suffered heavily from the warfare that went on between the two regions. The existence of a large French population was always a source of irritation, and of danger, to the English. Finally in 1758 the French were cleared out, about 6000 of them being distributed throughout the English colonies, and the remainder escaping to Canada. Those who came to the thirteen colonies suffered hardships, but on the whole were more humanely treated than were those who fled to their co-religionists in Quebec Province. The place of the exiled Acadians[1] was largely taken by New England emigrants.

The American population of Nova Scotia was further greatly augmented at the time of the Revolution by an influx of Loyalists. These came in such numbers as to disturb the colony seriously, but formed an invaluable addition of the best sort of British stock. This general trend has continued so that, even in 1921, of the foreign-born population of

---

[1] Acadie in the Micmac language means "place." Henry Wadsworth Longfellow's pathetic poem, "Evangeline," embodies the anti-English sentiments of the early nineteenth century in New England and is founded largely on an error of spelling, which made "Arcadia" out of the Indian word. The expulsion of the French in 1758 was by Bostonians under Colonel John Winslow, and was justified by the refusal of the French to accept loyally the rule of the English.

Nova Scotia, that which originated in the United States was twice as large as all the rest of the foreign-born population put together.

The Scotch immigration which has exercised such an important influence on the eastern counties of Nova Scotia began about 1760 with the arrival of Scots and Ulster Scots. In 1772 a contingent of Highlanders direct from Scotland took up land alongside an American group from Philadelphia. From then on until about 1820, a steady stream of Highlanders came into the region; Gaelic is still spoken in parts of the colony. Nova Scotia with the other Maritime Provinces still represents the most purely British of all the Canadian provinces, and as shown, an important part of its population came to it through the United States.

New Brunswick was established on August 16, 1784, out of a part of ancient Acadia. It also received an important number of Loyalists at the time of the Revolution—indeed it might be said to owe its existence to the arrival of some 10,000 expatriates from the United States. But the bulk of the population is Scottish with a strong Highland contingent. There are few foreign-born other than a small element from the United States.

Prince Edward Island is similar as to its population and is the most purely "native" of all, only one in each one hundred in this province being foreign-born. The Roman Catholics there include a considerable number of Scotch Highlanders and number nearly a half of the population.

Quebec is still the stronghold of the French-Canadians, more than half of whom are unable to speak the English language. The French stock still numbers one-fourth of the entire population of the entire Dominion of Canada. On the northern frontier of Quebec there was some mixture with the Indians, but the half-breeds are probably not numerous enough to form a substantial part of the old population. In addition to their great movement to New England the French-Canadians have spread into Ontario, New Brunswick, and Prince Edward Island to some extent.

The French-Canadian stock is the most highly inbred of any of the large groups of the New World. It is based on original immigrants who numbered a good many less than 10,000. In the course of three centuries this nucleus has multiplied to 3,000,000, with virtually no additions of fresh arrivals from abroad. They have lived a New World life longer than have most of the Whites of the Western Hemisphere, and must be put in a class by themselves. They are not French, in spite of their language—an archaic speech at which the true Frenchman laughs. In every way they differ from the present-day French, more indeed than New Englanders of Colonial descent now differ from the present-day Englishman. From the cradle to the grave they are surrounded by the influence of the Roman Catholic

Church to an extent almost as unknown to the present-day French as it is to the present-day Americans. Of late years not only those who have come to New England, but some of those living in Quebec Province have shown a disposition to break away from the church because of its heavy and inexorable taxation.

The French-Canadians, in Quebec and the neighboring provinces, were, to an extent, disloyal to the British Empire in the Great War. Under the influence of their priests they resisted the draft in several instances and there was bloodshed in Quebec on this account. As has been said elsewhere, these Frenchmen would not fight for the British Empire, which had guaranteed them extraordinary privileges as to their language and religion, nor would they fight for France, which they claimed as motherland, but which they now regarded as atheistic. Neither would they fight for Belgium, which is pretty nearly as clerical as they are. In short, their conduct during the World War was contemptible and in sharp contrast to the militant and effective patriotism of the more westerly provinces of Canada.

Ontario, called Upper Canada in distinction to French-speaking Lower Canada, received its first important population from the United States when Loyalist refugees, including many Highland Scots, mainly from northern and western New York, settled there and became known as the United Empire Loyalists. Among these immigrants, were the disbanded frontier regiments which had been organized by Sir John Johnson, including abundant Macdonalds from Glengarry and Inverness, together with Camerons, Chisholms, Fergusons, MacIntyres, Russells, and Hamiltons, who opened up the region constituting the present counties of Glengarry, Stormont, and Dundas.

In 1785, almost the entire parish of Knoydart, Glengarry, emigrated direct from Scotland and settled in a body in Upper Canada. In 1793 a contingent from Glenelg settled at Kirkhill. In 1799 came many Camerons from Lochiel, and in 1803 another delegation of Macdonalds arrived, with more people from Glenelg and Kintail. Thus Ontario, which in 1791 was set off from (French) Lower Canada and given its own government under the name of Upper Canada, became almost as much entitled to consider itself a "Nova Scotia," as did the Maritime Province of that name.

At the end of the American Revolution, Upper Canada was supposed not to contain as many as 10,000 inhabitants. By 1811 it had 83,000 and by 1817 it was estimated to have 134,000. While many Irish came at a somewhat later period, most of these eventually went on to the United States.

The interference with British immigration caused by the Napoleonic wars led to Upper Canada's offering special attraction to settlers from the United States. The lack of sympathy of these with the British Government during the War of 1812 was an embarrassment to Canada, just as the loyalty of the

United Empire group, which prevented Canada from being conquered by the United States, was in turn a serious annoyance to the American Government.

The later settlement of Ontario was largely from Scotland and the northern English counties, and was predominantly Presbyterian. There were enough Ulster Scots to make it an active center of the American Protective Association of forty years ago and it is definitely, at the present time, a Nordic territory.

During the present century it has received thousands of Austrians, Poles, and Italians, who introduced racial elements not easily assimilated.

Manitoba began to be settled shortly after the War of 1812, when Lord Selkirk established his Red River Colony. The Scotch Highlanders, Swiss, and others whom he planted there did not prosper, and many of them eventually drifted down into the United States, taking an active part in the formation of Minnesota. Around this nucleus, however, there gradually grew an incongruous and isolated settlement made up of three elements that had almost nothing in common; the Scotch, the French-Canadians, and the half-breeds. In 1849 the Red River Settlement was credited with 5391 people. With the establishment of steam navigation on the Red River, and the official creation of Winnipeg, both of which occurred in 1862, development began on a larger scale.

A provisional government was given to the territory in 1869, and from time to time land was generously allotted to the early white settlers, to the half-breeds, and to the Hudson's Bay Company. Thereafter the province grew slowly, from the natural increase of its founders and from a Nordic migration from Ontario and from the neighboring parts of the United States, until the mixed European immigration of the last half-century changed somewhat the character of the population. These latter now account for one-third of the whole.

The proportion of these non-Nordic Europeans, from southern or central Europe, is three times as great as the European immigration from either northern or western Europe. If this immigration continues in like proportions, Manitoba, like the other prairie provinces, is in danger of being lost to the Nordics.

Saskatchewan has a larger American-born population than Manitoba, one resident in every eight having first seen the light of day under the American flag. But it has a still larger recent European immigration amounting to nearly 40 per cent of the total population of the province. A bare half of the people of Saskatchewan are of British origin.

Alberta has both a somewhat smaller European element and the largest American-born contingent of any of the provinces amounting to one in six. Many English of a fine type have settled there.

In all the Prairie Provinces the French-Canadian

represents scarcely more than one in twenty of the population.

British Columbia has prided itself with justice on its British origin, and is exceeded in this respect only by the Maritime Provinces. Of its European immigrants (one in eleven of the whole), approximately equal numbers are Nordics from northern or western Europe, and Alpines or Mediterraneans from southeastern and central Europe. During the World War its young men showed great attachment to the mother country, and the loss from death was correspondingly great. Because of its great distance from the ports of entry, it was long avoided by immigrants. Not until about 1907 did it begin to get its fair share. Since then, it has held its own, about half of its new arrivals however coming from the United States.

The province also has its Asiatic problem, which has been the source of hard feeling on several occasions. One of the great hindrances to its more rapid development was shortage of labor, and it was natural that the Orient, which could reach British Columbia more easily and cheaply than could either Europe or even the Atlantic provinces of Canada itself, should be called upon to meet the need. Chinese soon began to enter, until stopped by a head tax of $500. Japanese came in considerable numbers, not merely in the fisheries but for day labor in railway construction. Some 6000 Hindus likewise found their way there. Orientals now amount to one in every seven of the total population. There is a real Asiatic question here and the Whites are beginning to look to the United States for protection.

Canada's immense arctic area, the Yukon and the Northwest Territories, may be neglected in this discussion because of the lack of population. Those who see in the mosquito-infested tundra of "The Land of Little Sticks," with its months of winter darkness, a future populous area of agricultural and livestock industry are destined to wait long for the realization of their dream.

So far as the British element in Canada is concerned, it has been pointed out above in several places that the country is to a certain extent an offspring of the United States. This contribution has continued up to the present time. During the 1880's there was another great period of migration from the Union to the Dominion. At that time nearly twice as many entered Canada from this country as from Great Britain, and six times as many as from the continent of Europe.

Not all of these Americans were of the old native stock. It has been calculated that at least half of this contingent was of British extraction, the other half being made up of various European nationalities who, after becoming acclimated to the New World in the United States, passed on to Canadian soil. Thus the contribution from the United States during that period did not represent a purely Nordic accession.

The 1890's represented a period of British immigration. But, with the turn of the century, Canada began to share in the great influx of miscellaneous peoples who were already deluging the shores of the United States. During the first twelve years of the twentieth century, Canada received 2,000,000 people, of whom 800,000 were British. About 700,000 others came from the United States, but more than a third of these are calculated to have been Continental arrivals who merely passed through the United States for convenience. In 1901 there were in Canada some 650,000 of "foreign stock"—that is, of neither British nor French origin. In 1921 there were more than twice as many. Since the beginning of the century Canada has acquired more than 100,000 Jews.

After the World War the Empire Settlement Act began to make itself felt, reducing markedly the proportion of immigrants from the United States into Canada while from 1900 onward Ireland began to figure heavily in the immigration statistics.

In 1930 there were, on the other hand, over 1,200,000 Canadian-born, both of British and French stock, in the United States and during the preceding eight years 300,000 had returned to Canada.

Not only have the western provinces, then, been thrown violently into a disequilibrium by the population changes of the last generation, but the stability of the whole Dominion has been menaced. Canada, like the United States, has taken on a great liability in the admission of the hundreds of thousands of non-Nordics, who will be hard to assimilate, even if it be assumed that they would become valuable when assimilated, which is by no means always the case. One of Canada's advantages, on the other hand, is the negligible proportion of Negroes, and it might well erect barriers even now against them, as it has already done against the Asiatics.

With its immense territory and more than 10,000,000 inhabitants, Canada is still to be credited to the Nordics, though, if the population trends that began with this century should continue, the balance would change rapidly. While the United States has contributed by far the largest number of foreign-born, Russia has contributed the second largest number of immigrants, Saskatchewan receiving more of these than any other province. Ontario, Quebec, and Manitoba have received about equal numbers, in each case one-third less than went to Saskatchewan. Those of Austrian birth, who are third in the list, are concentrated in the two provinces of Manitoba and Saskatchewan in about equal numbers, each of these provinces having almost twice as many Austrian-born as Alberta or Ontario. The Chinese stand fourth in numbers among the foreign-born of the Dominion, but most of them are concentrated in British Columbia. Ontario has almost as many Italians as all the rest of Canada put together, and it has also the largest number of Poles.

Because of the great body of French-Canadians, the Roman Catholic Church is proportionately twice as strong as in the United States.

The 1921 census showed the population to be made up as follows:

	PER CENT
British origin	55.40
French	27.91
Other European	14.16
Indian	1.26
Asiatic	.75

This computation distributes the immigrants from the United States according to their racial stock; thus the main part would be classified with those of British origin, a smaller part as "other European," and so on.

From the foregoing it is evident that Canada is now less than 60 per cent Nordic—probably less Nordic than the United States.

Canada has been the great obstacle to extending the American immigration quotas to the countries of the Western Hemisphere. The majority of its inhabitants are our own kinsmen, many of whom have already contributed elements of great value to our population. Others would be most welcome if they chose to come.

Our nation has been unwilling to put the slightest restriction on Canadian immigration, by applying a quota; and it was thought it would be invidious and discriminatory to apply a quota to the countries south of us, and not to the one to the north. That difficulty will have to be met firmly in the near future. One proposed solution has been to admit from Canada only those whose mother tongue is English.

XVII

OUR NEIGHBORS ON THE SOUTH

UNLIKE Canada on our north, the countries south of the Rio Grande have been relatively little influenced by Nordic culture, to say nothing of anything resembling a Nordic conquest. The outlying territories of Mexico which were annexed to the United States were nearly empty lands and present Mexican influences in the Southwest are matters of more recent date.

Latin America is one of the major divisions of the World, and from the present point of view should no more be discussed as a unit than could Europe or Asia. Its original population represents one of the great racial divisions of mankind. Its twenty different nations now speak several different languages, and embrace representatives of all the important races of both hemispheres.

The general area gets such unity as it possesses from the Latin and Roman Catholic aspect of its culture as contrasted with the Protestant, Anglo-Saxon culture of America north of the Mexican border. This Latin civilization was originally Spanish (in Brazil Portuguese), but since the era of the revolutions which threw off the Spanish yoke, the Spanish influence has become more and more negligible, and locally has been somewhat supplanted by the French, and, to a small extent, by the Italian influence.

Latin America was never colonized at all in the sense that North America was colonized. English settlers with their families came to the New World to found homes, but the early history of Latin America was that of a series of plundering and proselyting expeditions, and such of the adventurers as tarried were usually men without families who had no desire to stay a day longer than was necessary to acquire a fortune and return to Europe. Add to these the military forces who came under compulsion, and the missionaries, administrators, and concessionaires of all kinds and one has the bulk of the early European immigration.

Under these circumstances the number of women who came with their husbands was naturally small, and most of the Europeans took Indian wives, frequently several of them, thus laying the basis for the half-breed population of the present day. In Paraguay, for instance, some of the colonial rulers are said to have had fifty or a hundred native concubines. If every descendant of these matings carries the Spanish name but has married mainly with Indian stock in the ten or fifteen generations since, it is easy to understand that present-day families may bear the names of hidalgos, of whose genetic traits they have virtually none.

The number of European immigrants was never large. During the sixteenth century, a period of active exploitation, the entire movement from Spain to America is thought to have represented only about 1000 or 1500 persons a year. With a high death rate, and the disposition on their part to return as soon as possible, there was no opportunity for the Spaniard to establish the basis of a civilization built upon his own race.

By 1553 foundling half breeds numbered thousands in Spanish America and the viceroy Mendoza was obliged to establish an orphan school for them. Even at the end of the eighteenth century, when Humboldt visited Mexico City, he remarked that of the European-born Spaniards there, not one-tenth were women. The proportion of women must certainly have been still smaller in the provincial towns and on the frontiers.

So far as the present population goes back to the early days of Spanish dominion, it may be said to be Spanish by name and Indian by blood. The families, which in many Spanish American countries have social prestige, because of descent from the conquerors and rulers of the Colonial Period, must therefore attach all importance to the family name, and little or none to the many other lines of descent which have entered into the composition of their present generation.

Honorable exception should be made in almost every one of the Spanish American republics of a small group of Whites that has consistently maintained its racial integrity and upheld intelligent ideals of racial progress, under most difficult conditions.

In many of the countries, too, there are groups of far-seeing intellectuals who are working for the adoption of wise immigration policies, presenting sound and constructive measures of eugenic reform, and striving to awaken their fellow countrymen to the fact that a nation's capital is, in the last analysis, biological, and that permanent and satisfactory progress is possible only to a people with a healthy family life.

In many of the Latin American countries the Whites, or those who pass as such (for they have, in most cases, a large proportion of Indian blood) form an oligarchy or ruling caste occupying the higher positions in the political and ecclesiastical worlds. They also constitute the land-owning and professional classes, while commerce and industry are largely in the hands of foreigners or their descendants. In many cases these foreign immigrants marry into the best native families, and thus their children become a part of the ruling caste.

Mexico. The restriction of European immigration into the United States under the National Origins Quota cutting off what had been the principal source of unskilled labor had an unexpected and undesirable effect in encouraging immigration from nearby countries of the Western Hemisphere, which were not under the quota, and particularly from Mexico. Industries accustomed to depend upon cheap, ignorant, and docile workers from Mediterranean or Alpine countries turned to the illiterate

Indians on the South as a ready substitute. The stream of arrivals across the border, more illegal than legal, soon brought into the United States more than a million Mexicans. Only the unexpected depression beginning in 1929 stemmed this tide and apparently prevented Mexico from reconquering peacefully, by an immigrant invasion, the territory it had lost by the decision of war in 1848.

Since the sixteen million residents of Mexico are the nearest large body of people in a position to supply immigrants to the United States and ready to do so, a study of their composition is of the highest importance at the present time. Mexico at the time of the Spanish Conquest had seen the rise and fall of several relatively high native civilizations, and that of the Aztecs, which was destroyed by the Spaniards, had many noteworthy features. The combination of brutality and piety which dominated the conquerors led to the extermination as far as possible of every salient feature of the native culture. The country was, thereafter, exploited ruthlessly by the Spaniards, but the Spanish civilization, such as it was, did not succeed in establishing itself in this foreign soil. The history of the last four centuries has been a history of the gradual absorption of the foreigners by the Indian element. This is true alike of race and culture.

The large native population found here by the Spaniards was quickly reduced in numbers. A Spanish priest enumerates ten plagues which had decimated the people during his time, that is, during the

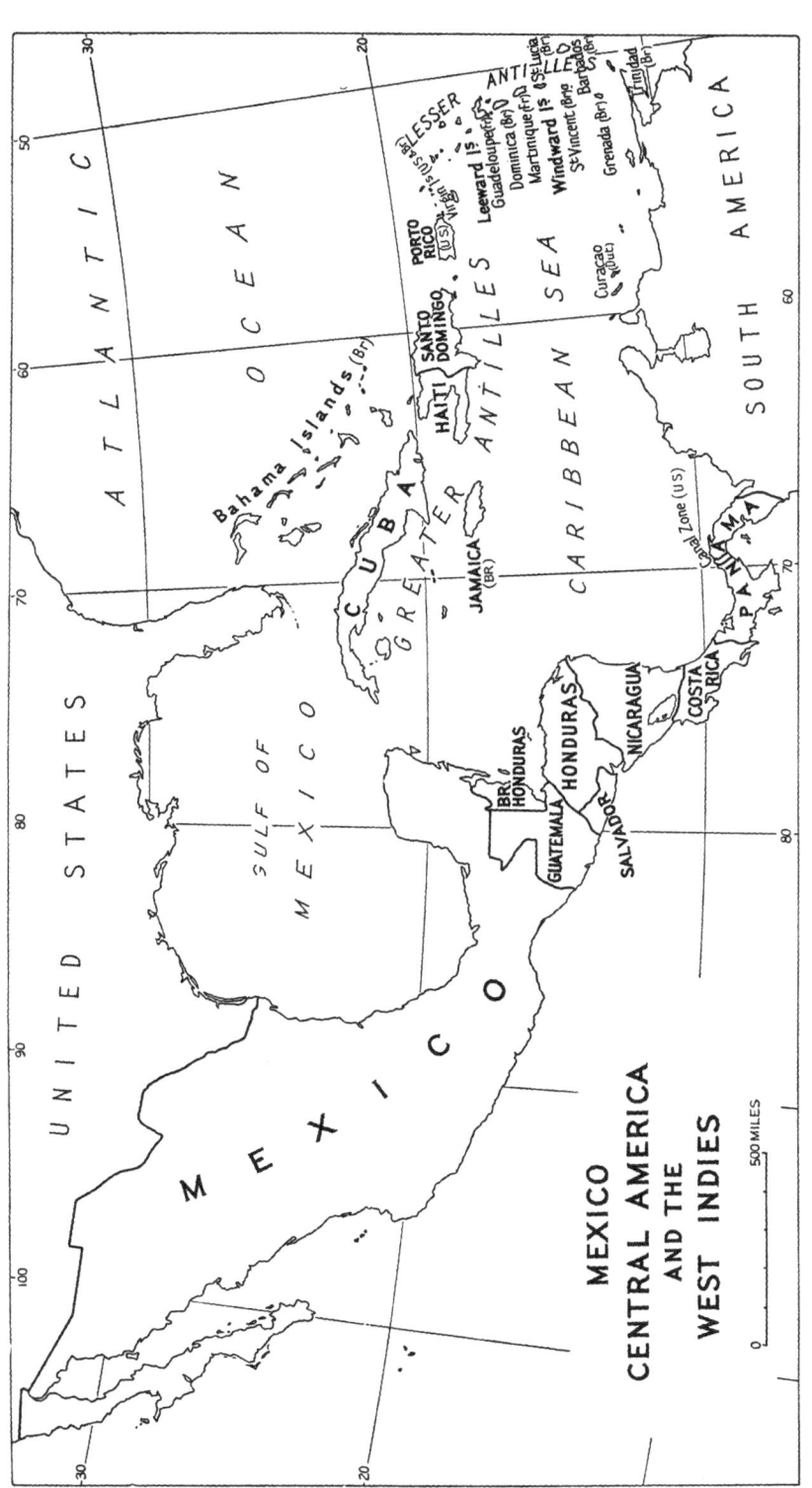

first quarter of a century after the conquest. First the smallpox, brought by a Negro in one of Narvaez' ships. It is said to have destroyed more than half of the people in many of the provinces. The others were: the slaughter in the capture of Mexico City, the famine resulting from the widespread warfare; the abuses of overseers of the towns given in vassalage; the heavy tributes; the tremendous abuses in connection with the mines; the reconstruction of Mexico City by forced labor; the traffic in branded slaves; the abuses of transportation, with Indians as human beasts of burden; and the factional warfare among the Spaniards themselves, in which the Indians bore the brunt of the fighting. To these should be added particularly the other infectious diseases that the Spaniards introduced, such as tuberculosis and syphilis, as to which the aboriginal inhabitants had not the slightest immunity or resistance, through previous racial experience.

Under such conditions the native population of the hemisphere was probably reduced by 50 or 75 per cent in a few generations, and in the West Indies it was exterminated. Since then it has been steadily regaining ground on the mainland, though not in the islands, in many of which the Negro has replaced it.

The number of Spaniards who came at any time to Mexico is placed at 300,000 at the outside. Many of these certainly did not remain in the country and few of them brought their families. Under the conditions that existed in Mexico and the other conquered territories, it was universally recognized that the situation was not suitable for a white woman. While the Spanish Government encouraged men to take their wives out from Spain, few of them cared to do so, and probably most of the men who came to the colonies were unmarried. Spain put insuperable difficulties in the way of unmarried women who wanted to emigrate, so that Spanish women throughout the history of Mexico were few. The resulting population is therefore made up of the offspring of the Indians and of a few Spanish men mated to Indian women. Most of the Mexican population is still pure or nearly pure Indian. There is a considerable hybrid element which does most of the talking, and a negligible element that can be considered white in the strict sense of the term.

Mexican statistics commonly designate about 10 per cent of the population as white. But most of these have much Indian blood, and recent students doubt whether 3 per cent are properly to be described as white. Much of this genuine white element is in Mexico City, though the various states have their local and reputable white aristocracies, of which that in Yucatan is conspicuous for the maintenance of high standards of racial integrity.

The Mexican revolution which began in 1810 dislodged the overseas Spanish and substituted exploitation by the local hybrid group. Since then the general trend has been toward the rise to control of the Indians. The last period of revolution, which began in 1910 and may be said to be still in progress, has been marked by attempts to take away from the hybrid oligarchy the immense land properties which it had obtained and to distribute them to the Indians. While this has met with many difficulties, and has been realized only to a small extent, it has been at least the avowed objective of most of the revolutionists in the past two or three decades.

During recent years there has been a glorification of the Mexican Indian and his culture by North American writers. No doubt the Mexican Indian is well suited to his environment, and his traditional habits are well suited to him. This does not mean, however, that either has any important contribution to make to the United States which would be realized by a northward mass migration of agricultural and industrial serfs. On the contrary, the Mexican immigration to the United States, which is made up overwhelmingly of the poorer Indian element, has brought nothing but disadvantages. It has created, particularly in the Southwestern States, an exploited peasant class unconformable with the principles of American civilization. This population, neither physically nor mentally up to the prevailing standards, is producing a large contribution to the future American race, since every one of its numerous children born in the States becomes an American citizen by birth.

Tests made in the schools of southern California, in which the language handicap was discounted as far as possible, indicate that the average Mexican child was about as far below the average Negro child in abstract intellect as the average Negro child was below the average white child.

Physically, the race is conspicuous by its low resistance to tuberculosis, which has exterminated so large a part of the native population of the Western Hemisphere during the last four centuries. The New World had not been subject to tuberculosis and therefore offered a fertile field for the germs of this disease. The population of the Old World had been ravaged by it for many centuries, and in each generation the low resistants had been killed off so that a more immune stock had been gradually produced by natural selection.

Such studies as have been made in the Southwestern States indicate that the average Mexican family is at least half again as large as the average white family. Thus there is every reason to expect that, without a sharp limitation of such immigration, the Southwest will become more and more Mexicanized.

By 1928 Los Angeles County had more than a quarter of a million Mexicans, and the City of Los Angeles had the largest Mexican population of any city in the world, with the exception of Mexico City. Whole industries and whole agricultural areas had come to think themselves largely dependent on Mexican labor, while millions of American citizens were out of employment in every State of the Union. The dependence of agriculture in the Southwestern States on cheap Mexican labor, largely of a migratory nature, is particularly disastrous from a racial point

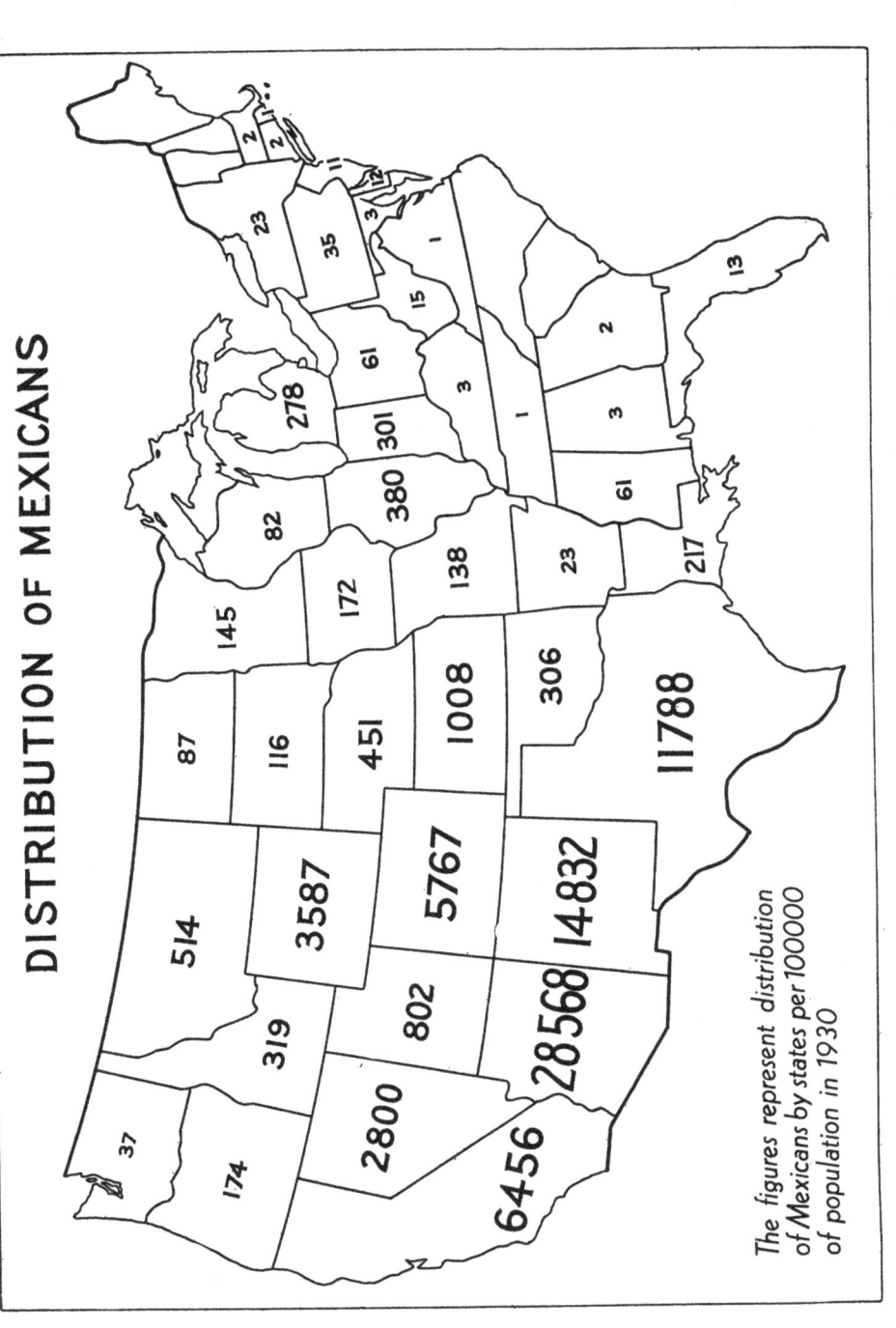

Distribution of Mexicans by States. Except in the border States Mexicans are chiefly concentrated in large urban centers.

of view, since the maintenance of American civilization depends largely on the maintenance of a healthy and prosperous farm population.

Nearly all of the Mexicans who came to the United States were seeking to better themselves economically and to avoid the murder and plunder that had been going on in their country for a score of years under the guise of revolution. Most of them intended to return home as soon as conditions became more satisfactory, but as conditions from year to year failed to improve, the Mexican population tended to become a permanent one. At the same time few of the Mexicans became American citizens, and in every community where they settled in racial groups there were unsatisfactory standards of education and sanitation.

Most of the Mexicans come with their families, thereby differing markedly from some of the other foreign groups, as the Bulgarians, Greeks, Spanish, and Filipinos, which consist mainly of unmarried men. These latter either return home after making money, or else intermarry with the other immigrant groups. The Mexican community, on the other hand, perpetuates itself and increases without much intermarriage with the other population.

Since the depression beginning in 1929 there has been a repatriation of a portion of the Mexican immigration of unknown size but undoubtedly considerable. Lack of work has led many to go home where they can live more economically and be among friends, and at the same time American authorities began to offer free transportation back to Mexico for those dependent on public charity, and willing to leave. Thus trainload after trainload returned, and at the same time a tightening of the immigration restrictions and procedures on the border cut down the flow of immigrants to almost nothing.

While the census of 1930 counted nearly a million and a half Mexicans in the United States, it is probable that the number has since then diminished, and it is of highest importance that it should not be allowed to increase. The Mexican Indian has no racial qualities to contribute to the United States population that are now needed, and if he has any cultural contribution to make it will not be made by the immigration of hundreds of thousands of illiterate and destitute laborers.

Guatemala. More than half of the population of Guatemala is still pure Indian, and the half breed class which plays such an important part in Mexico and other countries is relatively less conspicuous there. The inconsiderable white population is made up in part of the descendants of old Spanish families and in part from more recent immigrants, especially Germans.

The proportion of Teutonic names among the rulers of Guatemala during the last generation has been growing steadily. With two million population Guatemala is the most powerful of the Central American countries, but the Indians tend to be little more than a subject race exploited by others, and the general progress of the country is therefore in some ways slow.

Honduras suffers partly from its tropical situation but still more from the mixture of races, and the large amount of Negro blood in the population of the lowlands. By contrast with Guatemala the Indian element is here unimportant, and the people are Negroes and half-breeds, or a little of each. With its 600,000 population largely of mongrel origin, the Republic has been a backward member of the Central American group throughout most of its history. British Honduras is an unimportant area with much the same characteristics. The so-called Caribs along the coast are now scarcely distinguishable from pure Negroes.

Salvador. Smaller than the State of New Jersey, Salvador has an importance out of proportion to its size because of the dense population and large amount of cultivable land together with a smaller amount of Negro mixture than in the adjoining Republics. With a population estimated at a million and a half (such a thing as a real census is almost unknown in Latin American countries), its people are largely of mixed blood with the Indian predominating, but the number of pure-blooded Indians is not large compared with Guatemala.

Nicaragua, a synonym for turbulence in the minds of Americans, has also a population of highly mixed character. The Indians did not remain a distinct group as in Guatemala, nor were they largely exterminated as in Costa Rica. They were absorbed into a half-breed population of more than 600,000 which has also in the lowlands a large Negro admixture.

The upper classes of more or less remote European ancestry have maintained a semi-feudal political dominance that has been disastrous to the welfare of the country, and it is doubtful whether the Yankee influence, which during the last generation has been stronger in Nicaragua than in any of the other Latin American states except Panama, has been particularly useful.

Costa Rica has always prided itself on being the whitest of the Central American Republics, and its history of relative peace and prosperity reflects this fact. Apart from a fringe of Indians and Negroes in the lowlands, the population of nearly 500,000 is concentrated in a beautiful and healthful inland region. The Indians of the country having been driven out or destroyed at an early day, the settlers of Costa Rica were unable to live as parasites exploiting serfs as did the upper classes in some of the other Central American countries, but were forced to settle on the land and work out their own salvation. While they were therefore considered in colonial days to be in a pitiable situation, the result was highly advantageous in the long run, for it has given the country a more nearly genuine population of citizens prepared to contribute to the progress and welfare of the country.

A large part of the Spanish blood in Costa Rica is supposed to be Galician, and therefore to have a considerable Nordic infusion. The Gallegos, as natives of this part of the Iberian Peninsula are called, are one of the most law-abiding and hard-working of the numerous peoples that comprise the Spanish Republic, and their descendants in Costa Rica reflect credit on their origin. In most of the other Latin American countries the Spanish element is supposed to be largely from Andalusia and therefore quite different in makeup, with a noteworthy Moorish element.

Panama with its hybrid population of half a million, largely Negro in composition, is unimportant in the picture of Latin America. North American influence has transformed it economically, but cannot change mongrels into a sound and vigorous stock.

Colombia has large numbers of Negroes in the hot lowlands, but the bulk of the six million population is Indian with a slight infusion of European blood. The upper class of Colombia represents the results of geographical isolation, the region until recently having been inaccessible; and by virtue of a sort of intellectual inbreeding it has long been the most conservative and least touched by foreign influence of all the Latin American "aristocracies." The upper-class Colombian prides himself with reason on the purity of his Spanish blood, and still lives to a large degree in the memories of the ancient colonial period. In Bogotá there is an intense anti-Negro social sentiment. The isolation of the half-breeds in Colombia has come nearer to producing a new racial group than is to be found elsewhere in Latin America.

Venezuela, in spite of its nearly three million inhabitants, is an unimportant country, largely hybrid with extensive Negro infiltrations. As in many other Latin American countries, the number of Whites is officially put down as about 10 per cent, but as in most such instances it is doubtful whether one resident in fifty can properly be called a white man, except by courtesy.

Guiana. The three Guianas, British, French, and Dutch, represent one of the least attractive parts of South America in almost every way.

British Guiana has 300,000 inhabitants of whom one-third are Negroes, another third Orientals, mostly Hindu, and the remainder is largely made up of crosses between these two elements, of a few thousand native Indians, and of a handful of Whites.

Dutch Guiana has a population well under a hundred thousand, largely Orientals imported to furnish coolie labor and including Hindus, Javanese, and Chinese. There are many Negroes and a couple of thousand Whites.

French Guiana differs from the Dutch settle-

OUR NEIGHBORS ON THE SOUTH 335

ment mainly in being smaller, its population being not much more than 30,000, including many convicts or ex-convicts, for this has long been a French penal settlement.

Brazil with a territory larger than the continental United States differs from its neighbors in many striking ways, apart from the fact that it was settled by Portuguese, not Spanish, and that its language and culture are therefore Portuguese rather than Spanish.

The Indian population was killed off or driven westward by the early settlers just as in the United States, so that it is now confined largely to the untracked and almost unpopulated forests of the Amazonian Basin, where perhaps a couple of a million aborigines may still exist.

To provide labor the Portuguese imported slaves from Africa, and then fused with them to produce the present-day predominantly Negro population. The Portuguese here thus repeated the experience of the mother country. During the great years of Portuguese exploration and colonization in the fifteenth, sixteenth, and seventeenth centuries, it has been estimated that a million Portuguese, mainly young men, went to the tropics, and for the most part never came back. Negroes were imported to take their places and to do the work of the country. Intermarriage of these Negroes with the old population left Portugal with a larger amount of Negro blood than any other European country, and greatly impaired its ability to contribute to the progress of civilization. Thus Portugal, which, when dominated by the Nordics, had set an extraordinary example of progress in many ways, now contributes relatively little to such progress and only the rebirth of a reasonable pride of race, and the application of a sound eugenics program will enable it to regain a position of leadership.

History has repeated itself in Brazil. The salvation of Brazil has been the arrival during the past century of European immigrants. Thousands of Germans poured into the Highlands of the Southern States where large regions have an almost Teutonic civilization at the present time. If a false interpretation of the Monroe Doctrine had not helped to interfere with this process, the results for South America might have been most beneficial.

But the main currents of immigration have been from Latin countries of the Old World. During the past century Brazil has received more than four million foreigners, of whom a million and a half were Italians, a million and a quarter Portuguese, and half a million Spanish. Thus more than three-fourths of the immigration has been from the Latin countries, and only about a quarter of a million from Germany and Austria. Since the World War this overwhelming migration from the Latin countries has slowed down. The German migration has, on the contrary, increased.

Brazil thus consists of two distinct areas: a relatively small, fertile, and healthful highland region in the south, where the main activities of the country are carried on largely under the influence of Mediterranean and Alpine immigrants; and a huge tropical area given over mainly to the Negro and Mulatto element and the Indians.

With a population of somewhere around 30,000,000 Brazil is not only the largest of the South American republics, but nearly as large as all the rest of them put together.

The future of Brazil depends largely on the nature of its immigration policy during the next generation or two and on the acceptance of a workable program of eugenics. Fortunately, no South American country has taken up such a policy with more interest than has this great republic. It still possesses an aristocracy which has maintained its racial purity, but this is probably too small a nucleus alone to regenerate the whole body politic.

Uruguay. Crossing the boundary from Brazil to Uruguay, one sees a new picture. Uruguay is almost entirely white. Indeed, this whole region of La Plata is one of the future dominant areas of the New World. It contains less Negro blood than does, relatively, the United States. Not only have Negroes been largely kept out, but the remnants of Indian tribes have become inconspicuous, as on the plains of the Mississippi Valley, where the Indians, mere nomads with a negligible culture, were driven back by the march of civilization. The striking parallel between the settlement of this region and that of the Western States of North America is often pointed out. Each was a sheep and cattle country, and then farmers took up land and developed it into a region of prosperity and great potentialities.

Uruguay has a cosmopolitan population almost wholly of European origin. Since the World War it has attracted not only a large part of the Spanish emigration but also large numbers of Italians, French, Germans, and others. The earlier immigration was largely of North Italians, mainly of Alpine blood with slight Nordic infusion. The total population of the country is now well over a million and a half.

A wise selection of immigration from now on will still further increase the influence of this small republic, and set a good example for all of South America.

Argentina represents one of the striking examples of a nation built up rapidly by foreign immigration. Nearly 85 per cent of its people are foreign-born or the descendants of recent immigration, with Italians forming by far the largest group. Moreover, the Argentine Republic has attracted the vigorous population of North Italy, which racially is mainly Alpine but still has a Nordic element, and forms a striking contrast to the population of South Italian and Sicilian immigrants that have filled up the slums of North American cities. The North Italians are more akin to the Swiss and the South Germans than they are to the South Italians.

Non-whites do not amount to 5 per cent of the population. The total population of something like 10,000,000 makes the Argentine Republic second only to Brazil in size in South America, and in every respect, except size, it easily takes first rank.

The racial composition of this extraordinary nation with its ultra-modern civilization, and its get-rich-quick atmosphere, deserves more extended treatment than can be given here. The English, though not the most numerous, have taken the first place in its financial world. French immigrants, though fewer in number, have become a very important factor in the progress of its civilization. A hundred thousand Germans have settled in the country and form the backbone of many regions.

Since the war Argentina has been one of the principal destinations of citizens of the former Central Empires who were going overseas. The spirit of the civilization has attracted many Jews. More than 160,000 immigrants during the last two generations are credited to Russia, and almost an equal number to Turkey. These last, however, were Turks only by force and were actually Christian Syrians from the Lebanon who became so completely identified with the retail trade of the country that the colloquial name for a small grocery store is "Turco."

All of these elements together do not begin to measure in importance with the Spanish and Italian elements. But in recent years new currents have set in which, if continued, will profoundly modify the character of the country by introducing a large number of Slavs, particularly Poles, Yugoslavs, Czechoslovaks, and Lithuanians, together with the Slavic element among the Germans. Before the World War the immigration to Argentina was about seven-eighths from the Latin countries, but since then these have furnished only about two-thirds.

Argentina therefore represents a white population largely Alpine and Mediterranean with a considerable Nordic element. It is doubtful whether it stands to gain by allowing Alpines to increase, particularly if this brings in different types of culture and traditions. Argentina might well profit by the mistakes of the United States and immediately orient its immigration policy along sound logical and constructive lines.

Chile, unlike the Indo-Spanish countries just south of the United States, is also a white man's country. The pure Indians are a vanishing minority. The Spanish and dominant element is largely made up of Basques, but there has been a substantial addition of British, whose influence is important in commerce and industry, and of Germans, who have dominated the army and education, and have been an important factor in agriculture. Chile, with four million population, is therefore the least Latin of any of the countries south of the United States. The progressiveness and prosperity of the region have long attracted the attention of every traveller.

Bolivia is another of the predominantly Indian

countries which have made little contribution to the world. The number of Whites here is negligible. Immigration has never been important and the Bolivian has developed a provincial arrogance and hostility to foreigners which is as prejudicial to his own interests as it is unwarranted. Scarcely one-fifth of the people even speak Spanish in their daily life, and two-thirds are primitive Indians, the others being hybrids of varying degrees.

Paraguay is an Indian republic which has not only avoided the Negro influence common elsewhere but has almost escaped the infusion of white blood. There are scarcely any pure Whites. The Guarani Indians of this region were not highly civilized like the Mayas and Incas, and therefore took on a Spanish culture instead of retaining one of their own. It would have been extremely interesting to see what an Indian republic could amount to in the nineteenth and twentieth centuries. Unfortunately the course of experiment was obstructed by one of the most sanguinary wars in history (1864–69) in which Paraguay carried on a contest with Brazil and Argentina until the greater part of its male population was destroyed. At the beginning of the war, the population of Paraguay was officially said to be 1,-337,437. Even if this were extraordinarily inaccurate and exaggerated, the figures afterward were no less so, for the calculation after the close of hostilities credited the country with a loss of more than a million. More exactly, the population was returned as 221,709, of which 86,079 were children, 106,254 women, and only 28,746 men. Nothing like this situation has ever before been recorded in a large population. Whole regiments had been made up of boys under sixteen. In more than half a century since then, the country has not begun to recover. Even now its population is less than a million. Immigrants from Europe have always avoided it. Paraguay is in a class by itself.

Peru's four or five million inhabitants are mostly pure Indians, while the remainder are nearly all hybrids. Chinese and Japanese as well as Negroes have contributed to the mongrelization of the mass, and not one in ten even claims to be white, which here, as elsewhere in Latin America, by no means guarantees anything more than a homœopathic dose of European blood.

The aboriginal civilization is often described as remarkably high but seems to have been the work of peoples who antedated the Spanish by a long period; and the Conquerors themselves apparently considered the Peruvian Indians to be less intelligent than those they had encountered in Mexico. The number of Indians decreased during the early Spanish regime until some districts were almost depopulated and the loss of leaders especially was irreparable. Whether or not the present inhabitants are the descendants of the Incas, they have not been able to develop a strong and progressive state.

Ecuador is an isolated and unimportant re-

OUR NEIGHBORS ON THE SOUTH

gion inhabited largely by backward Indian tribes. Probably not less than two-thirds of the 2,000,000 population are pure Indian. The handful of Whites and the few hundred thousand hybrids rule the country. The Negro element, never large, is gradually being absorbed and is leaving its stamp on the whole population.

The West Indies are more important to the United States immigration policy than would be expected from their size, because of their close proximity to American ports of entry.

Cuba has always received its immigrants predominantly from Spain, and the imported Negro element, numbering about 800,000 of its three millions of population, is not increasing in importance. The island is considered less white than Puerto Rico, but more than a quarter of a million of the inhabitants are Spanish-born, these comprising nearly three-quarters of all the foreigners.

As in many other Latin-American countries, the Chinese have taken a strong hold, beginning nearly a century ago, and are intermarrying with the Whites.

Cuba does not represent a desirable or needed source of immigration to the United States, and should be put under a proper quota.

Puerto Rico has a population of nearly a million and a half. The fact that this dense population cannot make a living under the present and backward conditions on the island, and that it is continually exercising its right of entry to the United States, is one of the most serious features of the present immigration policy.

The Negro and Mulatto element makes up a majority of the population but is relatively losing ground—partly from high death rates and partly by absorption in the mass. The Indian stock is extinct. Immigration from abroad has been negligible for a long time.

As the island is a territory, the inhabitants are citizens of the United States and cannot be prevented from coming freely into the mainland. The number of Puerto Ricans in New York City was at one time estimated as high as 100,000. If economic conditions are attractive there is nothing to prevent half a million of them from migrating to the continent and adding their traits to the much-overloaded "melting pot."

It is now clear that the United States made a great mistake, after the war with Spain, in taking over territories that were already populated by aliens. Previously the territory that was acquired was largely empty and suitable for settlement by the old stock. What has been done is not easy to undo, but it may at least serve as an emphatic lesson against any further acquisitions of inhabited territory in the future. Meanwhile there is an embryonic movement for independence in Puerto Rico, which may have to,

OUR NEIGHBORS ON THE SOUTH 345

indeed should, be encouraged in order to give the United States protection from its own folly.

The Virgin Islands, which the United States bought from Denmark in 1917, have, like other West Indian islands, a population almost exclusively Negro or Mulatto.

The British West Indies are overwhelmingly black, though many of them, such as New Providence, Barbados, Bermuda, and the Bahamas, have substantial English aristocracies that guard jealously their racial heritage. These British islands, particularly Jamaica and Barbados (the latter one of the most densely populated spots in the whole world) have been fertile sources of black emigration to other islands and to the mainland.

Haiti is a purely Negro Republic, and offers a good illustration of what the Negro accomplishes if left to himself, even though given all the advantages of easy access to European civilization. The republic of Santo Domingo occupies the other part of the same island; its hybrid population has more Spanish and less Negro blood but it is not by any means civilized.

In general the islands of the West Indies now contain nearly 8,000,000 people, the descendants of Negro slaves with a very small but undiscoverable admixture of Indian blood and a somewhat larger but still unimportant admixture of European stock. They present a standing menace to the United States immigration policy, and afford one of the principal arguments for extending stringent restrictions to the Western Hemisphere. The whole Caribbean is in the process of becoming a Negro territory. Such a result may be inevitable, but adjacent nations which desire to remain white must protect themselves while there is time.

In broad outline, the picture of Latin-America is the picture of a diversified region occupied by some 80,000,000 people, mainly Indians, but with varying proportions of White and Negro blood, the former usually small in amount, the latter often large. The few countries that may properly be called white are not emigrant-exporting countries, and their inhabitants are for the most part non-Nordic, therefore not particularly well adapted to incorporation in the United States.

In conclusion, it may be remarked at this point that each successive revolution in Latin America has tended toward hastening the elimination of European blood and influence. It is usually the half-breeds who revolt and they, in turn, are subject to the increasing self-assertion of the pure native.

XVIII

THE NORDIC OUTLOOK

In the preceding chapters we have seen the unity of the nation greatly impaired in race and religion and threatened in language, but the country is still 70 per cent Nordic and 80 per cent Protestant, and no one foreign language seriously threatens our English speech. There are nearly 50 per cent of Old-Native American Whites in the country at large, although they have been swamped by aliens in New England and in the industrialized States of the Northeast.

The great majority of the senators of the United States are still of old American stock and so are the members of the House of Representatives. The leaders of the nation in science, education, industry, and in the Army and Navy are still overwhelmingly Nordic, so that with these elements in our favor we are still in a position to check the increase of the other elements and contend against their deleterious effects upon our institutions.

Much of the immigration during the last century has been identical with the old British stock in all respects. The English and the Scotch who have come over here, as well as the Scandinavians and most of the Germans, and perhaps some other elements, are to be regarded as reinforcements of the older stock. On the other hand, most of the people from southern and eastern Europe must be regarded as distinct menaces to our national unity.

The remedy is first and foremost *the absolute* suspension of all immigration from all countries; and the signs of the times indicate that such suspension is inevitable. Such a total suspension of immigration would remove all grounds for charges of discrimination against Asiatics, which now embarrass our foreign relations. At the very least, the same quota limitations should be imposed on the countries to the south of us as are enforced against Europe.

In view of the fact that during the great depression which began in 1929 we had millions of unemployed of our own people here, we should be deaf to sentimental pleas for the admission of relatives of any kind. If families are separated, it has not been through the fault of the American people, and the immigrant can return whence he came, if he wishes to join his family. As a matter of fact, it is only one or two groups which are so vigorously clamoring for the admission of relatives.

Not only should European immigration be entirely stopped but still more, all immigration of every sort from countries to the south of us should be barred. In the islands and on the coasts of the Caribbean, and in Mexico and in Central America, to say nothing of the countries farther south, we have a vast reservoir of Negroes, and of Indians in the interior, who sooner or later will be drawn toward

THE NORDIC OUTLOOK 349

the United States by the high wages of common labor. The strictest legislation at this time is necessary to prevent this impending invasion before it assumes the dimensions of a flood, such as has already happened in the case of the Mexican Indians. If immigration be not absolutely prohibited, at very least, no one should be allowed to enter the United States, unless a visitor or traveller, except white men of superior intellectual capacity distinctly capable of becoming valuable American citizens.

The law of 1790 providing that no one could become a citizen of the United States except free Whites was the law until the aftermath of the Civil War added the word "black" or "of African descent" to those who could be naturalized. This last provision should be repealed and the blacks with the South American and Central American Indians put on the same footing as the Orientals.

All Filipino immigration should be stopped before it becomes a serious menace. If possible, half-breeds from Hawaii should not be allowed entry and absolute restriction should be placed on the entrance of Negroes and Mulattoes from Puerto Rico. There are now swarms of them in the Harlem District of New York. This last is simple justice to the American Negroes.

The increasing use of machines calls for less and less common labor, and even in normal times there will be a surplus of man power for the factories and the farms. Why should outsiders be allowed to come in and take the jobs and lower the living standards of American labor? This is one of the greatest questions before the American people and the depression following 1929 has brought this truth home.

We have now in this country over five million aliens who are not citizens, more than a million of whom are said to be illegally here. These last should be deported as fast as they can be located and funds made available. There can be no better means of relieving unemployment present or future than by such wholesale deportation. We should begin with those aliens who have violated our laws or who have become public charges and all such, now in our penitentiaries and asylums, should be deported forthwith. When that has been done and done fully, it should be followed by the deportation of unemployed aliens.

Registration is necessary for the carrying out of any proper system of deportation. Why any one should object to registration as a proper means of identification is a mystery, unless there is a sinister motive behind the desire to conceal identity.

A storm of protest will arise from the vociferous and influential foreign blocs and from the radicals and half-breeds claiming to be Americans, who will all rush to the defense of their kind. It is strange to find how sensitive we are to any foreign criticism of things American, but how prone we are to listen respectfully to local aliens, who are urging their own interests at the expense of the national welfare.

In order to curb the influence of these aliens and to prevent their pernicious control by politicians, it would also be wise to suspend all naturalization for a generation at least. Our citizenship in the past has been made of little value by the absurd way that it has been thrust upon foreigners. Nothing can be more ill-advised politically than the Americanization programs of some worthy people. An American is not made by conferring upon him the franchise, but by the alien's voluntary and genuine acceptance of our language, laws, institutions, and cultural traditions.

Even though the foregoing program were put into effect, which would, possibly, be a "Counsel of Perfection," we would still have with us an immense mass of Negroes and nearly as many southern and eastern Europeans, intellectually below the standard of the average American. The proper extension to and use by these undesirable classes of a knowledge of birth control may be in the future of substantial benefit, and the practice of sterilization of the criminal and the intellectually unfit, now legally established in twenty-seven States, can be resorted to with good result.

The fundamental question for this nation, as well as for the world at large, is for the community itself to regulate births by depriving the unfit of the opportunity of leaving behind posterity of their own debased type. Our civilization has mercifully put an end to the cruel, wasteful, and indiscriminate destruction of the unfit by Nature, wherefore it is our duty, as exponents of that civilization, to substitute scientific control, that civilization itself may be maintained. Down to date the American stock has only just begun to intermarry with the immigrant stock. When this process has gone further—and it will go further—it will be more difficult to control the destinies of the nation. It is therefore the duty of all Americans, and such of the immigrant stock as are in sympathy with them, to face the problem boldly and to take all eugenic means to encourage the multiplication of desirable types and abate drastically the increase of the unfit and miscegenation by widely diverse races.

So much for our internal problems. The problems outside of our country are a different matter. In the last century the world has grown smaller, and, perhaps, in the long run America must take her part in international affairs.

The White Man's Burden

As Americans we are faced with the necessity of assuming our share of a burden which has been carried by Great Britain for the last three centuries—that is "the White Man's Burden,"—the duty of policing the world and maintaining the prestige of the white man throughout the Seven Seas. Due to the change in the industrial situation all over the world and to the spread of the fatal sentimentalism of the Anglo-Saxon, the lower races in Europe and elsewhere are beginning to assert themselves. Everywhere from one end of the world to the other is heard the cry of self-determination.

THE NORDIC OUTLOOK

Americans already have much the same problem in the Philippines.

The attitude of the Imperial Government in London toward the native races in its various Dominions has been in the past and still is not unlike that of the Federal Government in Washington toward the Negroes in our Southern States.

Americans must sympathize with the firm resolve of the handful of white men in South Africa (less than a million and a half) to control and regulate the Negro population there—numbering some seven millions and in the midst of which they live. The same problem arises in Australia and New Zealand where the Whites are determined that their civilization shall not be swamped by Orientals.

We must also sympathize with the Whites in Kenya Colony in their opposition to a filling of their country with cheap Hindu labor. As Americans we can understand the Negro and recognize his cheerful qualities, but we can have little sympathy with the Hindu whom we have expressly barred from our Pacific Coast. These Hindus, with the Chinese, have ruined the native races of many of the Polynesian Islands. They have been for ages in contact with the highest civilizations, but have failed to benefit by such contact, either physically, intellectually, or morally.

Similar dangers exist on the Pacific Coast of Canada. The struggle for the maintenance of the supremacy of the white man over the native, or for that matter over the non-European, until now has been maintained by Great Britain alone. Her ruling class has given the world the greatest example since the days of Rome, of a just, fearless, and unselfish government, but apparently the native does not desire such a government.

The old imperial instinct that enabled Great Britain to retain control of the white man's world appears to be coming to an end. The weary Titan seems willing to turn over the burden of government to the Dominions as fast as the latter demand it. This is evidenced also by the proposal to give up the naval base at Singapore. If this base is ever actually abandoned, it means England's withdrawal from the supremacy of the Pacific. In such event, whether we Americans like it or not—whether we intend it or not—the burden of the control of the Pacific will pass in great measure to America. The future lies in the Pacific rather than in the Atlantic, and with the completion of the Panama Canal, America is brought face to face with Oriental problems.

Australia and New Zealand, still more British Columbia, look for co-operation and leadership to the United States as well as to Great Britain, and we must be prepared to accept this responsibility.

We have our own troubles in respect to the Philippines. The swarming of the Filipinos into the Pacific States brings with it a repetition of the Chinese problem of sixty years ago. California is determined that the white man there shall not be replaced by the Chinese, the Japanese, the Mexican, or the Filipino. The Eastern States should face this problem understandingly, and recognize the simple fact that the white men on the Pacific Coast of the United States and Canada are determined to maintain a white ownership of the country, even though the East has been willing to see New England swamped by French-Canadians and Polaks, and the industrial centers of the North filled to overflowing with southern and eastern Europeans.

When we talk about the maintenance of the white man's ideals and culture and about the supremacy of the white man, we are talking about two distinct things. One is the determination of the white man to keep for himself his own countries, the United States, Great Britain, Canada, South Africa, Australia, New Zealand, and many of the smaller islands. With this determination Americans sympathize and sooner or later we may be called on to help protect the White race and the English language in these countries. It seems to be a part of our destiny. The other phase of white supremacy is the white man's effort to benefit the backward races and raise them to civilization by instilling his language, his religion, and his culture into Asiatics and Africans. This is the tendency of foreign missions, and it leads sooner or later to a challenge by the natives of the control of the Whites.

To rule justly, as the English have in India and Burma, is for the best interest of the native. For example, the United States should either firmly govern the Philippines, which, in the last analysis, is for the interest and enrichment of the Filipinos, or else abandon them to their own devices. If Japan ever gets hold of these islands, she will keep them without regard to the wishes or interests of the native, as that Empire is not greatly troubled with sentimentalists and native sympathizers such as flourish in the United States.

The Japanese, the Chinese, the Hindus, and the Moslems have cultures, customs, religions, arts, literatures, and institutions of their own, which for them may be, and in many cases probably are, as good as our own. The writer does not see any gain in destroying these native elements of culture or replacing them indiscriminately with the institutions of the white man to which those races are, for the most part, unfitted. Democracy is an excellent example. It simply will not work among Asiatics. In fact, its success is yet fully to be proven in the Western World.

But the other side of the problem—whether we, the White race, shall surrender our own culture, our own lands and our own traditions, good or bad, to another race—presents a very different question. Fortunately, in this case, Reason and Sentiment march hand in hand.

The prestige and strength of Europe and Great Britain have been greatly impaired since the World War and Western civilization sooner or later may be forced to hand on the Torch to America.

We see the Nordics again confronted across the Pacific by their immemorial rivals, the Mongols. This will be the final arena of the struggle between these two major divisions of man for world dominance and the Nordic race in America may find itself bearing the main brunt.

In the meantime, the Nordic race, that has built up, protected, and preserved Western civilization, needs to realize the necessity of its own solidarity and close co-operation. Upon this mutual understanding rest the peace of the world and the preservation of its civilization.

Let us take thought as to how we can best prepare for our share of the task before us—that is, bear our share of the White Man's Burden.

BIBLIOGRAPHY

Abbott, John S. C., *Peter Stuyvesant.* New York, Dodd, Mead & Co., 1898.
Adams, Alexander A., *The Plateau Peoples of South America.* (An Essay in Ethnic Psychology.) New York, Geo. Routledge & Sons, Ltd., 1915.
Adams, James Truslow, *The Founding of New England.* Boston, Atlantic Monthly Press, 1921.
———, *The March of Democracy.* New York, Charles Scribner's Sons, 1932-33.
———, *New England in the Republic,* 1776-1850. Boston, Little Brown, 1926.
———, *Provincial Society,* 1690-1763. New York, Macmillan Co., 1927. Vol. III of series entitled *A History of American Life.*
———, *Revolutionary New England,* 1691-1776. Boston, Atlantic Monthly Press, 1923.
Alsina, Juan A., *European Immigration to the Argentine,* 1898.
American Council of Learned Societies, *Report of the committee on linguistic and national stocks in the population of the United States.* Washington, D. C., 1932. (Reprint from annual report of the American Historical Association for 1931, pp. 107-441.)
Arber, Edw. (ed.), *Story of the Pilgrim Fathers.* Boston, Houghton Mifflin Co., 1897.
Arbois de Jubainville, M. H. d': 1. "Les Celts en Espagne," *Revue Celtique,* Vols. XIV and XV.
———, 2. "Les Celts et les langues celtiques," *Revue archéologique,* série 2, t. XLIII, pp. 87-96, 141-155.
———, 3. "Les Gaulois dans l'Italie du Nord," *Rev. Celt.,* Vol. XI.
Avebury, Lord (Sir John Lubbock), *Prehistoric Times,* 7th ed. New York, Henry Holt & Co.; London, Williams and Norgate, 1864-1913.
Avery, Elroy McKendree, *A History of the United States and Its People.* Cleveland, Burroughs Bros., 1905.

Babcock, Kendrick Charles, *The Scandinavian Element in the U. S.* Urbana, University of Illinois, 1914.

Baily, John, Esq., *Central America*. London, Trelawney Saunders, 1850.
Bancroft, Hubert Howe, *History of Arizona and New Mexico, 1530–1888*, Vol. XVII. San Francisco, The History Co., 1889.
——, *History of California*, 4 vols. San Francisco, A. L. Bancroft & Co., 1884, 1885, 1886.
——, *History of Oregon*, 2 vols. San Francisco, The History Co., 1886.
——, *History of Washington, Idaho, and Montana*. San Francisco, The History Co., 1890.
Barker, Eugene C. (ed.), *Readings in Texas History*. Dallas, Southwest Press, 1929.
Barker, Howard F., "The Founders of New England." American Historical Review 38 (4): 702–713. July, 1933.
Bassanovitch, I., *Materials on the Anthropology of the Bulgars: The Lomsk District*, pp. 3–186, 1891.
Beard, Charles and Mary, *Rise of American Civilization*. New York, Macmillan, 1927.
Beddoe, John: 1. *The Anthropological History of Europe*, 1893.
——, 2. "The Kelts of Ireland," *Journal of Anthropology*, 1870–1871, pp. 117–131.
——, 3. "On the Stature and Bulk of Man in the British Isles," *Memoirs of the Anthropological Society*, Vol. III, pp. 384–573. London, 1867–1869.
——, 4. *The Races of Britain*. Bristol and London, 1885.
Bertrand, Alexandre (with S. Reinach), *Les Celts dans les vallées du Pô et du Danube*. Paris, E. Leroux, 1894.
Binder, Julius, *Die Plebs*. Leipzig, G. Bohme, Deichert, 1909.
Biographical and Historical Memoirs of Northeast Arkansas. Chicago, Goodspeed, 1889.
Blackmar, Frank W. (ed.), *Kansas*. Chicago, Standard Pub., 1912.
Blegen, Theodore C., *Norwegian Migration to America*. Northfield, Minnesota, Norwegian American Historical Assn., 1931.
Boam, Henry J., *British Columbia*. London, Sells Ltd., 1912.
Boni, G. Roma, *Notizie degli Sclavi;* série 5, pp. 123 seq. and 375 seq., 1903.

BIBLIOGRAPHY

Bork, Ferdinand, *Die Mitanni Sprache.* Berlin, W. Peiser, 1909.
Boule, M., "Essai de paléontologie stratigraphique de l'homme," *Revue d'anthropologie*, série 3, t. III, pp. 129–144, 272–297, 385–411, 647–680, 1888.
Bourinot, Sir John G., *Canada under British Rule, 1760–1900.* Cambridge, Massachusetts, University Press, 1900.
Bracq, Jean Charlemagne, *The Evólution of French Canada.* New York, The Macmillan Company, 1924.
Breasted, James H.: 1. *Ancient Times, A History of the World.* Boston, Ginn & Co., 1916.
———, 2. "The Origins of Civilization," *Scientific Monthly*, vols. IX, nos. 4, 5, 6, and X, nos. 1, 2, 3.
———, 3. *A Survey of the Ancient World.* Boston, Ginn & Co., 1919.
———, 4. *History of Egypt,* and other writings.
Bresette, Linna E., *Mexicans in the United States: Report of a Brief Survey.* Washington, D. C., Natl. Catholic Welfare Conf., 1929.
Breuil, L'Abbé H., "Les peintures rupestres d'Espagne," (avec Serrano Gomez et Cabre Aguilo), *L'Anthropologie,* t. XXIII, 1912.
Brewer, Daniel Chauncey, *The Conquest of New England by the Immigrant.* New York, Putnam's Sons, 1926.
Brown, John Henry, *History of Texas,* 2 vols. St. Louis, L. E. Daniell.
Browne, William Hand, *Maryland, The History of a Palatinate.* Boston, Houghton Mifflin Co., 1890.
Bruce, Philip Alexander, LL.B., LLD., *History of Virginia,* 1607–1763, vol. I. Chicago and New York, American Historical Society, 1924.
———, *Institutional History of Virginia.* New York, G. P. Putnam's Sons, 1910.
Bruhnes, Jean, "Race et nation," *Le Correspondant.* Paris, September, 1917.
Bryce, George, *The Remarkable History of the Hudson Bay Company.* New York, Scribner, 1900.
Bryce, James, *The Holy Roman Empire.* Macmillan, 1904.
Buck, Solon, *Illinois in 1818.* Springfield, Illinois Centennial Commission, 1917.
Bureau of the Census: Reports on Population.

Burke, U. R., *A History of Spain*, 2d ed. London, Longmans, Green & Co., 1900.
Burrage, Henry S., D.D., *The Beginnings of Colonial Maine*, Portland, Me., Marks Printing House, 1914.
Bury, J. B., *A History of Greece*. Macmillan, 1917.

Cable, George W., *The Creoles of Louisiana*. New York, Charles Scribner's Sons, 1889.
Cahun, Léon, *Histoire de l'Asie*. Paris, Armand Colin et Cie., 1896.
Caldwell, Bishop R., *A Comparative Grammar of the Dravidian or South Indian Family of Languages*, 2d ed. London, K. Paul, Trench, Trübner & Co., 1913.
Campbell, Charles, *Introduction to the History of the Colony and Ancient Dominion of Virginia*. Richmond, B. B. Minor, 1847.
Candolle, Alphonse de, *Histoire des sciences et des savants depuis deux siècles*, 2me éd. Genève, H. Georg, 1806–1893.
Carpenter, Niles, *Immigrants and Their Children*. Census Monographs VII. Washington, D. C., Bureau of the Census, 1927.
Cartailhac, Émile, *La France préhistorique d'après les sépultures et les monuments*, 2me éd. Paris, 1903.
Castle, William E., *Genetics and Eugenics*. Cambridge, Harvard University Press, 1930. 4th ed.
Cattell, J. McKeen, "A Statistical Study of American Men of Science," *Science*, N.S., vol. XXIV, nos. 621–623, and vol. XXXII, nos. 827 and 828.
Chambers, Henry E., *Mississippi Valley Beginnings*. New York, G. P. Putnam's Sons, 1922.
Chantre, Ernest, "Recherches anthropologiques dans l'Asie occidentale," *Extrait des Archives du musée d'histoire naturelle de Lyon*. Lyon, 1895.
Claiborne, J. F. H., *Mississippi as a Province, Territory, and State*, vol. I. Jackson, Mississippi, Power & Barksdale, 1880.
Clay, Albert T., *The Empire of the Amorites*. Yale University Press, 1919.
Cleland, Robert Glass, Ph.D., *A History of California* (The American Period). New York, The Macmillan Co., 1930.
Clemenceau, Georges, *South America To-day*. New York and London, G. Putnam & Sons, 1911.

Coan, Charles F., Ph.D., *A History of New Mexico*, vol. I. Chicago and New York, The American Historical Society, Inc., 1925.
Cobb, Sanford H., *The Story of the Palatines*. New York and London, G. P. Putnam's Sons, 1897.
Cole, Arthur Charles, *The Era of the Civil War*. Springfield, Illinois Centennial Commission, 1919.
Cole, Cyrenus, *A History of the People of Iowa*. Cedar Rapids, Torch Press, 1921.
Collignon, R.: 1. "L'anthropologie au conseil de révision, etc.," *Bulletin de la Société d'anthropologie*, pp. 736–805, 1890. Also *Bull. Soc. d'anth.*, 1883.
———, 2. "Anthropologie de la France: Dordogne, Charente, Creuse, Corrèze, Haute-Vienne," *Mémoires de la Société d'anthropologie*, série 3, I, fasc. 3, pp. 3–79.
———, 3. "L'indice céphalique des populations françaises," *L'Anth.*, série I, pp. 200–224, 1890.
Committee on Immigration and Naturalization, House of Representatives. Hearings, especially 67th Cong., 3d session; 68th Cong., 1st session; 69th Cong., 1st session; 70th Cong., 1st session and 2d session; 72d Cong., 1st session. (A valuable series of reports, containing testimony of H. H. Laughlin and other experts.) Washington, D. C., Government Printing Office, 1923–1932.
Conklin, Edwin G., *Heredity and Environment*. Princeton University Press, 1929. 6th ed.
Cooke, John Esten, *Virginia, A History of the People*. Boston, Houghton Mifflin Co., 1887.
Cotterill, R. S., *History of Pioneer Kentucky*. Cincinnati, Johnson & Hardin, 1917.
Cowan, Helen I., *British Emigration to British North America, 1783–1837*. University of Toronto Library, 1928.
Coy, Owen Cochran, *The Great Trek*. Chicago, Powell Pub. Co.
Crawford, O. G. S., "Distribution of Early Bronze Age Settlements in Britain," *Geographical Journal*, XL, pp. 184 seq., 1912.

Darwin, Charles, *The Descent of Man*, 2d ed. London, John Murray, 1901.
Davenport, Charles B.: 1. *The Feebly Inhibited, Nomadism . . . Inheritance of Temperament*. Washington, D. C., Carnegie Institution, 1915.

——, 2. *Heredity in Relation to Eugenics.* New York, Henry Holt & Co., 1911.
Davidson, Alex., and Stuvé, Bernard, *A Complete History of Illinois* from 1673 to 1873. Springfield, Illinois Journal Co., 1874.
Davis, John, *Travels in Louisiana and the Floridas in the Year 1802.* New York, I. Riley Co., 1806.
Davis, Walter B., *History of Missouri.* St. Louis, Hall & Co., 1876.
Dawkins, W. Boyd, *Early Man in Britain.* London, Macmillan, 1880.
Deniker, J., "Les races de l'Europe, Note préliminaire," *L'anthropologie,* vol. IX, pp. 113–133. Paris, 1898.
Dill, Samuel, *Roman Society in the Last Century of the Western Empire,* 2d ed. Macmillan, 1906.

Eginhard, *Life of Charlemagne,* Glaister translation. London, George Bell & Sons, 1877.
Esarey, Logan, *A History of Indiana,* vol. II. Indianapolis, Bowen, 1918.
——, *A History of Indiana from Its Exploration to 1850.* Indianapolis, W. K. Stewart, 1915.

Fairbanks, *History of Florida,* 1512–1842. Philadelphia, J. B. Lippincott & Co., 1871.
Fanning, John William, Negro Migration. Bull. Univ. Georgia, June, 1930.
Farish, Thomas Edwin: 1. *History of Arizona,* vol. III. San Francisco, The Filmer Bros. Electrotype Co., 1916.
——, 2. *History of Arizona,* vol VI. San Francisco, The Filmer Bros. Electrotype Co., 1918.
Faust, Albert Bernhardt, *The German Element in the United States,* 2 vols. Boston and New York, Houghton Mifflin Co., 1909.
Feist, Sigismund, *Address to the International Congress at Gratz.* 1909.
Ferrero, Guglielmo, *The Greatness and Decline of Rome.* New York, Putnam, 1909.
Ferris, Jacob, *The States and Territories of the Great West.* New York, Miller, Orton & Mulligan, 1856.
Fish, Carl Russell, *The Rise of the Common Man, 1830–1850.* New York, Macmillan, 1927.
Fisher, George Park, *The Colonial Era.* New York, Charles Scribner's Sons, 1892.

BIBLIOGRAPHY

Fisher, H. A. L., *The Political History of England,* vol. IV. Edited by William Hunt and Reginald Poole. London, Longmans, Green & Co., 1906.

Fisher, Sydney George: 1. *The Making of Pennsylvania.* Philadelphia, J. B. Lippincott Co., 1896.

———, 2. *The Quaker Colonies.* New Haven, Yale University Press, 1921.

Fiske, John, *The Dutch and Quaker Colonies in America,* vols. I and II. Boston, Houghton Mifflin Co., 1899.

Fleure, H. J. (with James, T. C.), "Anthropological Types in Wales," *Journal of the Royal Anthropological Institute of Great Britain and Ireland,* vol. XLVI, pp. 35-154.

———, (with L. Winstanley), "Anthropology and Our Older Histories," *Jour. Roy. Anth. Inst.,* vol. XLVIII, pp. 155 seq.

Flint, Timothy, *History and Geography of the Mississippi Valley,* 2 vols. Cincinnati, E. H. Flint, 1832.

Flower and Lydekker, *Mammals, Living and Extinct.* London, Adam and Charles Black, 1891.

Foerster, Robert F., *The Racial Problems Involved in Immigration from Latin America and the West Indies to the United States.* Washington, D. C., U. S. Dept. of Labor, 1925.

Folwell, William Watts, *Minnesota.* Boston, Houghton Mifflin Co., 1908.

Ford, Henry Jones, *The Scotch-Irish in America.* Princeton University Press, 1915.

Fortier, Alcée, *A History of Louisiana,* 4 vols. New York, Manzi, Joyant & Co., 1904.

Fosdick, Lucian J., *The French Blood in America.* New York, The Baker & Taylor Co., 1911.

Frank, Tenney, "Race Mixture in the Roman Empire," *American Historical Review,* vol. XII, no. 4, July, 1916.

Freeman, E. A.: 1. *A Historical Geography of Europe.* Edited by J. B. Bury, 3d ed. London, Longmans, Green & Co., 1912.

———, 2. *Race and Language.* Historical Essays, series 3, pp. 173-230. New York and London, Macmillan, 1879.

Fritsch, Gustave, *Das Haupthaare und seiner Bildungsstatte bei den Rassen des Menschen.* Berlin, 1912.

Fuller, George W., *A History of the Pacific Northwest,* 3 vols. New York, Alfred A. Knopf, 1931.

Galton, Sir Francis, *Hereditary Genius.* London and New York, Macmillan & Co., 1892.
Garneau, F. X., *History of Canada,* vols. I and II. Montreal, John Lovell, 1862.
Gayarre, Charles, *Louisiana, Its History as a French Colony,* vol. II. New York, Wiley, 1852.
Geer, Baron Gerard de, "A Geochronology of the Last 12,000 Years," *Compte-Rendue de la session 1910, du Congrès Géol. Intern.,* vol. XI, fasc. 1, pp. 241–257.
Gibbon, Edward, *Decline and Fall of the Roman Empire.*
Gindley, Anton, *History of the Thirty Years' War.* New York, G. Putnam's Sons, 1884.
Gjerset, Knut, *The History of the Norwegian People.* New York, Macmillan, 1915.
Goodwin, John A., *The Pilgrim Republic.* Boston and New York, Houghton Mifflin Co., 1909.
Gosnell, R. E., *The Year Book of British Columbia.* Victoria, B. C., Librarian Legislature Assembly, 1897.
Gosney, E. S., and Popenoe, Paul, *Sterilization for Human Betterment.* New York, Macmillan, 1929.
Grant, Madison, "The Origin and Relationships of North American Mammals," *Eighth Annual Report of the New York Zoological Society.* New York, 1904.
——, *The Passing of the Great Race.* 4th ed. New York, Charles Scribner's Sons, 1921.
Green, John R., *A History of the English People.* New York, Harper, 1878.
Greene, Evarts B., and Virginia D. Harrington, *American population before the federal census of 1790.* New York, Columbia University Press, 1932.
Gregory, W. K.: 1. "The Dawn Man of Piltdown, England," *American Museum Journal,* vol. XIV. New York, May, 1914.
——, 2. "Facts and Theories of Evolution, with Special Reference to the Origin of Man," *Dental Cosmos,* pp. 3–19, March, 1920.
——, 3. "Studies on the Evolution of the Primates," *Bull. Amer. Mus. Nat. Hist.,* vol. XXXV, article xix. New York, 1916.
Griffis, William Elliot: 1. *The Story of New Netherland.* Boston and New York, Houghton Mifflin Co., 1909.
——, 2. *The Story of the Walloons.* Boston and New York, Houghton Mifflin Co., 1923.

BIBLIOGRAPHY 367

Gue, Benjamin F., *History of Iowa.* New York, Century History Co., 1903.

Guillaume, H., F. R. G. S., *The Amazon Provinces of Peru.* London, Wyman & Sons, 1888.

Haddon, A. C.: 1. *The Races of Man and Their Distribution.* London, Milner & Co.

——, 2. *The Study of Man.* New York, Putnam; and London, Bliss Sands, 1898.

——, 3. *The Wanderings of Peoples.* Cambridge University Press, 1912.

Haeckel, Ernst, *The Riddle of the Universe.* Harper, 1901.

Hale, Will, and Merritt, Dixon, *A History of Tennessee and Tennesseans,* vols. I and III. Chicago, Lewis Pub. Co., 1913.

Hall, H. R., *The Ancient History of the Near East,* 3d ed. London, Methuen & Co., 1916.

Hall, Prescott F.: 1. *Immigration,* 2d ed. New York, Henry Holt & Co., 1908.

——, 2. "Immigration Restriction and World Eugenics," *Journal of Heredity,* vol. X, no. 3, pp. 125–127. Washington, D. C., March, 1919.

Hamilton, Peter Joseph, *The Colonization of the South,* vol. III of *The History of North America,* edited by Guy Carleton Lee. Philadelphia, George Barrie & Sons, 1904.

Hanna, Charles A., *The Scotch-Irish,* or *The Scot in North Britain, Ireland, and America,* 2 vols. New York, G. Putnam's Sons, 1902.

Harper, Roland M., *The Population of Mexico: an Analysis.* Pan-American Magazine 44 (4): 269–278. Apl., 1931.

Harrison, J. P., "On the Survival of Racial Features in the Population of the British Isles," *Jour. Roy. Anth. Inst.,* vol. XII, pp. 243–258.

Hart, Albert B. (ed.), *Commonwealth History of Massachusetts.* New York, States History Co., 1927–28.

Hawley, James H., *History of Idaho,* vol. I. Chicago, The S. J. Clarke Pub. Co., 1920.

Henderson, Archibald, *Conquest of the Old Southwest.* New York, The Century Co., 1920.

Herodotus, *History of the World.*

Hewatt, *An Historical Account of the Rise and Progress of*

the Colonies of South Carolina and Georgia, 2 vols. London, Alexander Donaldson, 1779.
Hirt, Herman, *Die Indo-Germanen, ihre Verbreitung, ihre Urheimat und ihre Kultur.* Strassburg, Trübner, 1905.
History of Tennessee. Nashville, Goodspeed Publishing Company, 1886.
History of Welsh in Minnesota. Hughes, Edwards & Roberts, 1895.
Hittell, Theodore H., *History of California,* vol. III. San Francisco, N. J. Stone & Co., 1897.
Hodgkin, Thos., *Italy and Her Invaders.*
Holmes, S. J., and S. L. Parker, "The Stabilized Natural Increase of the Negro." *Journal of the Amer. Statistical Asso.,* June 1, 1930.
Holmes, S. J., "The Biological Trend of the Negro." *Univ. of Calif. Chronicle,* Jan., 1930.
Holmes, T. Rice, *Ancient Britain, and the Conquests of Julius Cæsar.* Oxford University Press, 1907.
Homer, *The Iliad; the Odyssey.*
Houck, Louis, *A History of Missouri,* vols. I, II, and III. Chicago, R. R. Donnelley & Sons, 1908.
Hulbert, Archer Butler: 1. *The Ohio River.* New York, G. P. Putnam's Sons, 1906.
———, 2. *Soil, Its Influence on the History of the United States.* New Haven, Yale University Press, 1930.
Human Betterment Foundation, *Collected Papers on Eugenic Sterilization.* Pasadena, Calif., 1930.
Huntington, Ellsworth: 1. *Civilization and Climate.* Yale University Press and Oxford University Press, 1915.
———, 2. *The Pulse of Asia.* Boston, Houghton Mifflin Co., 1907.
Hooton, E. A. R., *Up from the Ape.* Macmillan, 1931.

Jacobs, J., "On the Racial Characteristics of Modern Jews," *Jour. Roy. Anth. Inst.,* vol. XV, pp. 23–62, 1885–1886.
James, Bartlett Burleigh, *The Colonization of New England,* vol. V. Philadelphia, G. Barrie & Sons, 1904.
James, T. C. (with Fleure, H. J.), "Anthropological Types in Wales," *Jour. Roy. Anth. Inst.,* vol. XLVI, pp. 35–154, 1916.
Janson, Florence Edith, *Background of Swedish Immigration.* University of Chicago Press, 1931.
Jenks, Albert Ernest, *Indian-White Amalgamation.* Minneapolis, *Bulletin of Univ. Minnesota,* 1916.

Johnson, Charles S., *The Negro in American Civilization*. New York, Henry Holt & Co., 1930.
Johnson, Harrison, *History of Nebraska*. Omaha, 1880.
Johnson, Stanley C., *A History of Emigration* (from the United Kingdom to North America). London, George Routledge & Sons Limited, 1913.
Johnston, Sir Harry H.: 1. *The Negro in the New World*. London, Methuen & Co., 1910.
―――, 2. "On North African Animals, A Survey of the Ethnography of Africa," *Jour. Roy. Anth. Inst.*, vol. XLIII, pp. 375–422.
―――, 3. Various writings.
―――, 4. *Views and Reviews*. London, Williams and Norgate, 1912.
Jones, Frederick Robertson, *The Colonization of the Middle States and Maryland;* vol. IV of *The History of North America*. Philadelphia, George Barrie & Sons, 1904.
Jones, Howard Mumford, *America and French Culture*. Chapel Hill, N. C., University N. Carolina Press, 1927.
Jones, Sir J. Morris, "Pre-Aryan Syntax in Insular Celtic," Appendix B of Rhys and Jones, *The Welsh People*. London, Macmillan, 1900.
Jordanes, *History of the Goths*, Mierow translation. Princeton University Press, 1915.
Josephus, Flavius, *De Bello Judaico*, or *The Jewish War of Flavius Josephus*, translated by Robert Traill. London, Houlston & Stoneman, 1851.

Keane, A. H.: 1. *Ethnology*. Cambridge University Press, 1896.
―――, 2. *Man, Past and Present*. Also new edition by Ouiggin & Haddon. Cambridge University Press, 1900.
Keary, C. F., *The Vikings in Western Christendom*. London, T. Fisher Unwin, 1891.
Keith, Arthur: 1. *Ancient Types of Man*. Harper, 1911.
―――, 2. *The Antiquity of Man*. London, Williams and Norgate, 1915.
Kephart, Horace, *Our Southern Highlanders*. New York, Outing Publishing Co., 1913.
King, Grace, *New Orleans: The Place and the People*. New York, Macmillan Co., 1920.
Kingsford, William, *The History of Canada*, vol. I, 1608–1682; vol. II, 1679–1725. Rowsell & Hutchison, 1887.
Kuhns, Oscar, *The German and Swiss Settlements of Co-*

lonial *Pennsylvania:* Study of the So-Called Pennsylvania Dutch. New York, Henry Holt & Co., 1901.

Levering, Julia H., *Historic Indiana.* New York, G. P. Putnam's Sons, 1909.

Lockley, Fred, *History of the Columbia River Valley* (From The Dalles to the Sea). Chicago, The S. J. Clarke Pub. Co., 1928.

Lodge, Henry Cabot, *Short History of the English Colonies in America.* New York, Harper & Bros., 1881.

Louhi, E. A., *The Delaware Finns.* New York, Humanity Press, 1925.

Lyman, Horace S., *History of Oregon,* 4 vols. New York, The North Pacific Pub. Society, 1903.

MacDougall, D., *Scots and Scots' Descendants in America,* vol. I. New York, Caledonian Publishing Co., 1917.

Martin, François-Xavier, *The History of Louisiana.* New York, James A. Gresham, publisher, 1882.

Mathews, Lois Kimball, *The Expansion of New England* (The Spread of New England Settlement and Institutions to the Mississippi River, 1620–1865). Boston and New York, Houghton Mifflin Co., The Riverside Press, Cambridge, 1909.

Matthew, W. D.: 1. "Climate and Evolution." Published by the *New York Academy of Sciences,* vol. XXIV, pp. 171–318. New York, 1915.

McMaster, John Bach, *History of the People of the U. S.*

Merriam, John C., "The Beginnings of Human History Read from the Geological Record: The Emergence of Man," *Scientific Monthly,* vols. IX and X, 1919–20.

Metchnikoff, Elie, *Nature of Man.* Putnam, 1903.

Mexicans in California. Report of Gov. C. C. Young's Fact-Finding Committee. Sacramento, State Printer, 1930.

Meyers, Albert Cook, *Narratives of Early Pennsylvania, West New Jersey, and Delaware.* New York, Charles Scribner's Sons, 1912.

Miller, Gerrit S., "The Jaw of the Piltdown Man," *Smithsonian Miscellaneous Collections,* vol. LXV, no. 12. Washington, D. C., Nov., 1915.

Minns, E. H., *Scythians and Greeks.* Cambridge University Press, 1913.

Mommsen, Theodor, *A History of the Roman Provinces,* translated by William P. Dickson. Scribner, 1887.

Montelius, Oscar: 1. "Die Chronologie der altesten Bronzezeit," *Arch. f. Anth.*, Bd. 25, pp. 443 *seq.* 1900.
——, 2. *The Civilization of Sweden in Heathen Times*, translated by F. H. Woods. London, Macmillan, 1888.
——, 3. *La Civilisation primitive en Italie.* Stockholm, 1895.
——, 4. *L'Anthropologie*, série XVII, 1906.
Mortillet, G. de, *Formation de la nation française.* Paris, 1897.
Much, Mathæus, *Die Heimat der Indo-Germanen im Lichte der urgeschichtlichen Forschung.* Berlin, 1902.
Müller, Friedrich: 1. *Grundriss der Sprachwissenschaft.* Wien, 1884.
——, 2. *Reise der österreichischen Fregatte Novara um die Erde in den Jahren 1857–9, unter den Befehlen des Commodore B. von Wiellerstorf.* Wien, Ubair-Linguistischer Theil, 1867.
Müller, Sophus: 1. *L'Europe préhistorique*, tr. du Danois, . . . par Emmanuel Philipot. Paris, J. Lamarre, 1907.
——, 2. *Nordische Alterthumskunde.* Strassburg, 1897.
Munro, Dana Carleton, *A Source Book of Roman History.* Boston, New York and Chicago, D. C. Heath & Co., 1904.
Munro, John, *The Story of the British Race.* New York, D. Appleton & Co., 1907.
Munro, R.: 1. *The Lake-Dwellings of Europe.* London, Cassell & Co., 1890.
——, 2. *Palæolithic Man and the Terramara Settlements.* Macmillan, 1912.
——, 3. Discussion in *Jour. Roy. Anth. Inst.* for 1890.
Myres, J. L., "A History of the Pelasgian Theory," *Jour. of Hellenic Studies*, vol. XXVII, pp. 170–226, 1907.

Nansen, Fridtjof, *In Northern Mists.* New York, Frederick A. Stokes, 1911.
Nason, Elias, *A Gazetteer of the State of Massachusetts.* B. B. Russell, 1874.
Nordenskiöld, Erland, "Finland: The Land and the People," *Geographical Review*, vol. VII, no. 6, pp. 361–375, June 1919.

Oman, Sir Charles: 1. *The Dark Ages.* London, Rivington's Press, 1905.
——, 2. *England before the Norman Conquest.* London, Methuen & Co.; or New York, Putnam, 1913.

Origin, Birthplace, Nationality, and Language of the Canadian People. Dominion Bureau of Statistics, Ottawa, 1929.
Osborn, Henry Fairfield: 1. *Men of the Old Stone Age*, 2d edition. New York, Scribner, 1918.
———, 2. *The Origin of Life*. New York, Scribner, 1917.
Owen, Thomas M., *History of Alabama*, vol. II. Chicago, Clarke Publishing Co., 1921.

Palfrey, John Gorham, *A Compendious History of New England*, vol. IV. Boston, Houghton Mifflin, 1893.
Palgrave, Sir Francis, *The Rise and Progress of the English Commonwealth*. London, 1832.
Parkman, Francis, *The Old Régime in Canada*. Boston, Little, Brown & Co., 1905.
Parrish, Randall, *Historic Illinois*. Chicago, A. C. McClurg, 1905.
Parsons, F. G., "Anthropological Observations on German Prisoners of War," *Jour. Roy. Anth. Inst.*, vol. XLIX, 1919.
Paxson, Frederic L., *History of the American Frontier*. Boston, Houghton Mifflin & Co., 1924.
Payne, Edward John, *A History of the New World Called America*. Oxford Press, vol. I, 1892; vol. II, 1899.
Peake, H. J. E., *Memorials of Old Leicestershire*. 1911.
Pearl, Raymond, "The Sterilization of Degenerates," *Eugenics Review*, April, 1919.
Peck, J. M., *A New Guide for Emigrants to the West*. Boston, Gould, Kendall & Lincoln, 1836.
Penck, Albrecht, "Das Alter des Menschengeschlechts," *Zeitschr. f. Eth.*, Jahrg. 40, Heft 3, pp. 390–407. 1908.
Penka, K., *Die Herkunft der Arier*. Wien, 1886.
Petrie, W. M. F., "Migrations," *Jour. Roy. Anth. Inst.*, vol. XXXVI, pp. 189–233. 1906.
Pickett, Albert James, *History of Alabama*, vol. II. Charleston, Walker & James, 1851.
Pliny, *Natural History*.
Plutarch's *Lives*, Langhorne translation. London, Frederick Warne & Co.
Pollard, A. F., *A Political History of England*, vol. IV. London, Longmans, Green & Co., 1915.
Polybius, *History*.

Popenoe, Paul, "One Phase of Man's Modern Evolution," *19th International Congress of Americanists*, pp. 617 seq. Washington, D. C., 1915.
Popenoe, Paul, and Johnson, Roswell H., *Applied Eugenics*. 2d ed. New York, Macmillan, 1933.
Popular History of New England, 2 vols. Boston, Crocker & Co., 1881.
Priestly, Herbert Ingram, *The Coming of the White Man, 1492–1848;* A History of American Life, vol. I. New York, The Macmillan Co., 1929.
Procopius, *A History of the Wars*, translated by H. B. Dewing, Loeb Classical Library. New York, Putnam; and London, Wm. Heinemann, 1919.
Pumpelly, Raphael, *Explorations in Turkestan*. Washington, D. C., Carnegie Inst., 1905 and 1908.

Ramsey, J. G. M., *The Annals of Tennessee*. Kingsport, Tenn., Kingsport Press, 1853.
Ranke, Johannes, *Der Mensch*. Leipsig, 1866–7.
Ratzel, Friedrich, *The History of Mankind*. Macmillan, 1908.
Reade, Arthur, *Finland and the Finns*. New York, 1915.
Reid, Sir G. Archdall: 1. *The Laws of Heredity*. London, Methuen & Co., 1910.
——, 2. *The Principles of Heredity*. London, Chapman & Hall, 1905.
Reinach, Salomon, "Inscription attique relative à l'invasion des Galates en Grèce," *Rev. Celtique,* série 11, pp. 80–85.
Reisner, George A., *The Early Dynastic Cemeteries of Naga ed-Dêr*. University of California publications, 1908; Leipsig, J. C. Hinrichs, 1905.
Retzius, G.: 1. *Anthropologia Suecica, Beiträge zur Anthropologie der Schweden*. Stockholm, 1902.
——, 2. *Crania Suecica Antiqua*. Stockholm, 1900.
——, 3. "The So-Called North European Race of Mankind," *Jour. Roy. Anth. Inst.,* vol. XXXIX, pp. 277–314. 1909.
Rice, Holmes T.: 1. *Ancient Britain and the Conquests of Julius Cæsar*. Oxford, Clarendon Press, 1907.
——, 2. *Cæsar's Conquest of Gaul*. Oxford, Clarendon Press, 1911.
Ridgeway, Sir William: 1. *The Early Age of Greece*. Cambridge, 1901.

———, 2. *The Origin and Influence of the Thoroughbred Horse.* Cambridge University Press, 1905.
———, 3. "Who Were the Romans?" *Proceedings of the British Academy,* 1907–1908.
Riegel, Robert E., *America Moves West.* New York, Henry Holt & Co., 1930.
Ripley, William Z., *The Races of Europe.* New York, D. Appleton & Co., 1899.
Robinson, Edward, *University of Minnesota Studies in Social Sciences,* no. 3.
Robinson, Will H., *Story of Arizona.* Phœnix, The Berryhill Co., 1926.
Roosevelt, Theodore, *Winning of the West,* vol. IV. New York, G. P. Putnam's Sons, 1896.
Rossiter, William S., *Increase of Population in the United States,* 1910–1920. Washington, D. C., Bureau of the Census, 1922.
Rowland, Dunbar, *Mississippi, the Heart of the South,* vol. II. Chicago, S. J. Clarke, 1925.
———, *Mississippi, the Heart of the South,* vol. I. Chicago, S. J. Clarke, 1925.

Savigny, Friedrich Karl, *Geschichte des römischen Rechtes im Mittelalter.*
Sayce, Archibald Henry, *The Ancient Empires of the East.* Scribner, 1898.
Scharf, J. Thomas, *History of Delaware* (1609–1888), vol. I. Philadelphia, L. J. Richards & Co., 1888.
Schrader, Oscar, *Die Indo-Germanen.* Leipsig, 1911.
Sclater, W. L. and P. L., *The Geography of Mammals.* London, Kegan Paul, Trench, Trübner & Co., 1899.
Secret History, or The Horrors of Santo Domingo, in a series of Letters Written by a Lady at Cape François to Colonel Burr (late Vice-President of the United States) Principally during the Command of General Rochambeau. Philadelphia, Bradford & Inskeep, R. Carr, printer, 1808.
Sergi, G.: 1. *Africa: Antropologia della Stirpe Cannitica (Specie Eurafricana).* Torino, 1897.
———, 2. *Arii e Italici.* Torino, 1898.
———, 3. *Italia: le Origini.* Torino, Fratelli Bocca, Editori, 1919.
———, 4. *The Mediterranean Race.* New York, Scribner; and London, Walter Scott, 1901.

BIBLIOGRAPHY

Shaler, N. S., *Kentucky.* Boston, Houghton, Mifflin & Co. 1893.

Skeat, W. W., *The Wars of Alexander,* translated chiefly from *Historia Alexandri Magni de preliis.* London, N. Trübner & Co., 1886.

Smith, G. Elliot: 1. *The Ancient Egyptians.* Harper, 1911.

——, 2. "Ancient Mariners," *Journal of the Manchester Geographical Society,* vol. XXXIII, parts 1-4, pp. 1-22, 1917. Manchester and London, April, 1918.

Soane, E. B., *To Mesopotamia and Kurdistan in Disguise.* Boston, Small, Maynard & Co.

Southern Historical Publication Society, *The South in the Building of the Nation—a History of the Southern States.* Richmond, Virginia, 1909.

Spangler, J. M., *Civilization in Chile.* San Francisco, H. G. Parsons, 1885.

Speranza, Gino, *Race or Nation?*

Stanard, Mary Newton, *The Story of Virginia's First Century.* Philadelphia, J. B. Lippincott Co., 1928.

Stark, James H., *The Loyalists of Massachusetts.* W. B. Clark Co., 1910.

Stella, Antonio M. D., *Some Aspects of Italian Immigration to the United States.* New York and London, G. P. Putnam's Sons, 1924.

Stoddard, Lothrop, *The French Revolution in San Domingo.* Boston, Houghton Mifflin Co., 1914.

Sykes, Mark, "The Kurds," *Jour. Roy. Anth. Inst.,* vol. XXVIII, pp. 45 *seq.,* 1908.

Tacitus, *Germania,* translated by M. Hutton, Loeb Classical Library. New York, Macmillan; and London, Wm. Heinemann, 1914.

Taylor, Isaac Canon: 1. *The Origin of the Aryans.* London, Walter Scott, 1890.

——, 2. *Words and Places,* edited by A. Smythe Palmer. New York, E. P. Dutton & Co.; and London, Routledge & Son.

Taylor, Paul S., *Mexican Labor in the United States: Migration Statistics.* Univ. of Calif. Pubs. in Econ. 6 (3): 237-255. Berkeley, 1929.

Thomas, William Roscoe, *Life Among the Hills and Mountains of Kentucky.* Kentucky, Standard Printing Co.

Thomson, J. Arthur, *Heredity*. New York, Putnam; and London, John Murray, 1926. 5th ed.
Topinard, P.: 1. "Carte de la couleur des yeux et des cheveux en France," *Rev. d'anth.*, série 3, IV, pp. 513-530.
——, 2. *Éléments d'anthropologie générale*. Paris, Delahaye et Lecrosnier, 1885.
Trevelyan, Sir George, *George III and Charles Fox*. London, Longmans, Green & Co., 1914.

Utley, Henry M., *Michigan as a Province, Territory and State*. The Publishing Society of Michigan, 1906.

Van der Zee, *The British in Iowa*. Iowa City, State Hist. Society, 1922.
Van Tramp, John C., *Prairie and Rocky Mountain Adventures*. Columbus, Segner & Condit, 1867.
Villari, Pasquale, *The Barbarian Invasions of Italy*, translated by Linda Villari, 2 vols. Scribner, 1902.
Von Luschan, F.: 1. "The Early Inhabitants of Western Asia," *Jour. Roy. Anth. Inst.*, vol. XLI, pp. 221-244.
—— (with E. Petersen). *Reisen in Lykien, Milyas und Kibyratis*. Wien, 1889.

Wallis, B. C.: 1. "The Rumanians in Hungary," *Geographical Review*, Aug., 1918.
——, 2. "The Slavs of Northern Hungary," *Geo. Rev.*, Sept., 1918.
——, 3. "The Slavs of Southern Hungary," *Geo. Rev.*, Oct., 1918.
——, 4. "Central Hungary: Magyars and Germans," *Geo. Rev.*, Nov., 1918.
Weeden, William B., *Early Rhode Island*. New York, The Grafton Press, 1910.
Wertenbaker, Thomas: 1. *Patrician and Plebeian in Virginia*. Virginia, The Michie Co., 1910.
——, 2. *The First Americans* (1607-1690). New York, The Macmillan Co., 1927.
Whitney, Orson F., *History of Utah*, vol. I. Utah, Geo. Q. Cannon & Sons Co., 1892.
Willcox, Walter F., *International Migrations*, vols. I and II. New York, National Bureau of Economic Research, Inc., 1929 and 1931.
Wilser, L., *Die Germanen*. Eisenach u. Leipsig, 1904.

Wilstach, Paul, *Tidewater Virginia*. Indianapolis, The Bobbs-Merrill Co., 1929.
Winsor, Justin: 1. *The Mississippi Basin. The Struggle in America between England and France*. Boston, Houghton, Mifflin & Co., 1895.
——, 2. (ed.) *Narrative and Critical History of America*. Boston, Houghton Mifflin Co., 1894.
Wisconsin in Three Centuries, 4 vols. New York, Century History Co., 1906.
Wissler, Clark, *The American Indian*. New York, Douglas C. McMurtrie, 1917.
Woodruff, C. E.: 1. *The Effect of Tropical Light on White Men*. New York and London, Rebman Co., 1905.
——, 2. *The Expansion of Races*. New York, Rebman Co., 1909.
Woods, Frederick Adams: 1. *Heredity in Royalty*. New York, Henry Holt & Co., 1906.
——, 2. *The Influence of Monarchs*. Macmillan, 1913.
——, 3. "Significant Evidence for Mental Heredity," *Jour. of Hered.*, vol. VIII, no. 13, pp. 106-112. Washington, D. C., 1917.
Work, Monroe N., *Negro Year Book*, 1931-32 (Negro Census by States), vol. VIII. Tuskegee Institute, Ala. Ala. Negro Year Book Pub. Co.
Wortham, Louis J., LL.D., *A History of Texas* (From Wilderness to Commonwealth). Fort Worth, Wortham-Molyneaux Co., 1924.

Yoakum, H., Esq., *History of Texas* (Its First Settlement in 1685 to Its Annexation to the U. S. in 1846). New York, Redfield, 1856.

Zaborowski, M. S.: 1. "Les peuples aryens d'Asie et d'Europe" (part of the *Encyclopédie scientifique*), Octave Doin, Éditeur. Paris, 1908.
——, 2. "Relations primitives des Germains et des Finnois," *Bull. Soc. d'anth.*, pp. 174-79. Paris, 1897.
——, 3. *Les races de l'Italie*. Paris, 1897.
Zeuss, J. K., *Die Deutschen und die Nachbarstamme*. München, 1837.

INDEX

Aberdeen, 136.
Abolitionists, 210.
Acadia, 308, 309.
"Acadie" (Nova Scotia), 308.
Achæans, invasions into Greece, 26; Nordics in West as, 39; Osco-Umbrians, kin to, 39.
Africa, Negro slaves in, 9; Christianity in, 14; (Ethiopia) early races in, 19, 20.
Alabama, settlement in, 183, 184; heart of Cotton Kingdom, 184; Scotch and English blood in, 184; 1930 census native population, 242.
Alans, the, 44, 45, 46.
Alaska, 90.
Albanians, 36.
Albany (N. Y.), 102, 110, 168; Ulster Scots in, 108; increase in Negroes in, 237.
Albemarle, 138.
Alberta, 314, 318.
Alemanni, the, 42, 51, 52.
Alemannish dialect, 79, 166.
Alexander the Great, 23.
Alien Act of 1798, 268.
Aliens, public sentiment in America, 1; attitude toward, 268; restrictions of, 269; opposition to restrictions of, 269; literacy test for, 269; Quota Act of 1921, 270, 271; National Origins Act, 272, 274, 278.
Alleghanies, Ulster Scots west of, 123; "poor whites" in, 135.
Allentown (Pa.), 121.
Alpine race, characteristics of, 29, 30; origin of, 29; similarity to Mongols, 29; extent of domain, 31; Turanians, 31, 32; Armenians, 32; increase in Central Europe, 33; in United States, 153.
Alpine Slavs, 15.
Alsace, 50, 116.
Amazonian Basin, 335.
America, Catholics in, 4; Jews in, 4, 224–227; South Germans in, 8; relative diminution of Anglo-Saxon blood in, 10; whites and blacks in, 12, 13; origin of American Indians in, 19; Norman element in, 55; Ulster Scots in, 60; sentiment for France in, 71; naval war with France in 1798, 71; motive of early settlers in, 65; migration from Leinster to, 76; "Scotch Irish" of, 92; emigration from Ireland to, 93; Huguenot migration to, 96; North German Nordics in, 143; opportunities for British race in, 156; migration toward Pacific Coast, 158; emigration of Scottish farmers to, 159; emigration of Southern England farmers to, 159; emigration of Irish to, 159; emigration of Germans to, 161, 162; South Irish Catholics in, 218; freedom of speech and press in, 219; waste in, 221; ratio of criminals in, 224; alien invasion in, 223–234; migration following the Revolution, 256; migration with panic of 1819, 256; migration at time of land speculation by Andrew Jackson, 256; minority of women among recent immigration groups in, 275; solutions of Negro elimination in, 285 ff. See also under United States.
American colonies, Nordics in, 77.
American Indians, Mongols and Alpines ancestors of, 30; Mongolian blood in, 37.
American Protective Association, 313.
American Revolution, the influence of Massachusetts during, 99; loss of population during, 100; increase in migration following, 101; New York State after, 108; migration after, 109; troops from New York and Massachusetts, 111; Calvinistic, 121.
Amerinds, 26, 27.
Amish, 79.
Andalusia, 188, 333.
Andover, 94.
Angles, the, 59.
Anglicans, Quakers become, 121.
Angora, 41.
Annapolis, 127.
Apache Indians, 291.
Apennines, the, 41, 51.
Appalachian valleys, 74, 78; lawlessness in, 67.
Apulia, 39.
Arabia, 22, 27; the Mediterraneans of, 24.
Arabs, in Spain, 46, 49; race mixture among, 49; period of expansion, 49; ruined by Negro women, 49
Aral Sea, 34.
Argentina, 338; racial composition of, 339, 340.
Argonauts, the, 216.
Argyllshire, 159.
Arians, 46.
Arius, 46.
Arizona, 152, 213, 214; Mexicans in, 162, 262; separated from New Mexico, 262; Mormons in, 262; Texans in, 263; Indians in, 289.

379

Arkansas, 243; settlement in, 189, 190; growth of, 190; British stock in, 190.
Arkansas River, 189.
Armenians, 32.
Armorican language, 58.
Aryan language, Centum group, 24–25; Satem group, 24–25.
Ashkanazim Jews, 225.
Asia, Christianity in, 14; Mongoloid tribes of northeastern, 19; expansion of civilization in southeastern, 23.
Asia Minor, Nordic Gauls in, 41; Turks in, 50.
Asiatics, 356.
Assyria, 22.
Assyrians, cruelty of, 156.
"Asylum for the Oppressed," 268.
Atlas Mountains, 45.
Attila, 44, 51.
Aurora (N. Y.), 110.
Austin, Moses, 209.
Australia, 20, 303, 353, 354; Negroids in, 28; racial tangle in, 28.
Australoids, the, 20, 21, 28; compared to Alpines, 30.
Austria, 116.
Austrian Empire, languages in old, 5.
Aztecs, the, 324.

Babylonia, 22.
Bactria, 23.
Bahamas, the, 345.
Baltic Sea, 35, 56.
Baltimore (Md.), growth of, 129; cosmopolitan population in, 239.
Baltimore, Lord, 125, 126, 128.
Barbadoes, 85, 86, 345.
Basques, 340.
Bath (N. Y.), 110.
Baton Rouge (La.), 187, 245.
Bavaria, Alpines in, 36.
Bay of Chaleurs, 296.
Beaker Makers, 57.
Belcher, Thomas, 105.
Belfast, 95.
Belgæ, the, 41, 42, 43, 58.
Belgium, languages in, 5; the Flemings of, 52.
Beothics, the, 307.
Berbers, the, 24; in Atlas Mountains (North Africa), 39.
Berkeley, Governor (Virginia), 126, 132, 135.
Berkshire, 84.
Bermuda, 85, 345.
Bethlehem (Pa.), Moravians in, 117.
Bigot, 46.
Binghamton (N. Y.), 109.
Black Hawk Purchase, 198.
Black Hawk War, 198.
Black Hills, gold in, 254.
Blacks, the, 12, 20; advance in America, 13

Blue Ridge, the, 137, 138.
Bogota, 334.
Bohemia, Czechish in, 5; rise of nationalism in, 14; Mongolian characters in, 37.
Bolivia, population of, 341.
"Bonnie Prince Charlie," 140.
Boone, Daniel, 123, 145.
Boone, Daniel Morgan, 200.
"Boone's Lick," 191.
Boston (Mass.), 71, 82, 101, 105; Huguenots in, 97.
Braddock, General, 137.
Bradford (postmaster), 83.
Brandenburg, 181.
Branford (N. J.), 113.
Brattleboro (Vt.), 89.
Brazil, Portuguese in, 335; European immigrants in, 336; size of, 337.
Bristol, 307.
Britain, Celts in, 41; invaded by Saxons, 59; invaded by Angles and Jutes, 59; Norman conquest in 1066, 60, 61.
British Columbia, 297, 354; Asiatic problem in, 315, 316.
British Commonwealth, 303.
British Empire, abolition of slavery in, 11.
British Honduras, 331.
British Islands, mixture of Nordics and Mediterraneans in, 33.
British Isles, racial composition of, 57.
British West Indies, 345.
Brittany, Armorican language in, 58.
Bronze Age, 57; Alpines in, 31.
Brooklyn (N. Y.), 105.
Brythons, the, 41, 42, 43, 58.
Buckingham, 84.
Buffalo (N. Y.), 177; increase in Negroes in, 237.
Burgundians, the, 42, 46, 50.
Burlington (Iowa), 197.
Burlington (N. J.), 112.
Burma, Sanscrit in, 25; English rule in, 355.
Burnett Act, 270.
Bushmen, the, 20.
Byrd, Colonel, 136.
Byzantine Empire, 54.

Cabot, John, 307.
Cæsar, Julius, 221; campaigns in Gaul, 41.
Caithness, 55.
"Cajans," 6.
Calabria, 39.
Calhoun, John C., 168.
California, 152, 173; Mexicans in, 162; Indians and Spaniards in, 214; annexed to United States, 215; Spanish blood in, 215; increase in Americans in, 215, 216; gold in, 215, 263; Chinese in, 216; contrasted with other United

INDEX

States frontiers, 217; foreigners in, 263–267; migration to, 263, 264; Nordic element in, 264; decline of Chinese in, 265; vote against Chinese immigration, 265; racial problems in, 265, 266; Indians in, 289.
California gold rush, 199.
Camoens, 48.
Campbelltown, 139.
Canada, French language in, 5; migration of Loyalists to, 100, 110; annexed to the Union, 111; divisions of, 296, 297; Maritime Provinces, 296, 300; Quebec, 297–301; Upper Canada, 297, 302; inducements to immigrants, 302; population in 1840, 304; Irish Catholics in, 304; population in 1871, 305; British and French in, 305; Mounted Police in, 305; Indians in, 306; migration from United States to, 316–319; British immigration in, 317; "foreign stock" in, 317, 318; Jews in, 317; few Negroes in, 318; Nordic element in, 318; strength of Roman Catholic Church in, 318; 1921 census, 319.
Canandaigua (N. Y.), 109, 110.
Canary Islands, 188.
Cape Cod Bay, 82.
Cape Fear River, 139.
Cape May, 112.
Caribbean Sea, 12, 155, 348.
Caribs, 331.
Carlisle (Pa.), 122.
Carpathians, the, 31.
Carroll, Jesuit John, 151.
Carter, Colonel John, 137.
Caspian Sea, 34.
Caucasus, the, 44; beauty of women in, 50.
Cayuga, 110.
Celtiberians, 40.
Celtic Nordics, 36; conquest of Spain by, 40; in British Isles, 40.
Celtic-speaking tribes, 42.
Celtic tribes, in Gaul and Britain, 40, 41; "Q" and "P," 57, 58.
Central America, 294, 330 ff., 348.
Central Asia, 17, 44.
Central Pacific Railway, 265.
Cervantes, 48.
Chaldea, 22.
Chalons, 44; Battle of, 52.
Champlain, 300, 301.
Charlemagne, 31; the Franks under, 54; conquest of Saxons, 54.
Charles I, 126, 135.
Charleston (S. C.), 41, 42; Ulster Scots enter colonies through, 77, 78.
Charlestown (Mass.), 82.
Chesapeake Bay, 73.
Chester, 114.
Cheyenne (Wyo.), 259.

Chicago (Ill.), 196, 229.
Chickasaw Indians, 291.
Chile, white races in, 340.
China, rise of nationalism in, 14; Mongols of, 19.
Chinese, the, 353; in California, 265.
Choctaws, 291.
Christian Syrians, 339.
Christianity, Unitarian form of, 46; orthodox, 46.
Christy, Howard Chandler, 3.
Cid Campeador, 48.
Cimbri, 42.
Cincinnati (Ohio), 161, 164, 248.
Circassians, the, 50.
Cisalpine Gaul, 41, 51.
City of Brotherly Love (Philadelphia), 114.
Civil War, 2, 3, 12, 138, 158, 169–176, 193, 199, 200, 207, 212, 214, 220, 223, 229, 241, 254, 262, 267, 349; Irish in, 161; influence of "Solid South" after, 282.
Civilization, development of, 22 ff.
Clark, General George Rogers, 163, 167, 168, 171.
Clay, Henry, 87, 211.
Cleveland (Ohio), 165.
Coast cities, inhabitants richer than frontiersmen, 75.
Colbert, 299.
Coligny, 141, 192.
Coligny, Admiral, 96.
Collinson, Peter, 117.
Colombia, population of, 333.
Colonial times, racial population in, 2; religion in, 4; intermarriage during, 8.
Colonies, original racial complexion of, 75; Ulster Scots in, 78.
Color, 26, 27.
Colorado, 173, 203; Daniel Boone's grandson in, 123; Southeastern, 213; gold in, 258; Nordics in, 259; Mexican population in, 292.
Columbia River, 260.
Columbus, Christopher, 48, 56, 208.
Commonwealth, Puritans under the, 66.
Comstock Lode, 261.
Confederate Army, 260.
Congregationalists, hostile to Presbyterians, 94.
Conkling, Senator Roscoe (quoted), 288.
Connecticut, 94, 108; early settlement of, 72, 86, 87; growth of, 101; Western Reserve of, 164, 165; foreign-born in, 218; 1930 census native population, 236.
Connecticut River, 90; migration to, 72.
Connecticut River Valley, 82; "forts" of Dutch in, 104.
Constitution of the United States, 155.
Constitution of 1835, 177.
Continental Congress, religion of, 69.

Continentals, the, 139.
Convention of 1787, 7, 155.
Cornwall, 58.
Corsica, Vandals in, 45.
Costa Rica, population of, 332, 333; Nordic infusion in, 333.
Creek Indians, 183.
Creeks, the, 246.
Crefeld, 116.
Creoles, French spoken by, 6.
Crete, 22.
Crimea, the, 44.
Cromwell, Oliver, 93, 125; and Irish Rebellion, 133.
Crown Point, 108.
Crusades, the, 53.
Cuba, 211; population of, 343.
Cumberland Gap, 145, 146
Cumberland Presbyterian Church, 122.
Cymric, 58.

Dacia, 44.
Dacian Plains, 39.
Dakota, 197; rush into, 253.
Dante, 48.
Danube, the, 44.
Da Vinci, Leonardo, 48.
Davis, John (quoted), 187, 188.
Dayton (Ohio), 164.
Declaration of Independence, 101; religion of signers, 69.
Dedham, 81.
de Lapouge, Count, 33, 49.
Delaware, 73, 125; 1930 census native population, 239.
Delaware River, 111; English settlers along, 73; French Huguenots along, 73; surrounding land colonized by Quakers, 112.
Democracy, 356.
Denmark, 22, 59, 345.
de Saussure, 141.
Detroit (Mich.), 176, 229.
Devonshire, 307.
Dippers, 115.
District of Columbia, residents of, 239; Negroes in, 239, 240.
Dorchester (Mass.), 82, 87, 144.
Dorchester Society, 144.
Drummond, James, the Earl of Perth, 113.
Dubuque, John, 197.
Duke of Liegnitz, 53.
Duke of York, 125.
Dundas (Ontario), 312.
Dunkards, 79.
Dutch East India Company, 102.
Dutch settlement, 102 ff.

East Anglia, Puritan emigration from, 84.
East Jersey, 112; stronghold of Scotch Presbyterians in, 113.

Ecuador, Indian tribes in, 343.
Edict of Nantes, 127, 139; revocation of, 96.
Egypt, 22, 25; rise of nationalism in, 14; Libyans in, 39.
Elbe, the, 31, 54.
Electoral College, 282.
Elizabeth (N. J.), 77.
Elizabethtown (N. J.), 113.
Elizabethtown Association, the, 113.
Emigration Society Land Company, 212.
Emmet, Robert, 159.
Emmet, Thomas A., 159.
Empire Settlement Act, 317.
England, Norman element in, 55; Norsemen in, 59; Puritan emigration from, 82; Palatines in, 107; population at time of Revolution, 154.
English Quakers, 77.
English Whigs, 70.
Episcopalians, strength of, 69.
Ericson, Leif, 56.
Erie Canal, 105, 106, 110, 168, 172, 177.
Erse language, 57.
Eskimos, 307.
Ethiopia (Africa), 27; early races in, 19, 20; true Negroes in, 28.
Euphrates, Valley of the, 22.
Eurasia, 18, 19; development of civilization in southwestern, 22; racial groupings in, 27; Negroids in, 27; Negritos in, 28.
Europe, intermingling of peoples in, 21; racial mixtures in, 36; saved from Mongols, 53; Nordics in, at time of discovery of America, 61; monopoly of land ownership in, 65.
Evangeline (Longfellow), 186.

Fairfield (Conn.), 87.
Fall Line, the, 73.
Falmouth, 101.
Fayetteville, 139.
Federal Children's Bureau, 275.
Federal Government, 163.
Federal Supreme Court, 277.
Filipinos, 224, 294.
Finland, Ural-Altaic language in, 24.
Finlanders, 111.
Firbolgs, the, 62.
Flemings, in New York, 76.
Florida, 152; Spanish in, 117; South Carolinians in, 142; settlement in, 192–194; ceded by Spain to England, 193; second Nordic invasion of, 193; slow development of, 193; small population in, 193, 194; Negroes in, 193; 1930 census native population, 241.
Forbes, General, 138.
Foreign missions, 355.
Fort Orange (N. Y.), 102.
Fort Schuyler (N. Y.), 110.
Fort Snelling, 196.

INDEX

Fort Stanwix (N. Y.), 110.
Founders of the Republic, 237.
France, races in, 4, 5; unity of national feeling in, 4; Alpines in, 15; decrease of Nordics in, 33, 49; Alpines in, 42; as a Nordic land, 42; eldest son of the church, 46, 47; (southern) Gothic names in, 48; variety of names in, 49.
Franklin, Benjamin 84, 124; (quoted), 118–120.
Franks, the, 42, 46; in Gaul and western Germany, 52; had support of Roman Church, 52; in Belgium, 52; in northern France, 53; conquer Franconia, 54; seize northern Italy, under Charlemagne, 54.
Frederick County (Md.), 129.
Free State Catholics, 273.
Freehold (N. J.), 77, 112.
French, the, Nordics and Alpines among the, 36; in Quebec province, 301; emigration from Quebec to New England, 301.
French Canadians, 355; influence of Roman Catholic Church on, 311.
French Huguenots, in New England, 73; in New York, 76; in South Carolina, 80; in North Carolina, 139.
Friesland, 116.
Frontier, the, character of, 68; history of, 156, 157; effect of Indians on, 157.

Gadsden Purchase, 210.
Gaelic, spoken in Scotland, 58; spoken in Nova Scotia, 309.
Galatia, 41, 45; Gothic blood in, 47.
Galatians, 41, 42.
Galena, 196.
Galicia, Mongolian characters in, 37.
Gallegos, the, 333.
Garvey, the Negro, 287.
Gaul, 221; Celts in, 41; remnant of Visigoths in, 46.
Gauls, the, 42.
Gelderland, 103.
Gendron, 141.
Geneva (N. Y.), 110.
Genoa, 48, 231.
"Genoese," 231, 264.
Genseric, 45.
"Gentiles," the, 261.
Georgia, racial complexion in, 80; Palatines in, 116, 117; settlement of 143, 144; benefited after Revolution, 145; 1930 census native population in, 241; idle farming in, 243.
Georgians, the, 50, 145.
Gepidæ, the, 44.
German Jews, 226.
Germans, among Roman Catholics in the colonies, 70; forced to the West, 73; in Pennsylvania, 73; in the colonies, 79.
Germantown (Pa.), founded by Mennonites, 115.
Germany, quota of immigrants from, 2; races in, 4; Nordics in eastern, 14; Revolution of 1848, 161, 181; immigrants in America, 161, 162; peak of emigration in, 228, 229.
Gettysburg (Pa.), 122.
Ghetto population, 227.
Glenelg, 312.
Glengarry (Ontario), 108, 312.
Gloucestershire, 84.
Gobi desert, 23.
Goidelic, the, conquer the Neolithic Mediterraneans in Ireland, 62.
Goidels, 40, 57.
Gold, discovered in California, 215; caused increase in California population, 216.
Gothia Septimania, 46.
Goths, the, 43, 250; in South Russia, 44.
"Great American Desert," 155.
Great Britain, emigration from New England to, 86; "White Man's Burden" in, 352, 354.
Great Lakes, the, 163.
Great Salt Lake, 204.
Great Wall of China, 34.
Greece, 22; invasions of Achæans into, 26; Nordic conquest of, 39.
Green Mountain Boys, 90.
Greenwich (Conn.), 104, 105.
Guadalquivir, the, 46.
Guarani Indians, 341.
Guatemala, population of, 330, 332.
Guiana (British), 334; (Dutch), 334; (French), 334, 335.
Guilford (N. J.), 113.
Gulf of California, 210, 211.
Gulf of Mexico, 12, 287.
Gulf of Saint Lawrence, 296.
Gulf States, extermination of Indians in, 291.

Habitants, the, origin of, 298; physical type of, 299; effect of decline in birthrate on, 302.
Haiti, 287; loss of white control in, 11, 12; barbarism in, 12; Negro Republic, 345.
Hamatic language, 24.
Hamburg, 116.
Hampshire, 84, 159.
Hamptons, the, 105.
Hansen, Professor, 152.
Hartford (Conn.), 87.
Hawaii, 349; Japanese element in, 295; possible source of undesirable immigration, 295.
Hawaiians, 294.
Henry, Patrick, 136.

384 INDEX

Henry VII, 307.
Highlands, the, mixture of races in, 61.
Hindus, the, 27, 353; Aryan speech among, 27.
Hittites, 32, 39.
Holland, 103, 116; Palatines in, 107.
Holland (Mich.), 178.
Holstein, 59.
Holston settlement, the, 148.
Homo sapiens, 20.
Honduras, population of, 331.
Hottentots, the, 20.
Hudson, Henry, 102.
Hudson (N. Y.), 109.
Hudson River, New Englanders and Germans along, 73; Dutch settlements along, 102.
Hudson River valley, 110; Dutch in, 102, 103, 105; growth of towns in, 109.
Hudson's Bay Colony, 314.
Huger, 141.
Huguenot French, during the Revolution, 7.
Huguenots, migration to America, 96, 97.
Humboldt, 322.
Hungary, 50; Ural-Altaic language in, 24.
Huns, 31, 44.
Hunter, Governor (N. Y.), 106.
Hussites, 79.

Iberian Peninsula, 333.
Iberians, 40, 61.
Iberville (French explorer), 291.
Idaho, first settlement in, 205; part of Washington territory, 205; growth during Civil War, 260; Nordic strength in, 260.
Illinois, 149, 164, 175; settlement of, 170–176; boom in, 171; Erie Canal access to, 172; lead mines in, 172; dominated by Ulster Scots, 173; population at beginning of Civil War, 173; represented in Westward migration, 173; Germans in, 175; Irish in, 175, 176; English in, 176; Mormons in, 176; Scandinavians in, 176; Mexican population in, 293; native population in, 249; Negroes in, 249.
Illinois Central Railway, 174, 176.
Immigration Commission (1907), 269.
Incas, 341.
India, rise of nationalism in, 14; Sanscrit in, 25; Aryans in, 25; passing of Nordics in, 26; Pre-Dravidians of, 27; English rule in, 355.
Indian War of 1855–1856, 207.
Indiana, 164; Southerners in, 167; Ulster Scots and Quakers in, 167; "Underground Railroad" in, 167; settlement of, 167–170; Nordic influence in, 169, 170; population in, 169, 170; influence of Germans in, 181; native population in, 248, 249.
Indianapolis (Ind.), 169, 170.
Indians, American, 22, 66; origin of, 19; culture of, 19; cruelty of, 156; effect on the frontier, 157; 1930 population in United States, 289; distribution in United States, 289; on Pacific Coast, 290; on Atlantic Coast, 291; lived as hunters, 291, 292; intermarriage with Whites, 292.
Indus, Valley of the, 25.
Inquisition, the, 227.
Inverness, 108, 312.
Inverness-shire, 159.
Invincible Armada, 208.
Iowa, 175, 195, 197; delay in settlement, 198; Southerners in, 198; foreign immigrants in, 198; entered Union as a State, 200; Nordic and Anglo-Saxon, 200; native population in, 252; agricultural, 252.
Iranian, division of Aryan languages, 25; distribution in Asia, 26.
Ireland, quota of immigrants from, 2; Erse in, 5, 6, 57, 58; potato famine in, 7; rise of nationalism in, 14; attacked by Norse and Danes, 55; Norsemen in, 59; Neolithic Mediterraneans in, 62; the Goidelics in, 62; Norse and Danes in, 62; English language in, 63; religion in, 63; the Reformation in, 63; Protestants in, 92, 93; emigration to North America from, 159, 160.
Irish Free State, 273.
Irish Rebellion in 1652, 133.
Iroquois Five Nations, 300, 301.
Iroquois Indians, 73, 291.
Isle of Man, 58.
Italians, immigration in United States, 231; high birth-rate of, 276.
Italy, races in, 4; invasions of Osco-Umbrians in, 26, 39; Ostrogoths in, 44; northern, 116; emigration from, 231.

Jackson, Andrew, 70, 256.
Jamaica, 345; results of abolition of slavery in, 11.
James I, 63, 92, 93.
James II, 127.
James River, 130.
Jamestown (Va.), settlement of, 130, 297; Negroes in, 131.
Japan, Christianity in, 14; "gentlemen's agreement" with United States, 266.
Japanese, in California, 266.
Jefferson, Thomas, 70, 208, 237, 245.
Jews, 46.
Johnson, Honorable Albert, 1 n.; 270.
Johnson, Sir John, 108, 312.
Johnson, Sir William, 108.

INDEX

Johnston, Gabriel, 140.
Johnston, Sir Harry H., 6.
Jordanes, 43.
Judaism, 225.
Jutes, the, 59.
Jutland, 59.

Kansas, 173; slavery in, 12; Daniel Boone's son in, 123; Kansas-Nebraska settlement, 200; battleground for slavery and free-soil elements, 201; few New England settlers in, 202; increase in emigration from Free States, 202; of British complexion, 202, 203; native population in, 255; settlement of, 256; Mexican population in, 292.
Kassites, 39.
Kearney, Dennis, 265.
Kent, 84, 159.
Kentaro, Baron Keneko, 9.
Kentucky, 72, 157; Boone in, 123; settlement of, 145, 146; growth of, 146; English atmosphere in, 147; admitted as a State, 147; Alpines in, 153; 1930 census native population, 242.
Kenya Colony, 353.
Khozars (Alpine), 225.
King Philip's War, 88.
Kingston (Ontario), 110.
Kintail, 312.
Kirkhill, 312.
Klondike gold rush, 130, 305.
"Know Nothings," 218; principle of, 219.
Knoydart, 312.
Korea, 31.
Krim, Götisch, 44.
Kurds, the, 50.

Labadists, the, 116.
Labrador, 308.
Lafayette, 12, 71.
Lake Champlain, 90, 109, 300.
Lake Erie, 110; first steamboat on, 177.
Lake George, 108.
Lake Ontario, 110.
Lancaster (Pa.), 79, 121, 124.
Land Act (1818), 189.
Languages, in West Indies, 23, 24; Hamitic, 24; spoken by Alpines, 24; Aryan, 24 ff.; Erse, 57. *See also under* various languages.
Lanier, 141.
La Plata, 337.
Latin America, 320, 321, 333, 334, 342, 346; Amerinds in, 26; Indians in, 321, 322; Whites in, 322, 323.
Laud, Archbishop, 85.
Laurens, 141.
Law, John, 187.
League of Nations, 294.
Lebanon (Pa.), 121.
Lebanon, the, 339.

Lee, Richard, 135.
Lehigh Valley, Germans in, 120–121.
Leicester, 84.
Leinster, 7, 63.
Leinster Protestants, 93.
Le Serrurier, 141.
Liberty Loans, 3.
Libyans, in Egypt, 39.
Liegnitz, Battle of, 53.
Lincolnshire, 83.
Literacy test, for aliens, vetoed by President Wilson, 269; passed over veto, 270.
Lithuania, 236.
Lithuanian language, 25.
Liverpool, 204.
Lochiel, 312.
Lombards, 46, 50, 250; in Italy, 51; overthrown by Franks, 51.
London, Puritan emigration from, 84; Imperial government in, 353.
Londonderry, 94.
Lone Star Republic, 211.
Long Island, 103, 105, 110.
Lord Baltimore, 80.
Los Angeles (Calif.), Mexicans in, 328.
Los Angeles County, Mexicans in, 328.
Louis XIV, 79, 106.
Louisiana, 152; French language in, 6; settlement in, 186–189; French in, 186; Acadian refugees in, 186; Nova Scotians in, 186, 187; cosmopolitan population in, 243, 244; religious groups in, 244; illiteracy test, 244, 245.
Louisiana Purchase of 1803, 149, 152, 185, 187, 188, 189, 191, 195, 208.
Lower California, 210.
Loyalists, 65, 68, 108, 146, 158; Episcopalians as, 69; expulsion in the North, 69; in Boston, 71; leave colonies for Canada, England, and English West Indies, 71; flee from colonies, 100; migration from New York State after the Revolution, 110; in New York State during the Revolution, 110; Scotch Highlanders as, 139; United Empire, 311.
Lynn (Mass.), 82.

Magna Græcia, 232.
Maine, 101; scattered settlements on coast of, 87; 1930 census native population, 235.
Malay Peninsula, Negroids in, 28.
Malays, the, 30, 294; in the Philippines, 31; in Japan, 31.
Man, ancestry of, 17.
Manhattan, Negroes in, 237.
Manhattan Island, 102, 111.
Manitoba, 195; Riel Rebellion in, 306; settlement of, 313, 314; Russians in, 318.

Mann, Elizabeth, 137.
Manx, 58.
Marcellus (N. Y.), 110.
Marietta (Ohio), established by New England Company, 164.
Maritime Provinces, 309, 315; Nordic element in, 296; population in, 300.
Maryland, 73, 127, 146; settlement of, 80; religious groups in, 127, 128; Negroes in, 128; Acadians in, 128; population at time of Revolution, 129; thoroughly Anglo-Saxon at time of first census, 129; Alpines in, 153; 1930 census native population, 239; attitude toward aliens, 268.
Mason and Dixon line, 172.
Massachusetts, first inhabitants of, 81; expansion in, 84; naming of cities in, 84, 85; population pushed westward, 88; as parent of all New England, 89; settlement west of Connecticut River in, 89, 90; influence during Revolution, 99; loss of population in, 100; growth in interior of, 101; Revolutionary troops from, 111; cosmopolitan population in 1930, 236; attitude toward aliens, 268.
Massachusetts Bay, early permanent settlements around, 72; Governor Winthrop's fleet in, 82.
Massachusetts Bay Colony, antecedents of, 82; social status of English founders of, 83, 84.
Mather, Cotton, 94.
Maverick, Rev. John, 85.
Mayas, 341.
Maynard, Lord, 85.
Medford (Mass.), 82.
Mediterraneans, the, 24, 57, 59; characteristics of, 29; range of, 29; in southern Italy, 39; Celtic-speaking, 40; on British Isles, 57.
Melanesia, Negroids in, 28; racial tangle in, 28.
Mendoza, 322.
Mennonites, 79; in Germantown, 115.
Mesopotamia, 22, 25, 39.
Mexican Indians, 327, 349.
Mexican revolution, in 1810, 326; in 1910, 326, 327.
Mexican War, 165, 208, 213; California annexed to United States as result of, 215.
Mexicans, in California, 216; in Southwestern States, 292; lack of intelligence, 327, 328; in United States, 327–330.
Mexico, 323, 348; Nordics in, 209; Spaniards in, 324, 325; Indian blood in, 326.
Mexico City, 325, 328; Humboldt in, 322.
Michaelangelo, 48.

Michigan, 164; French atmosphere in, 177; State Constitution, 177; population in 1836, 177; Dutchmen in, 178; native population in, 250; Canadians in, 250; Indians in, 289; Mexican population in, 293.
Micmacs, the, 307.
Middle Atlantic States, powerful section of America, 237.
Middlefield (Mass.), varied population in, 109.
Milan, 51.
Milford (N. J.), 113.
Milledgeville (Ala.), 183.
Milwaukee (Wis.), 161, 250, 251; Germans in, 251.
Minnesota, 313; settlement in, 195; treaties with Indians, 195; first official census in, 195; Scandinavians in, 196; Germans in, 196; Anglo-Saxon in character, 197; Scandinavians in, 251; Indians in, 289; native population in, 238.
Miocene, 17.
Mississippi, heart of Cotton Kingdom, 184; settlement in, 184–189; Negroes in, 185; 1930 census native population, 243.
Mississippi Bubble, 187.
Mississippi River, 73; territories west of, 195–207.
Mississippi Valley, 149; Norway and Sweden immigration to, 229; settlement of, 256.
Missouri, 87, 172, 175; Boone in, 123; settlement in, 190–192, 201; Kentuckians in, 191; Nordic American stock in, 201; native population in, 252; Negroes in, 252.
Mitanni, 30.
Mobile (Ala.), 183.
Mohammedan Arabs, 45.
Mohammedanism, and the Negro, 49.
Mohawk River, 107, 108; Loyalists and Scotch along the, 76.
Mohawk Valley, 109, 110.
Mohawks, the, 299.
Mohenjo-Daro, 25.
Mongolia, 23.
Mongoloid race, physical characteristics of, 37; as distinguished from Alpine race, 37.
Mongoloid tribes, 19.
Mongoloids, the, 28, 64, 294.
Mongols, the, 21, 53; similarity to Alpines, 29; traits in, 30; ancestors of American Indians, 30; Asiatic, 31; confront the Nordics, 356.
Monongahela country, 165.
Monroe, James, 136.
Montana, 254; few settlers in, 205; mining industry and growth of, 260;

admitted to statehood, 261; foreign stock in, 261; Indians in, 289.
Montcalm, overthrown at Quebec, 99.
Montgomery (Ala.), 183.
Moors, 49.
Moravia, 79; Mongolian characters in, 37.
Moravian Brothers, in North Carolina, 80.
Moravians, in Georgia, 117, 144.
Mormon Church, 204.
Mormon Utah settlement, converts from England, 204.
Mormonism, 67.
Mormons, 176; in Nebraska, 203; in Utah, 203.
Morocco, 231.
Moscovia, 54.
Mulattoes, 131, 283; in Virgin Islands, 11; migration northward, 237; intelligence of, 284.
Myjerka, 103.
"Myth of the Melting Pot," 1.

Naples (N. Y.), 110, 231.
Napoleonic Wars, 302, 312.
Nashville (Tenn.), 147.
Natchez (Ala.), 183.
Natchez (La.), 188.
National Origins Act, 272, 274, 278.
National Origins provision, 2.
National Origins Quota, 323.
Navajo Indians, 291.
Naval war in 1798, 71.
Neapolitan, the, 264.
Nebraska, 173; settlement in, 203; Mormons in, 203; transients in, 203; permanent settlers in, 203, 204; attracted pioneers after Civil War, 254; Bohemians in, 254; Nordic influence in, 255.
Negrillos (or Pigmies), 20.
Negritos, 31; in Eurasia, 28.
Negro slavery, 134, 144.
Negroes, the, 21; in Virgin Islands, 11; and Mohammedanism, 49; among Roman Catholics in the colonies, 70; increase in New York State, 237; manual labor in South by, 281; in United States according to census, 282; in the North, 282; treatment by Southerners, 282, 283; in the North, 283; tendency toward Communism, 283; advantages of "white blood," 284; in Central American countries, 330 ff.
Negroids, in Eurasia, 27; in Melanesia, 28; in Tasmania, 28.
Neolithic Mediterraneans, in Ireland, 62; conquered by the Goidelic, 62.
Nevada, 254; discovery of silver in, 205, 261; growth of, 261; admitted as a State, 262; decrease in population, 262.
Nevis, 85.
New Amsterdam (Manhattan Island), 102.
New Bern, 139.
New Brunswick, Scottish population in, 309; French-Canadians in, 310.
New Brunswick (N. J.), 113.
New Castle County (Del.), 116; Scotch settlements in, 122.
New England, Pilgrim and Puritan migration to, 65; early religions in, 67; Episcopalians as Loyalists in, 69; at war with France and Canadian Indians, 71; early settlements in, 72; natural increase in population of Whites in, 86; emigration to Great Britain and West Indies from, 86; Nordic character in, 90, 91; Indian population of, 97, 98; smallpox in, 98; golden age of, 99; vigor of Nordics in, 155; French-Canadians in, 218; increase of Anglo-Saxon stock in, 219, 220; decline in white stock birth rate in, 220.
New England Company, 164.
New England Emigrant Aid Company, 201.
New Hampshire, 72, 94; settlements in, 88, 89; growth of, 101; 1930 census native population, 235.
New Iberia, 188.
New Jersey, 72; settlement of, 77; small Dutch element in, 77; English in, 77, 111–114; East Jersey, 112; West Jersey, 112; population at time of Revolution, 114; Alpines in, 153; foreign-born in, 218; 1930 census native population, 238.
New London (Conn.), 87.
New Mexico, 152; Spanish language in, 6; native and Mexican Indians in, 213; population in, 213, 214; Mexicans in, 263; Indians in, 289.
New Netherland, Dutch settlement of, 102.
New Orleans (La.), 168, 171, 186.
New Providence, 345.
New Rochelle (N. Y.), 76, 106.
New York City, 112; inferiority of, at time of Revolution, 105; beginning of commercial greatness of, 105, 106; arrival of French Huguenots in, 106; Puerto Ricans in, 344.
New York State, 72, 229; small Dutch population in, 73; French Huguenots in, 73, 76; foreigners in, 75; Flemings in, 76; as unimportant colony, 105, 108; New England colonization of, 105; Palatines in, 107; invasion of New Englanders after the Revolution, 108; Ulster Scots in, 108; Loyalist

388 INDEX

migration from New York State after the Revolution, 110; large quantity of Revolutionary troops from, 111; Alpines in, 153; foreign-born in, 218; increase in Negroes in, 237; race mixture in, 237; Indians in, 289.
New York Tribune (quoted), 216.
New Zealand, 303, 353, 354.
Newark (N. J.), 72, 113.
Newark Bay, 113.
Newfoundland, 296, 307, 308.
Newport (R. I.), 88.
Newton, 87.
Nicaragua, population of, 331, 332.
Niebelungenlied, the, 51.
Nile, valley of the, 22.
Nordic Frisians, 76.
Nordic race, peculiar characteristics of, 34, 35; red-haired branch of, 35, 36; importance in United States, 153; necessity of close co-operation by, 357.
Nordics, 21; jealousy of, 15; originators of Aryan group of languages, 24, 26; in India, 25; and the caste system, 26; passing of, in India and Persia, 26; expansion of Alpines at expense of, 31; development of, 33; mixture with Mediterraneans in British Islands, 33; question as to homeland of, 33, 34; as aggressors, 34; in Scandinavia, 35; around Baltic and North Seas, 35; Celtic, 36; Teutonic, 36, 42, 46, 50; in West as Achæans, 39; in Mesopotamia, 39; in Italy, 51; in France, 52; and the Crusades, 53; Goidels, 57, 62; in American colonies, 77; weakened as a race, 150; in Mexican territory, 209; favored in Quota Act of 1921, 271; confronted by the Mongols, 356, 357.
Norfolk, 56; the Angles in, 61.
Norman conquest in 1066, 60.
Normandy, religion in, 60.
Normans, the, 52.
Norse, 59; in Scotland, 55.
Norsemen, 59, 60.
North, the Revolution in the, 69.
North Africa, the Berbers of, 24.
North Carolina, 134, 146; extended to Mississippi River, 74; Scots in, 74; Moravian Brothers in, 80; English and Ulster Scots in, 80; Boone in, 123; settlement of, 138; varied races in, 138–140; 1930 census native population, 240; Indians in, 289.
North Dakota, native population, 238; admitted as a State, 253; Nordic element in, 253; Indians in, 289.
North German Nordics, in America, 143.
North Sea, 35.
Northampton (England), 84.

Northamptonshire, 83.
Northern Abolitionists, 12.
Northern Pacific Railway, 253.
Northmen, the, in Scotland, 55; as Danes, 55; conquer Normandy, 55.
Northwest Territory (old), 163–182; French in, 162; Mexicans in, 162; Ohio, 164–167; Indiana, 167–170; Illinois, 170–176; Michigan, 176–178; Wisconsin, 178–182.
Norwalk (Conn.), 87.
Nova Scotia, the French in, 308; Loyalists in, 308; Gaelic spoken in, 309.

Offnet race, 32.
Oglethorpe, Governor, 116, 143, 145.
Ohio, 150; migration to, 109; settled by New England Company, 164; Pennsylvania emigration to, 165; Nordics and Pennsylvania Dutch in, 166; German and Irish immigrants in, 166; settlers of northern Indiana in, 168; native population in, 248; Canadians in, 248.
Ohio Legislature, 165.
Ohio River, 145, 146, 164, 167, 168.
Oklahoma, pride of Indian blood in, 98; cosmopolitan population in, 245, 246; Indians in, 246, 289–292; Canadians in, 246.
Old Charles Town, 141.
Old Pretender, the, 139.
Oneida Community, 67.
Ontario, 303; Roman Catholic Scotch Highlanders in, 108; "United Empire Loyalists" in, 111; French-Canadians in, 310; Loyalist refugees in, 311; increase in population, 312; Nordic element in, 313; Poles and Italians in, 318; Russians in, 318.
Orange County, Ulster Scots in, 107.
Oregon, settlement in, 206, 207, 256; native population in, 267.
Oregon Trail, 259.
Orient, revolt against European control in the, 15; missionaries in, 15.
Osco-Umbrians, 39; invasions into Italy, 26.
Ostrogoths, 44, 51.
Ottawa, French language in, 5.
Ottawa River, 297.

Pacific Coast, 155; migration westward to, 158, 217, 218; restless population on, 257; Indian population on, 290; immigration of Filipinos on, 293, 294.
Pacific States, America's future in, 354; Philippines in, 354.
Palatinate, the, 116, 228.
Palatine Germans, along the Hudson River and Mohawk valleys, 76.
Palatines, the, 8, 106; in Holland and

INDEX

England, 107; in New York State, 107, 117; in Pennsylvania, 107; in Georgia, 116, 117.
Paleolithic Period, 32.
Palmer, 94.
Palmyra (N. Y.), 110.
Panama, population of, 333; North American influence in, 333.
Panama Canal, 354.
Papua, racial tangle in, 28.
Paraguay, 321; population of, 341, 342; war with Brazil and Argentina, 341.
Paris, 186.
Peace of Paris, the, 99.
Pelham, 94.
Penn, William, 114, 115, 121, 123, 125.
Pennsylvania, 146; French Huguenots in, 73; settlement of, 77; Germans in, 79; Palatines in, 107; religious denominations in, 115; invasion of Palatinates in, 117, 122, 124; English alarmed over Palatine invasion, 120; Ulster Scots in, 121–122; increase in population, 123; races in, at end of Colonial period, 124; Delaware part of, 125; foreign-born in, 218; 1930 census native population in, 238; attitude toward aliens, 268.
Pennsylvania Dutch, 123, 124, 137.
Pennsylvanische Deutsche, 115.
Perpetual Emigrating Fund, 204.
Persia, passing of Nordics in, 26; Negro admixture in, 27.
Persians, Islamized, 49.
Perth Amboy (N. J.), 77, 113.
Perthshire, 159.
Peru, Indian race in, 342.
Peruvian Indians, 342.
Philadelphia, 105, 112, 114, 155, 309; English Quakers and Welsh around, 77; Ulster Scots enter colonies through, 77; strength of Church of England in, 121; as metropolis of United States, 123.
Philippines, the, 294; rise of nationalism in, 14; American problem in, 353; in Pacific States, 354; United States should govern, 355, 356.
Phrygia, Nordic conquest of, 39.
Picts, 58, 61.
Piedmont, 173.
Piedmont (Italy), 143.
Pigmies (or Negrillos), 20.
Pike's Peak, 258, 259.
Pilgrim Fathers, 82.
Piscataqua (New Brunswick, N. J.), 113.
Pittsburgh, Ulster Scots in, 123.
Pleistocene glaciation, 34.
Plymouth, 98.
Plymouth colony, settlers of, 81; antecedents in, 82.
Plymouth Rock, 82.

Po valley, as Cisalpine Gaul, 41.
Polaks, 355.
Poland, rise of nationalism in, 14; migration of German Jews into, 225.
Polish Jews, 224–226.
Polk, James K., 210.
Polygamy, as racial curse, 49, 50.
Polynesia, Malay blood in, 30.
Polynesian Islands, 353.
Pomerania, 181.
Port of New York, Dutch population outside, 77.
Portland (Maine), 101.
Portsmouth (R. I.), 88.
Portugal, 47, 48, 335, 336.
Portuguese, in Brazil, 335.
Prairie Provinces, 314.
Prince Edward Island, native population of, 309; French-Canadians in, 310.
Princeton University, 113.
Protectorate, the, 133.
Protestant Episcopal Church, the, 69.
Protestant House of Orange, 127.
Providence (R. I.), 88; Huguenots in, 97.
Prussia, 116, 170.
Pueblo Indians, revolt against Spanish, 291.
Puerto Ricans, 294.
Puerto Rico, 343, 349; results of abolition of slavery in, 11; population of, 343, 344.
Puget Sound, 267.
Puritan emigration, from England, 82.
Puritans, New England, 66; as refugees in Virginia, 135.
Putnam, General Rufus, 164.

"Q" Celts, 62.
Quakers, 93, 125; along Delaware River, 112; become Anglicans, 121; in Albemarle, 138.
Quebec, 229, 304; French language in, 5; "Habitat" French of, 8; intermarriage of French and Indians, 9; overthrow of Montcalm at, 99; stronghold of French Canadians, 310; Russians in, 318.
Quebec Province (Lower Canada), 301; French settlement of, 297; physical characteristics of settlers, 297, 298; language in, 298; domination of Jesuits in, 299; centre of French population, 301.
Quota Act of 1921, 270, 271; favored the European Nordic, 271.

Race, in United States during Colonial times, 2 ff.; at present time, 6; definition of, 21 ff., 36; distinction between language and, 24; Mediterranean, 28, 29; Alpine, 28, 29; Nordic, 29; Alpine

390 INDEX

Slavs, 31; Mongols, 36; in Ireland, 62, 63. *See also under* various races.
Railroads, 175.
Ravenal, 141.
Reading (Pa.), 121, 123.
Red River, steam navigation on, 313.
Red River Colony, 195, 313.
Red River country, 253.
Reformation, the, 42; lack of hold on Ireland, 63.
"Refuge for the Oppressed," 227.
"Regulators," rebellion in North Carolina, 70.
Reuter, E. B., 284.
Revolution, the American, hatred in New England of mother country during, 68; political and social, 70; loss of Nordic blood in America during, 71; and expulsion of Iroquois Indians, 76; Germans unloyal during, 79; Protestants in United States after, 152; Nordic invasion of Florida during, 193; migration following, 256.
Revolution (French), 179.
Revolution of 1689, 128.
Rhode Island, settlements in, 88; source of colonization, 89; 1930 census native population, 236.
Richelieu River, 301.
Richmond (N. Y.), 110.
Richmond (Va.), 136.
Riel Rebellion, 306.
Rio Grande, the, 154, 320.
Robinson (clergyman), 83.
Rochester, increase in Negroes in, 237.
Rock Island and Pacific Railway, 196.
Rocky Mountain States, 257; varying population in, 258.
Roderick, 46.
Roman Catholic church, growth in America, 162; hostility of Know Nothing Party to, 219; strength in Canada, 318.
Roman Catholics, population in the colonies, 69, 70; Negroes and Germans among, 70; many colonies legislated against, 70.
Rome, 22; sacked by Gauls, 41.
Roosevelt, Theodore, 4, 269.
Roxbury (Mass.), 82.
Royalists, in Virginia, 135.
Russia, Varangians in, 56.

Sahara Desert, 26.
Saint Croix, 85.
Saint Kitts, 85, 86.
Saint Lawrence River, 300, 301.
Saint Louis (Mo.), 161, 171, 196; as French outpost, 190; marked German tinge in, 191, 192.
Saint Mary's (Md.), 126, 128.
Saladin, 50.
Salem, 112.

Salvador, population of, 331.
Salzburg, 144.
San Antonio (Texas), 212.
San Francisco (Calif.), 216; Oriental laborers in, 265.
Sanscrit, in Burma, 25; in India, 25.
Santo Domingo, 287, 345; loss of white control in, 11, 12; barbarism in, 12.
Saracens, at Tours, 53.
Saskatchawan, 314; Russians in, 318.
Savannah (Ga.), 144.
Saxons, 41, 51; invaded Britain, 59.
Scandinavia, 42; first Nordics in, 35; Nordic immigration from, 227, 229.
Schenectady, 103.
Schuylkill valley, Germans in, 121.
Schwankenfelders, 79.
Scituate, 82.
Scotch Highlanders, importation of Roman Catholics, 108.
"Scotch Irish," 63.
Scotch Rebellion of 1670, 133.
Scotland, 58; Nordic population in, 59; invaded by Danes, 59.
Scrooby, 82.
Sedgmoor, Battle of, 134.
Sedition Act of 1798, 268.
Selkirk, Lord, 313.
Seneca Falls (N. Y.), 110.
Seneca Lake, 110.
Sephardim, 227.
Seven Seas, the, 352.
Seven Years' War, 193.
Sevier, 141.
Shakers, 67.
Shawneetown, 172.
Shays's Rebellion, 70, 90.
Sheffield, 90.
Shenandoah Valley, 74, 137, 146; Scotch Germans in, 122.
Sicily, 231, 232.
Sidonius, Appollonius, 51.
Sierra range, the, 155.
Silesia, 53.
Singapore, 354.
Sioux Indians, 291.
Skrellings, 98.
Slavery, 12; results of abolition on British Empire, 11; in South Africa, 11; in Jamaica, 11; in Puerto Rico, 11; and the Civil War, 12, 13; in South Carolina, 142.
Slavs, Alpine, 31.
Smith, Captain John, 90.
Société des Amis des Noirs, 12.
Sogdians, 23.
"Solid South," 282.
Somaliland, 29.
Somerset, 159.
South, the, religion in, 69; decline of leadership in, 175.
South Africa, 353; results of abolition of slavery in, 11.

INDEX 391

South Carolina, 168; racial complexion in, 80; settlement of, 141; large-scale agriculture in, 141; Ulster Scots in, 142; slavery question in, 142; Nordics and loyalists in, 142; Dorchester Society in, 144; Negroes outnumbered whites, 185; 1930 census native population, 240, 241.
South Dakota, rush in 1876 in, 254; Indians in, 289.
South Irish Catholics, 7.
South Italy, Negroid element in, 9.
South of Portugal, Negro slave element in, 9.
South Russia, Aryan language in, 24; the Goths in, 44.
"South Sea," the, 162
Southern frontiersman, religion of, 67.
Southwest, 183–194; Alabama, 183, 184; Mississippi, 184–189; Louisiana, 185–189; Arkansas, 189–190; Missouri, 190–192; Florida, 192–194.
Soviet Russia, Alpines in, 15.
Spain, conquered by Celtic Nordics, 40; Visigoths in, 45; ceded Florida to England, 193.
Spaniards, in Mexico, 324, 325.
Spanish Conquest, 324.
Spanish Main, the, 98.
Spencer, Herbert (quoted), 9, 10.
Stamford (Conn.), 87.
Statehood, 258, 261, 262.
Steamboat, first on Lake Erie, 177.
"Stony Mountains," 155.
Stormont (Ontario), 312.
Straits of Gibraltar, 45.
Stratford (Conn.), 87.
Suevi, the, 42, 45, 51.
Suffolk, the Angles in, 61.
Sumner, Senator, 288.
Surrey, 159.
Susquehanna River, 110.
Swabia, 228.
Sweden, 44, 45.
Swedes, 111.
Switzerland, 50; national unity in, 5; various languages in, 5.
Symmes, Judge T. C., 164.
Syracuse, increase in Negroes in, 237.
Syria, 231.

Tasmania, 20; Negroids in, 28.
Taunton (Mass.), 82.
Tennessee, 72, 146, 157; Scotch and Germans in, 122; settlement of, 147–149; Alpines in, 153; racial make-up of, 242.
Teutonic, branch of the Nordic race, 42; as a term, 43.
Teutonic Nordics, 36, 42, 43.
Teutons, 42; collapse of Roman Empire under, 43; physical characteristics of, 43.

Texas, 152, 174; Mexicans in, 162, 208; American settlement in, 209; importance as slave-holding territory, 209; growth of population at time of Mexican War, 212; Negroes in, 212; German emigration (Alpines) in, 212; foreign elements in, 246; Nordic absorption of, 256.
The Chronicle, 260.
"The Land of Little Sticks," 316.
"The Provisional State of Deseret," 204.
"The Refuge of the Oppressed," 1.
Theodoric, 44.
Thirteen Colonies, the, 163.
Thirty Years War, 127.
Thomson, David, 88.
"Three Notch Road," 184.
Tioga River, 110.
Tokarian language, 25.
Toulouse, 48.
Tours, the Saracens at, 53.
Transcontinental Railway, 203.
Treaty of Paris, 163.
Trenton (N. J.), 115.
Troubadours, 48.
Tucson (Ariz.), 214.
Turanians, 31.
"Turco," 339.
Turkestan, Ural-Altaic language in, 24.
Turks, race mixture among, 50; in Asia Minor, 50.

Ukraine, the, 54.
Ulster, 95; Presbyterians in, 63.
Ulster Presbyterians, 93.
Ulster Scots, 7, 92, 93, 96; in America, 60; hatred of England, 67; forced to the West, 73; in North Carolina, Kentucky and Tennessee, 74; in California, 78; in Ireland, 78; in Orange County, 107; established church in Albany, 108; west of Alleghanies, 123; in Pittsburgh, 123; in Maryland, 129; in South Carolina, 142; in Georgia, 144; animosity during Revolution, 150.
Union, the, requirement for admission to, in 1818, 173.
Union Pacific Railway, 259.
Unitarian form of Christianity, 46.
"United Empire Loyalists," 111, 311, 313.
United Irishmen, 159.
United States, mixture of racial groups in, 2; effect of sentimentalism on Nordic survival in, 12; slavery in, 12; first census, 49; distribution of free land in, 65; little Dutch blood in present population of, 104; population at time of first census, 149, 152, 153; Protestant majority in, 151, 154; Catholic hierarchy in, 151, 152;

INDEX

Nordic race in, 153; Alpine race in, 153; census of 1860, 158, 162; German settlement in, 180, 181; Nordics in, 220, 226, 234; national unity in, 222; Nordic immigration from Scandinavia, 227–230; Alpines in, 227, 228; European immigration to, 228; early Germans in, 228; Norwegians in farming land of, 230; immigration of English and Irish in, 230; immigration of Italians, 231; percentage of alien emigration and immigration in, 233; "gentlemen's agreement" with Japan, 266; white population in 1920, 278; percentage of Protestants in, 279; percentage of Nordics in, 279, 280; loss of unity in, 281; Negroes in, 282; increase of electoral vote in the South, 282; 1930 Indian population, 289; distribution of Indians in, 289; Mexicans in, according to 1930 census, 293; Hindu immigration prevented in, 295; Irish Catholic migration from Canada to, 304; Mexicans in, 324; disadvantages of Mexican immigration to, 327, 329; percentage of Nordics and Protestants in, 347; immigration during last century, 347, 348; restriction of immigration, 348 ff.; aliens in, 350; international affair, 352; "White Man's Burden" in, 352, 357; trouble with Philippines, 354; should govern Philippines, 355.
Upland (Chester), 114.
Upper Canada, 297; immigration from British Isles to, 302, 303; increase in population, 312.
Ur, 25.
Ural mountains, 54.
Uruguay, white races in, 337; cosmopolitan population in, 338.
Utah, Mormons in, 176, 204, 205, 256; Nordic population in, 204, 205; native population in, 261; foreign stock in, 261.
Utica, increase in Negroes in, 237.

Vaal River, 11.
Valens, 44.
Valley of the Syr-Daria, 22.
Van Buren, Martin, 256.
Vandals, 45, 46.
Varangians, 56, 59.
Varini, the, 52.
Venezuela, population of, 334.
Vermont, dispute over ownership of, 72; settlement of, 89; as a frontier, 90; migration from Massachusetts to, 90; as an independent state, 90; growth of, 101; 1930 census native population, 235.
Victorian Era, 281.
Vigot (or Bigot), 46.

Vincennes (Ind.), 149, 168.
Virgin Islands, 192; Negroes and Mulattoes in, 11, 345.
Virginia, 116, 117, 146, 220; early settlements, 72; Mother of States in Colonial times, 73; tidewater population, 73, 74; extended to Mississippi River, 73; English settlement, 80; natural increase in population of whites, 86; Pocahontas tradition in, 99; as exploitation of adventurers, 130; mixed classes of immigrants in, 132 ff.; Cavaliers in, 133; refuge of Puritans during Stuart period, 135; Royalists in, 135; Kentucky veterans in, 164; 1930 census native population, 240; surplus population, 242.
Virginia City (Nevada), 261.
Visigoths, 46, 52; in Gaul, 44; in Spain, 45, 49.
Vistula, the, 44, 54.
Von Bismarck, chancellor, 282.

Waldenses, 143.
Wales, 58, 59; Norsemen in, 59; Iberians in, 61.
Walker's Law, 276.
Walla Walla Valley, 207.
Walloons, 102.
War of 1812, 166, 171, 177, 208, 312, 313; causes of, 163.
Warwick (R. I.), 88.
Washington, 289; an independent territory, 207; native population, 267; population increased by railways, 267; Nordic element in, 267.
Washington (D. C.), 239.
Washington Bicentennial in 1932, 6.
Washington, George, 125, 148.
Watauga settlement, the, 148.
Watertown (Mass.), 81, 82, 87.
Welsh, in England, 41.
Wends, 31, 54.
Wessex, Puritan emigration from, 84.
West Central Asia, 64; origin of civilization in, 22, 23.
West India Company, 103.
West Indies, 208, 294, 325, 343; languages in, 23, 24; Nordic settlement, 85, 86; Negroes in, 86; Loyalists flee to, 100; South Carolinians in, 142; fate of colonists in, 154, 155.
West Jersey, 112, 113.
West Scotland, high stature in, 62.
West Virginia, 138; 1930 census native population, 241, 242.
Wethersfield (Conn.), 87.
Whiskey Rebellion, 70, 125.
"White Man's Burden," 352, 354, 357.
Whites, the, 12, 20; slaves injurious to, 13.
Whitesborough, 109.
Whitman, Marcus, 206.

INDEX

Wilderness Road, 145.
William III, 63.
Williams, Roger, 88.
Wilmington (Del.), 115, 139.
Wilson, Woodrow, 14, 269, 270.
Wiltshire, 84.
Windsor (Conn.), 87.
Winnipeg, 313.
Winthrop, Governor, arrival of fleet in Massachusetts Bay, 82.
Wisconsin, 164, 175, 195; lead mines in, 172, 178; settlement of, 178–182; growth, 178, 179; foreign element in, 179; climate, soil, and forest lands, 179, 180; Germans in, 179–181; non-Nordic population, 182; native population, 238; foreign element in, 250, 251; waning of wheat industry, 254; Indians in, 289.
Woodbridge (N. J.), 113.
Worcester, 94.
World, the, racially, 26 ff.
World War, 15, 116, 185, 212, 231, 246, 247, 252, 269, 283, 315, 336, 338, 340, 356; immigration law as result of, 1, 2; foreigners in draft list, 3; immigration from Scandinavia since, 229.
Wright, J. K., (quoted), 40 n.
Würtemberg, 268.
Wusuns, 34.
Wyoming, admitted to Union, 259; native population, 259; foreign stock in, 259.
Wyoming Valley of Pennsylvania, 101.

Yadkin valley, 123.
Yarmouth, 82.
Yiddish (language), 225.
York (Pa.), 79, 122.
Yorkshire, 82.
Young, Brigham, 204, 205.
Young Pretender, the, 139.

Zuyder Zee, 103.

www.ingramcontent.com/pod-product-compliance
Lightning Source LLC
Chambersburg PA
CBHW022111080426
42734CB00006B/94